GLASGOW HARBOUR

GRAEME SMITH
&
MIKE McCREERY

AMBERLEY

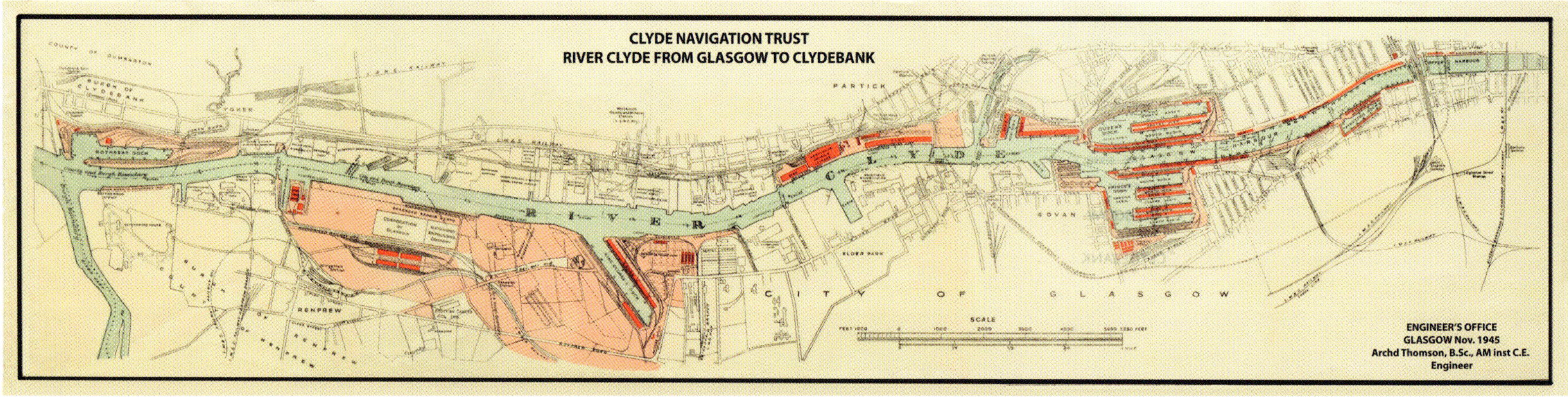

A map of the River Clyde from Glasgow to Clydebank, 1945, published by Clyde Navigation Trust.

First published 2025

Amberley Publishing
The Hill, Stroud
Gloucestershire, GL5 4EP

www.amberley-books.com

ISBN 978 1 3981 2237 6 (print)
ISBN 978 1 3981 2238 3 (ebook)

British Library Cataloguing in Publication Data.
A catalogue record for this book is available from the British Library.

Typesetting by SJmagic DESIGN SERVICES, India.
Printed in the UK.

EU GPSR Authorised Representative
Appointed EU Representative: Easy Access System Europe Oü, 16879218
Address: Mustamäe tee 50, 10621, Tallinn, Estonia
Contact Details: gpsr.requests@easproject.com, +358 40 500 3575

CONTENTS

Acknowledgements	4
Introduction	5
Freedom of the River	7
Invention and Innovation	23
Navigating a Future	69
Shipbuilding Companies	85

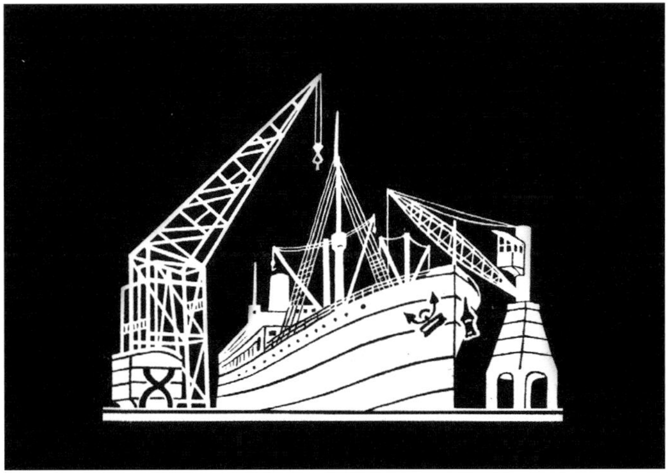

ACKNOWLEDGEMENTS

Writer Graeme Smith and photographer Mike McCreery are grateful to all who have contributed on the journey to creating this book. From past generations to current generations, from shippers, shipbuilders, mariners and families. Special thanks to Ian Johnston (shipbuilding), Suzanne di Paolo Bruce (business regeneration), Douglas Lindsay (drone photography) and to many more, including John Park, Peter Fraser, George Allison (naval drone photography), Graham Lappin, Fraser McHaffie, Charles Miller and Allan Milligan.

Also, the Royal Navy, BAE Systems, UK Defence Journal, Fairfield Heritage, the Mitchell Library City Archives, University of Glasgow Library, Strathclyde University Library, National Trust for Scotland, Royal College of Physicians and Surgeons of Glasgow and privately held archives.

About the Authors

With experience in building new towns and the renewal of cities and economies, Graeme Smith writes and illustrates city life, growth and changes involving businesses, international trading, education and entertainment. His family has included sea captains, engineers and a marine superintendent. Lifelong photographer and engineer Mike McCreery revitalises historic city images and creates challenging contemporary ones. This is the third book they have prepared jointly. Website: blythswoodsmith.co.uk.

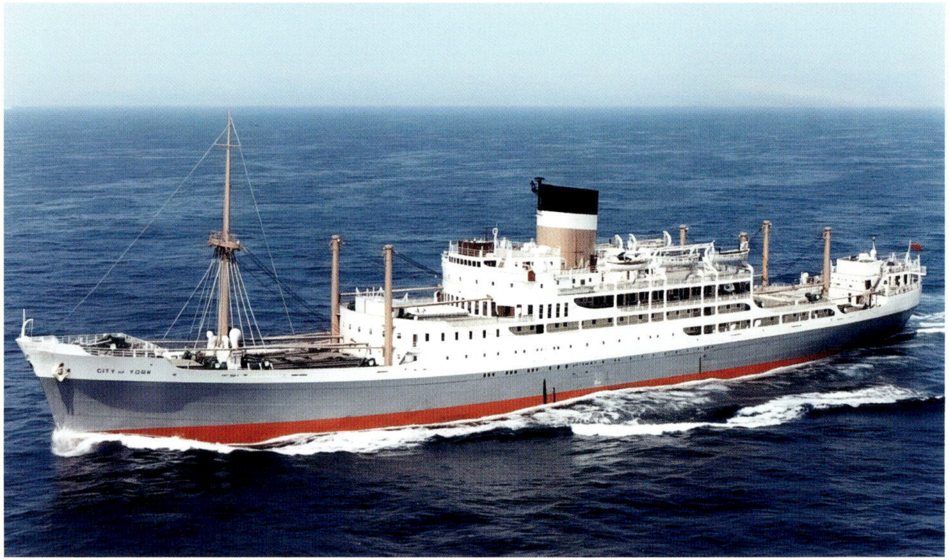

SS *City of York*.

INTRODUCTION

Opening onto the oceans of the world, the beautiful Firth of Clyde – with its mountains, lochs and islands – takes its name from the River Clyde, which rises over 100 miles south of Glasgow and wends its way through Lanark from its source in the Lowther Hills near Leadhills. It is the second longest river in Scotland. In pre-historic times the meandering river came through a vast shallow sea on the eastern flanks of Glasgow, resulting in sandbanks and shoals with a depth in places, including Glasgow Bridge, of only 15 inches at low tide.

From ancient origins and some 160 years after becoming a royal burgh in 1611, Glasgow adopted new methods to deepen and engineer the river to make it more useful as it wandered towards the deep sea water of the Firth. The largest and most advanced docks were built with eventually some 12 miles of busy quayside lining the river and over 500 miles of railway. Glasgow made the Clyde, and the Clyde made Glasgow.

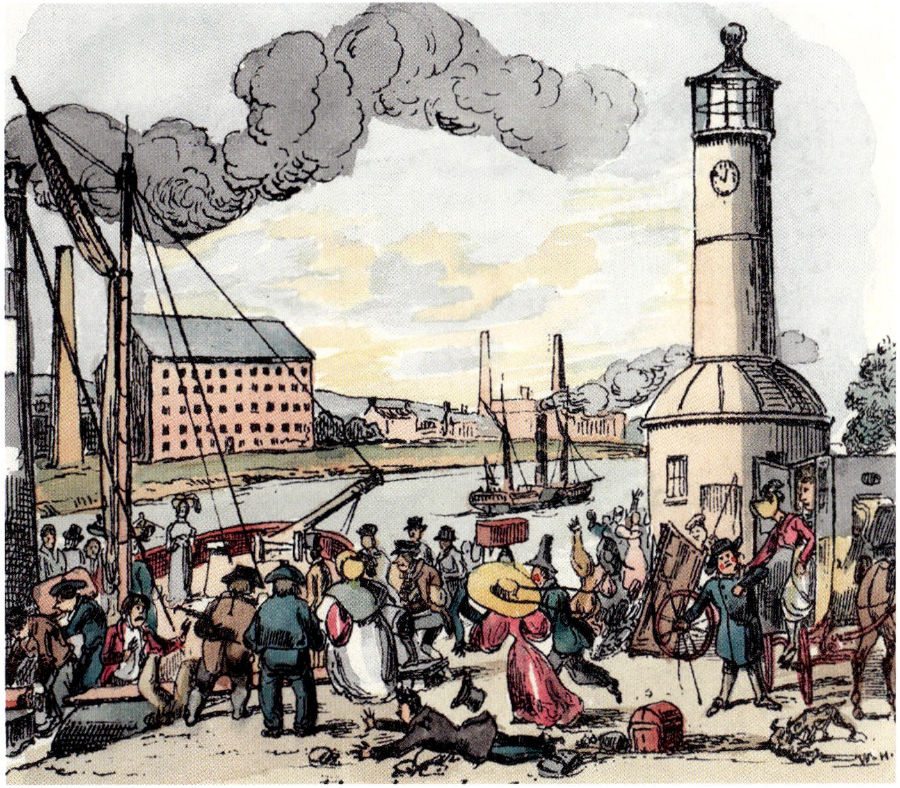

Passengers at the Broomielaw scrambling to embark on a steamboat bound for Liverpool. The Broomielaw Lighthouse is on the right. From the *Looking Glass*, 1825.

Earlier shipping using Irvine in Ayrshire; Greenock in Renfrewshire, buying land at Newark – nearer than Greenock – and building Port Glasgow; and Port Dundas on the very new Great Canal.

Ideas, philosophy and education expanded. Science, invention and art co-mingled. Glasgow and its hinterland became the birthplace of the Industrial Revolution. Soon, Glasgow and the Clyde became the undisputed world centre of shipbuilding, and the greatest centre of locomotive building in Europe. The city thrived nationally and internationally through its companies and headquarters, including shipping, shipbuilding, railways, locomotives, engineering, bridge-building, coal, steel, oil, chemicals and explosives; cotton, textiles, leather and furniture; tobacco, whisky, brewing and food manufacturing; printing and publishing; banks and insurance.

Glasgow Harbour, extending from Glasgow Green to the River Kelvin, and beyond to Clydebank, became the greatest port in Scotland and one of the largest in Britain. Glasgow transformed itself from being a town on a 'shallow Scottish salmon river' into a modern global port.

The largest and finest ships – and the fastest – in the world were built on the Clyde with the best craftsmanship available to owners worldwide. Owners transporting passengers and cargoes, and countries requiring navies.

The Clyde from Glasgow to Greenock and down to Ayr has designed and built more than half of the tonnage of ships made in the British Isles. Of the Clyde's sixty-five major shipbuilding firms over two centuries, this book highlights ten of the internationally famed shipyards, including the largest in the world of their time.

More than 100 major shipping lines operated from the city, and many of the company house flags and funnels are illustrated and celebrated in this book.

Here we tell the story of Glasgow Harbour.

FREEDOM OF THE RIVER

Already the largest town on the Clyde by the thirteenth century, with its cathedral high above Castle Street and joined in 1451 by its university – the fourth oldest in Britain – Glasgow had full trading rights and privilege of use of the river westward till it met the sea, 27 miles downstream. This was later confirmed in a Royal Charter signed by King James VI in 1611, granting 'freedom of the river from Broomilaw to the Clochstane', where today's Cloch Lighthouse would be built, past the villages of Greenock and Gourock.

To the east, the tide reached Cambuslang, beyond Rutherglen – a royal burgh before Glasgow became one. At Glasgow the river could be forded at low tide when the depth was only about 15 inches. The normal tidal rise was between 3 and 4 feet. Glasgow Brig, over the Clyde at the Stockwell, was made of timber until it was replaced in 1345 by a stone bridge that survived more than 500 years until Victoria Bridge took its place in 1857.

From the 1400s onwards, the town's merchants increased their export and import trades around the coasts of Scotland, England, Ireland, France, Norway, the Baltic states and Holland. Goods traded included wines, brandy, salt, timber, iron, cloth, pickled salmon and herring. But the river remained stubbornly shallow in too many places, meandering and with countless creeks, carrying more and more silt to the Tail of the (sand) Bank where the Firth begins. Frequently, the Clyde overflowed its natural shores on both sides and submerged adjoining streets. Exceptionally high tides and torrents brought floods up to 20 feet higher than the normal river levels. Severe winters brought ice flowing down the river, damaging bridges and the few wooden coastal boats in the town. Often, these were moored mid-stream because the River Wharf near Stockwell Street was too shallow.

Levies were placed on goods arriving at the wharf and tolls on the use of the bridge by carters and packmen. A 'little custom house' was built at the end of the bridge in 1601. For a time, half of the money taken was used to maintain the cathedral and the other half to maintain the bridge, removing sand from the river, building defences for the Green, removing stones, stobs and obstructions from the channel and repairing fords.

The river had seven islands (or 'inches'), the larger ones towards Renfrew. They changed size and shape with the tides and floods. The smallest one sat between the Stockwell and Gorbals. An architect builder landed his cargoes of timber on it for storage. It also had three haystacks and was a meeting place for young lads from each bank who engaged in stone fights, before the magistrates intervened.

Frustrated by the difficulties of directly sailing to and from the city, merchants used other ports such as Irvine, but the cost and time of packmen coming overland with cargoes was too great. Also, the sweeping westerly winds from the Atlantic frequently closed the harbour there with sand. Its healthy position was where Glasgow University moved to when the city was hit with plague in the 1640s. Very large sailing vessels arriving at the mouth of the Clyde transhipped their goods onto smaller boats and lighters to move upstream, taking many days, subject to tides, wind (if any) and running aground.

For small boats that could make it up the Clyde 'ane little Key and weigh-hous was builded' in 1663 at the Broomielaw, using oak from the cathedral and topped with stone. There was also a fountain and crane. Levies were charged on goods landed, including 'on herring and ling, potatoes and timber'.

Needing a Larger Port

The citizens wanted to have a port nearer the mouth of the Clyde. The magistrates prepared to buy land for an extensive harbour at Dumbarton. That burgh declined the idea. Instead, the city magistrates looked to the other side of the river. In 1662 they purchased 13 acres of ground west of Newark Castle and created a new town and harbours. A dry dock was added in 1762, the first in Scotland. This was Newport, Glasgow, soon being known as Port Glasgow. The city built its main custom house here.

However, most goods still needed to be transhipped into lighters and sailed, rowed or poled up to Renfrew and were then towed up to the harbour, some 6 miles away. In 1740 the council bought 'a flat-bottomed boat to carry off the sand and shingle from the banks'. In the second half of the eighteenth century, engineers John Golborne and James Watt, followed by John Rennie and Thomas Telford, advised on improvements required. Golborne was highly successful in forming over 100 jetties or groynes at right angles from both sides to 8 miles below Glasgow. This quickened the river, scouring the sand and deepening the water. Vessels drawing 6 feet of water now came up to the Broomielaw at high tides. The jetties were later adjusted in angle and number, dykes added and low rubble walls inserted to secure a continuous, more uniform channel.

The Forth & Clyde Canal, with a constant depth of 8 feet of water, opened in 1790. Linking the Forth at Grangemouth and the Clyde at Bowling, this was a crucial development for the foundries at Falkirk and trade in Glasgow. More land was bought and a larger basin opened in the city, being Port Dundas. Shipping cargoes increased there, especially grain, coal, sugar, timber, iron, coffee, herring and salt.

James Watt

In May 1765, on one of his walks on Glasgow Green, James Watt, polymath, instrument-maker and scientist at the nearby university, conceived his idea of a major improvement, by having a separate condenser, to increase the energy, efficiency and uses of earlier steam engines. He wrote:

> I was thinking upon the engine at the time when the idea came into my mind ... as steam was an elastic body, it would rush into a vacuum, and if a communication were made between the cylinder and an exhausted vessel, it would rush into it and might be condensed without cooling the cylinder ... I had not walked further than the golf-house when the whole thing was arranged in my mind.

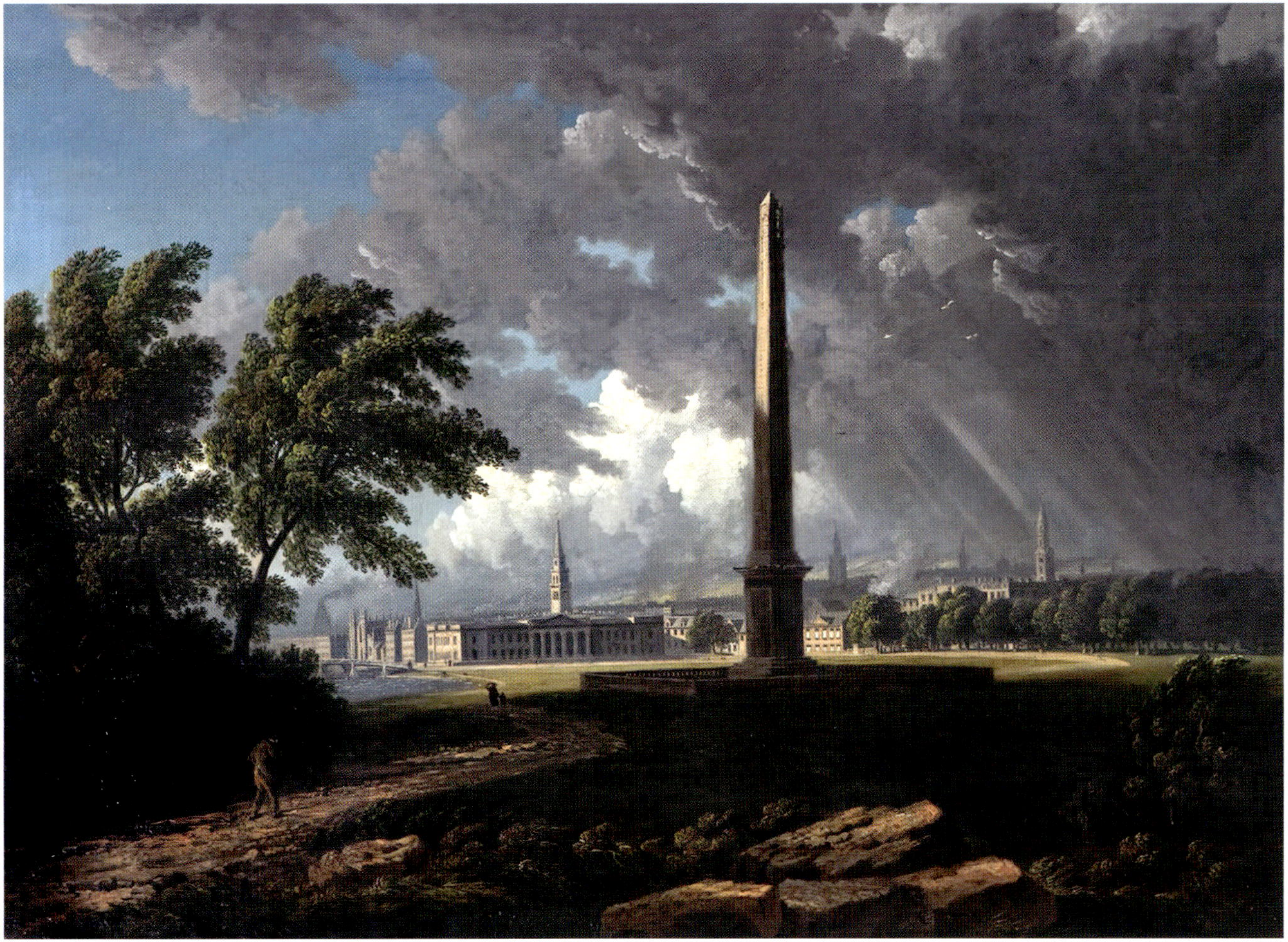

Glasgow Green and a Passing Storm, painting by John Knox around 1818. Nelson's Monument was erected in 1806.

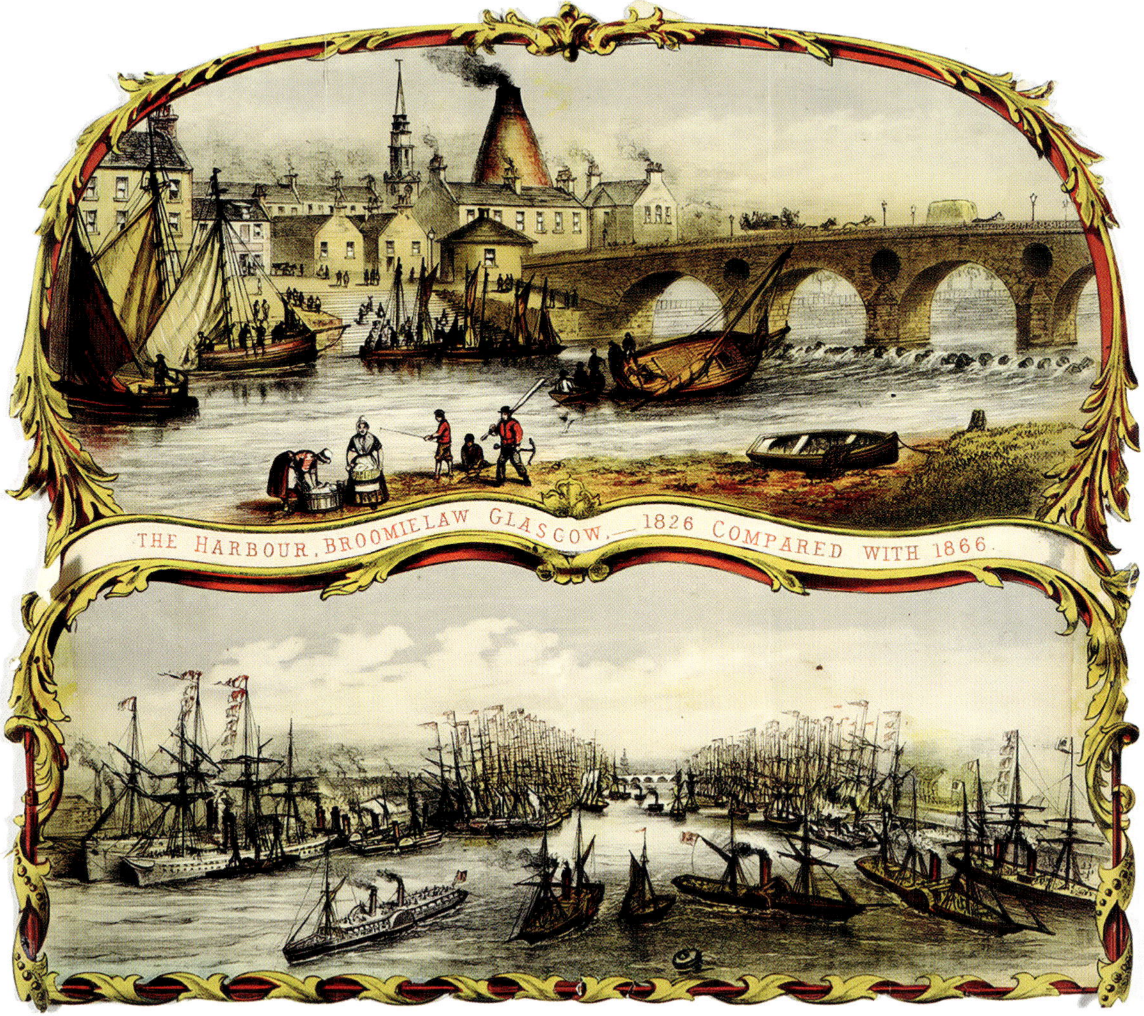

The Broomielaw in 1826 and in 1866.

Watt had defined power and enabled powered motion by his new steam engine. The Industrial Revolution had begun.

James Watt – 'early exercised in philosophic exercise, increased the power of Man, and rose to an eminent place amongst the most illustrious followers of science and the real benefactors of the World' – was laid to rest in Westminster Abbey.

At the end of the eighteenth century and into the early nineteenth century Britain's naval victories over France and its allies ensured the restoration of open seas and international trade, so important to Glasgow.

From 1806 a towing path, 20 feet wide, was built from Tradeston to Govan and on to Renfrew. This allowed horses, replacing men, to tow or track laden craft, where all else failed. This became a right of way but was extinguished in around 1913, to the relief of shipbuilders on the south side.

In 1812 Henry Bell's small paddle steamer, *Comet*, sailed from the city to Port Glasgow, demonstrating for the first time in Europe the power of steam-engine ships at sea. By 1820 Glasgow was the largest city in Scotland.

Soon the river at Glasgow Harbour had a depth of 17 feet at high tide, and increasing depth downstream. More depth to around 44 feet at high tide and regular width would be engineered. Steamships, dredgers and railway networks were opening up vast new horizons. The best and largest ships in the world would be built, from yachts and trawlers to cargo ships and passenger liners; from dredgers to battleships.

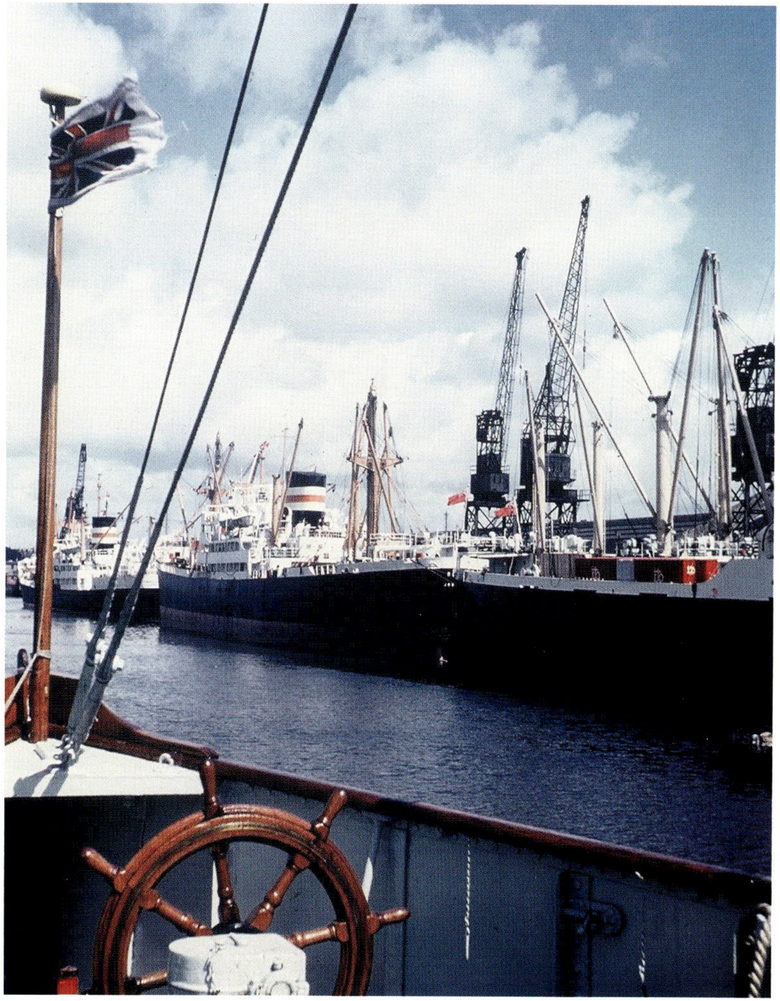

Sailing down the Clyde past City Line cargo passenger ships at Stobcross Quay, Queen's Dock, 1960s.

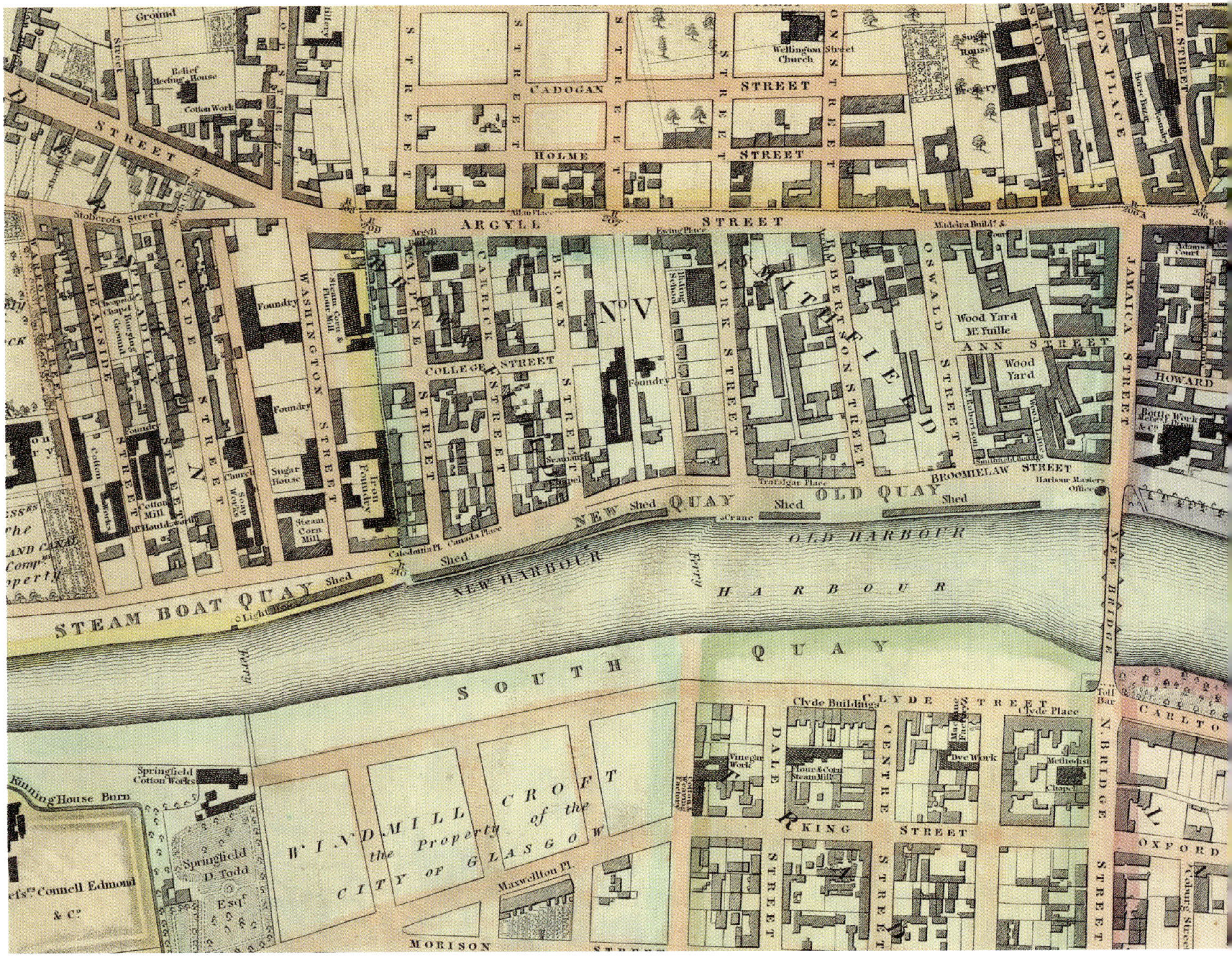

Relief Meeting House
Cotton Work
Wellington Church
CADOGAN
STREET
HOLME
STREET
ARGYLL
STREET
Stobcross Street
Argyll
Allan Place
Ewing Place
Madeira Build.
JAMAICA STREET
CHEAPSIDE
CLYDE STREET
WASHINGTON STREET
Foundry
Foundry
Sugar House
Steam Corn Mill
Iron Foundry
Soap Works
Church
Cotton Works
McHouldsworth
ALPINE STREET
CARRICK STREET
BROWN STREET
YORK STREET
COLLEGE STREET
No V
Foundry
ROBERTSON STREET
OSWALD STREET
BROOMIELAW STREET
ANN STREET
Wood Yard
Mr Tuille
Wood Yard
Harbour Masters Office
Trafalgar Place
HOWARD
Bottle Work
Shed
NEW QUAY
Shed
OLD QUAY
Shed
Crane
OLD HARBOUR
Caledonia Pl.
Canada Place
Shed
NEW HARBOUR
STEAM BOAT QUAY
Shed
Light
Ferry
Ferry
HARBOUR
SOUTH
QUAY
NEW BRIDGE
Toll Bar
Clyde Buildings
CLYDE STREET
Clyde Place
DALE STREET
CENTRE STREET
Vinegar Work
Flour & Corn Steam Mill
Dye Work
Methodist Chapel
KING STREET
N. BRIDGE STREET
CARLTON
OXFORD
Springfield Cotton Works
Kinning House Burn
Springfield D. Todd Esqr
Messrs Connell Edmond & Co
WINDMILL CROFT
the Property of the
CITY OF GLASGOW
Maxwellton Pl.
MORISON

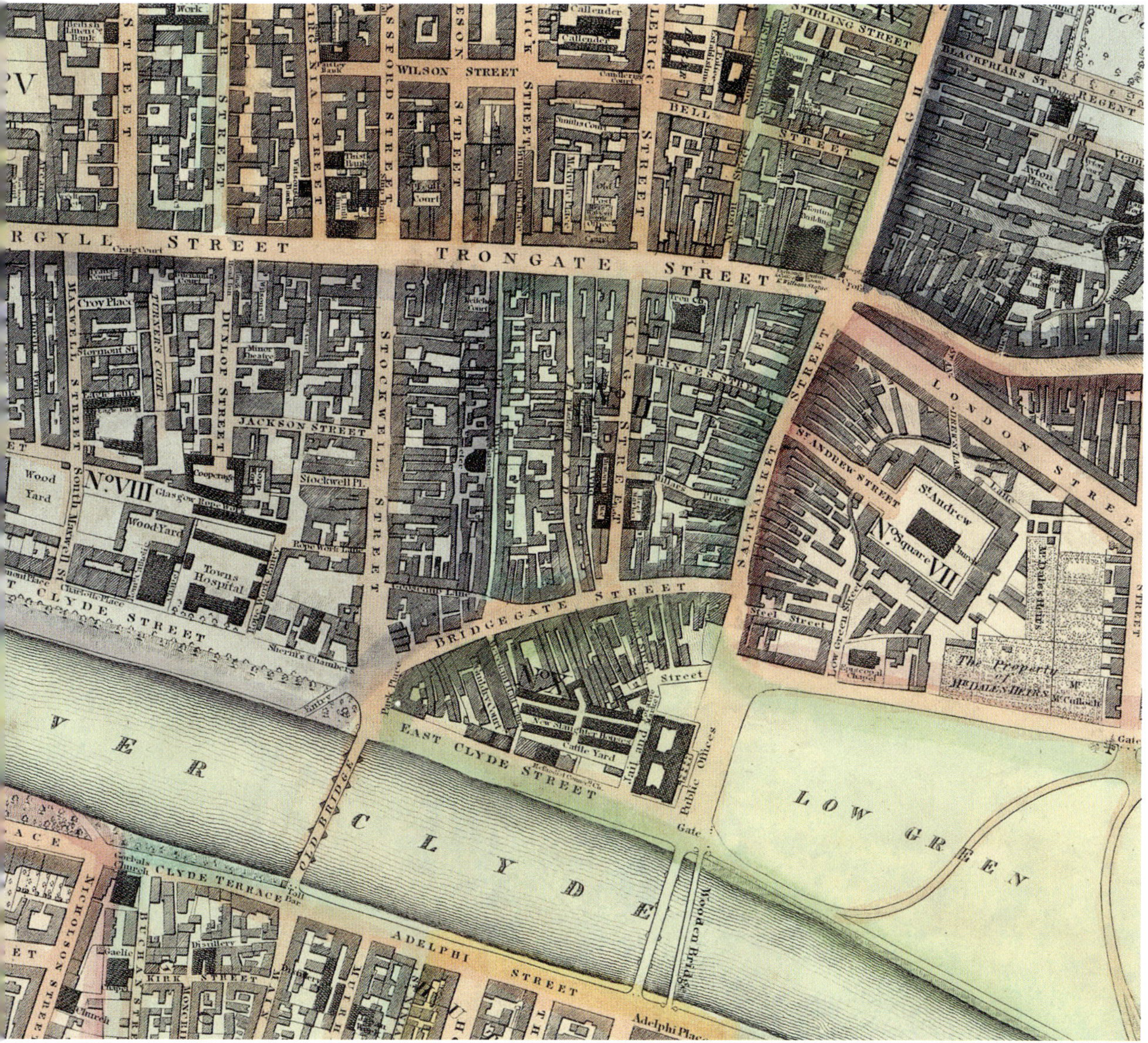

The riverside and quays in a Glasgow street map by David Smith, 1828.

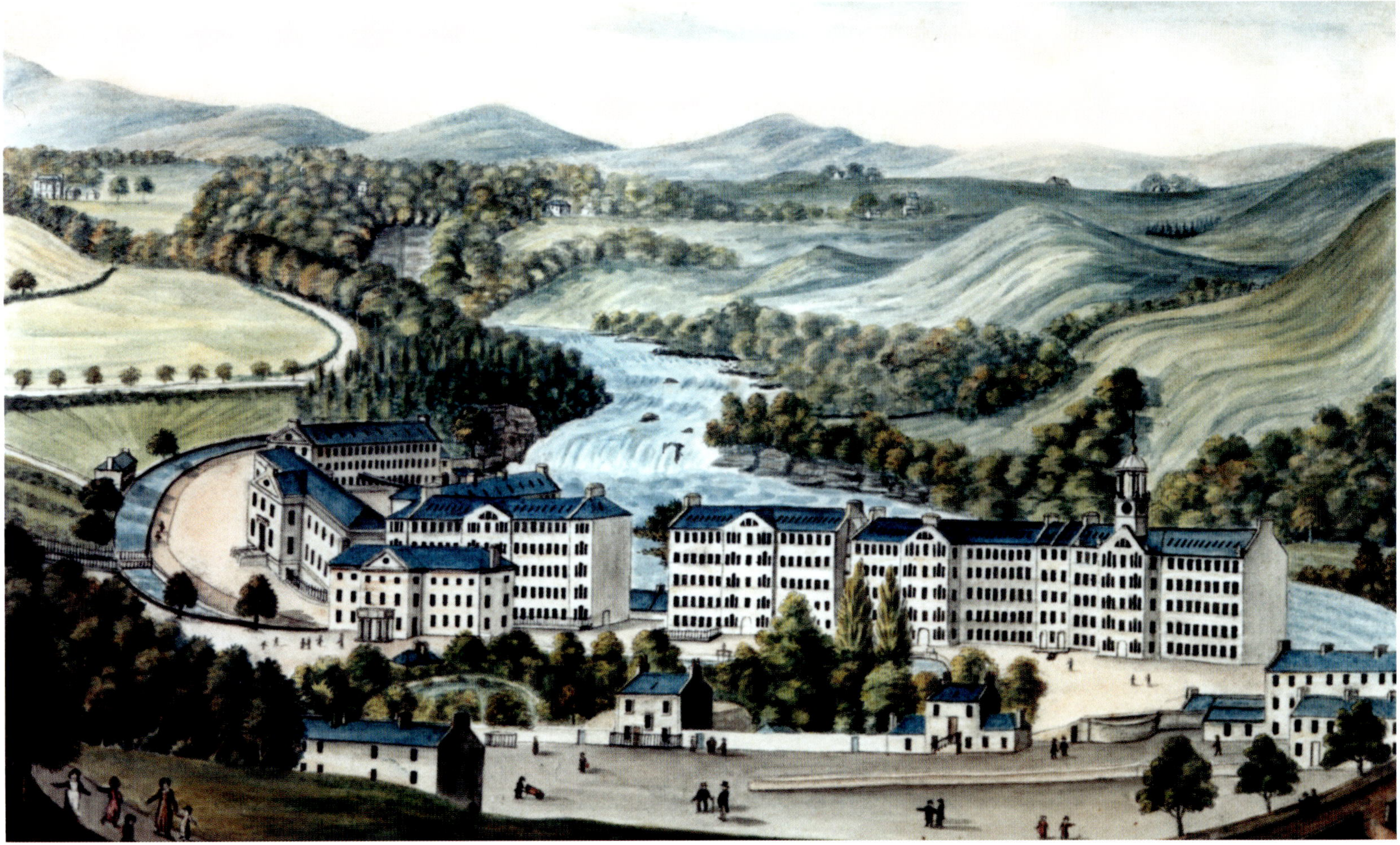

The cotton mill town of New Lanark harnessing the Clyde, a painting by John Winning, 1818. Over 130 mills were centred on Glasgow.

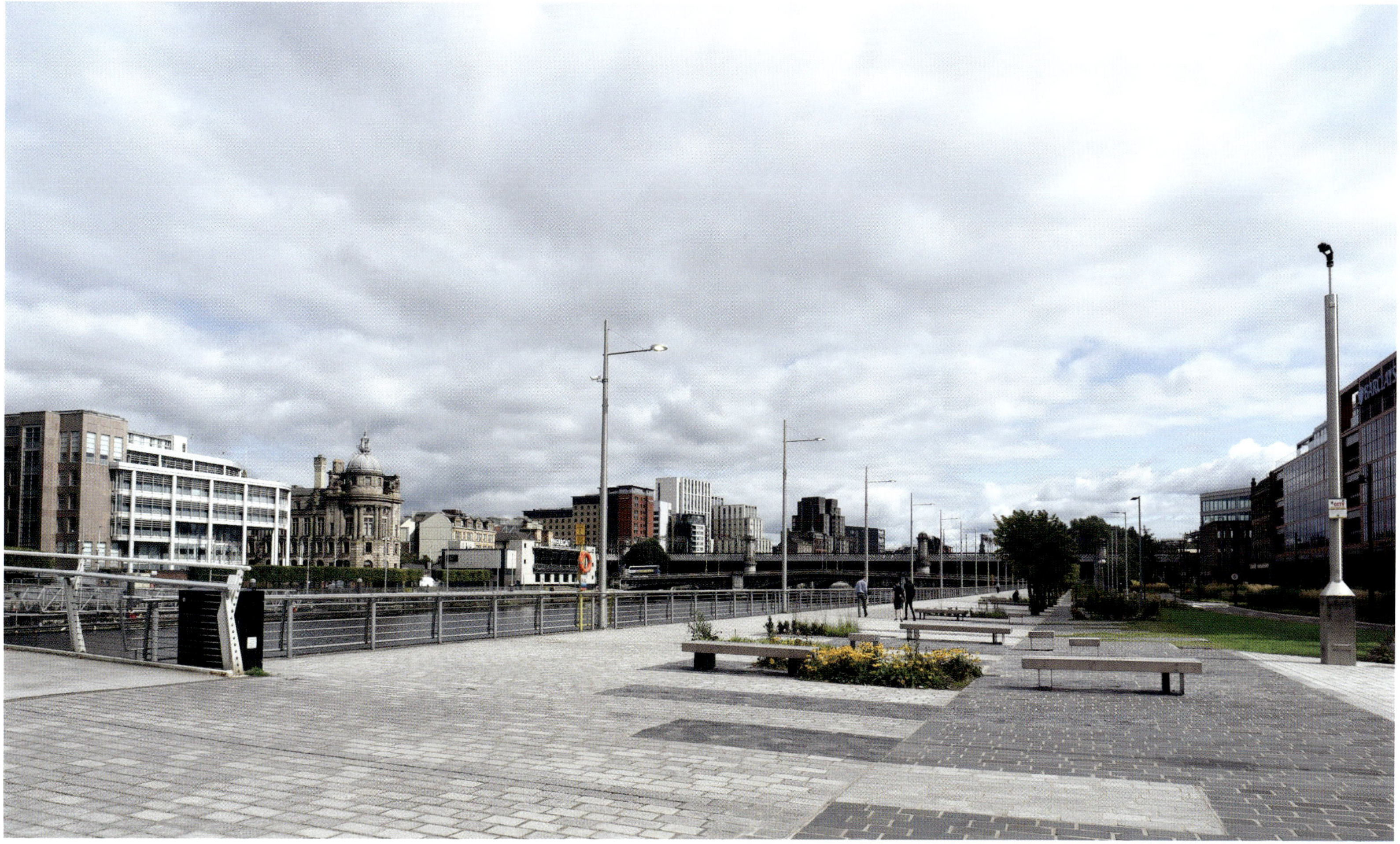

Tradeston looking towards the Broomielaw today.

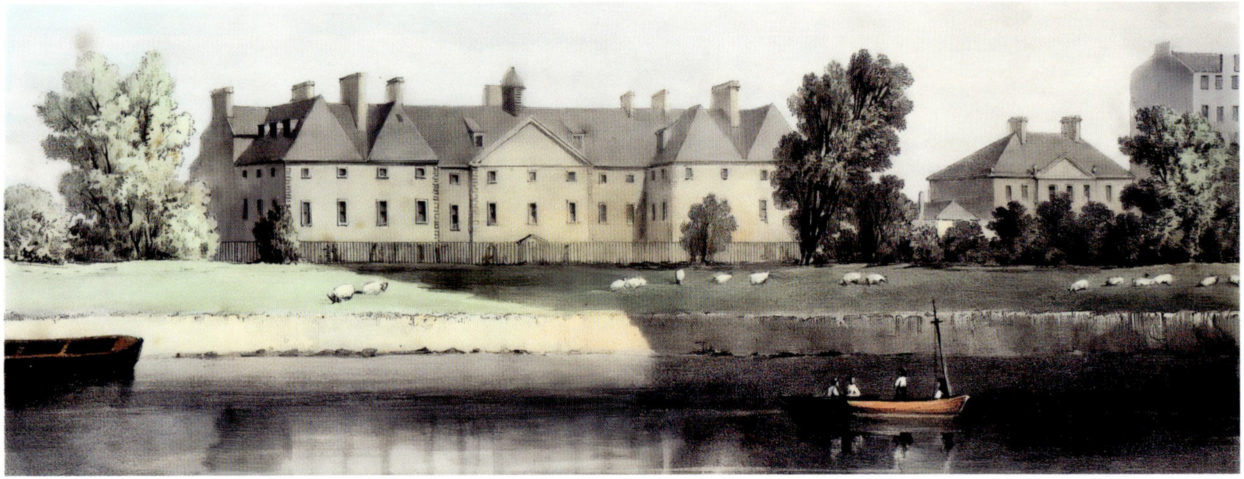

The Town's Hospital on Doocot Green, 1733, painting by Thomas Fairbairn. This was later fronted by Customshouse Quay.

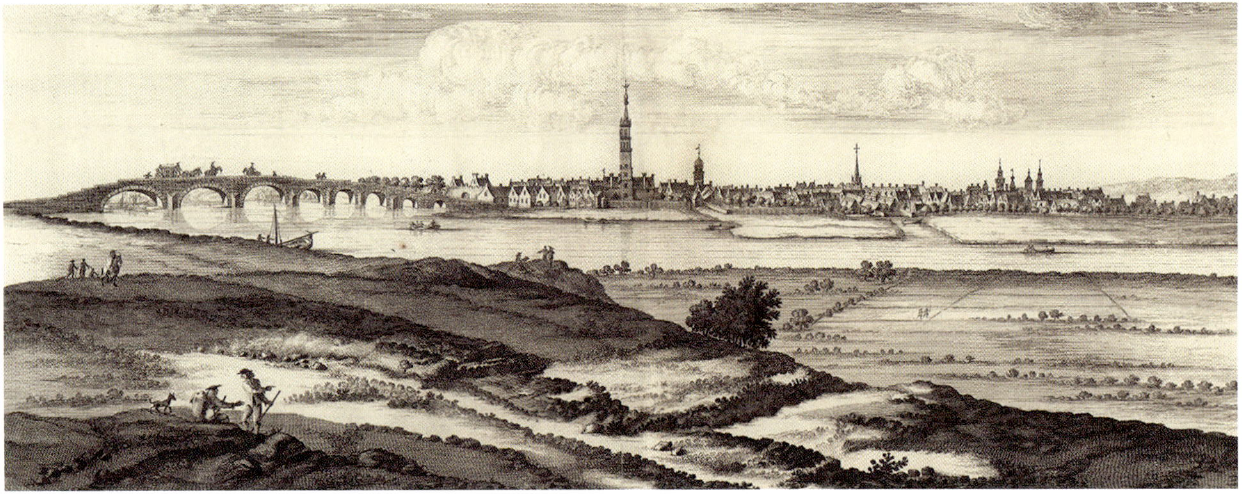

The Prospect of Ye Town of Glasgow from Ye South, drawing by John Slezer, 1693.

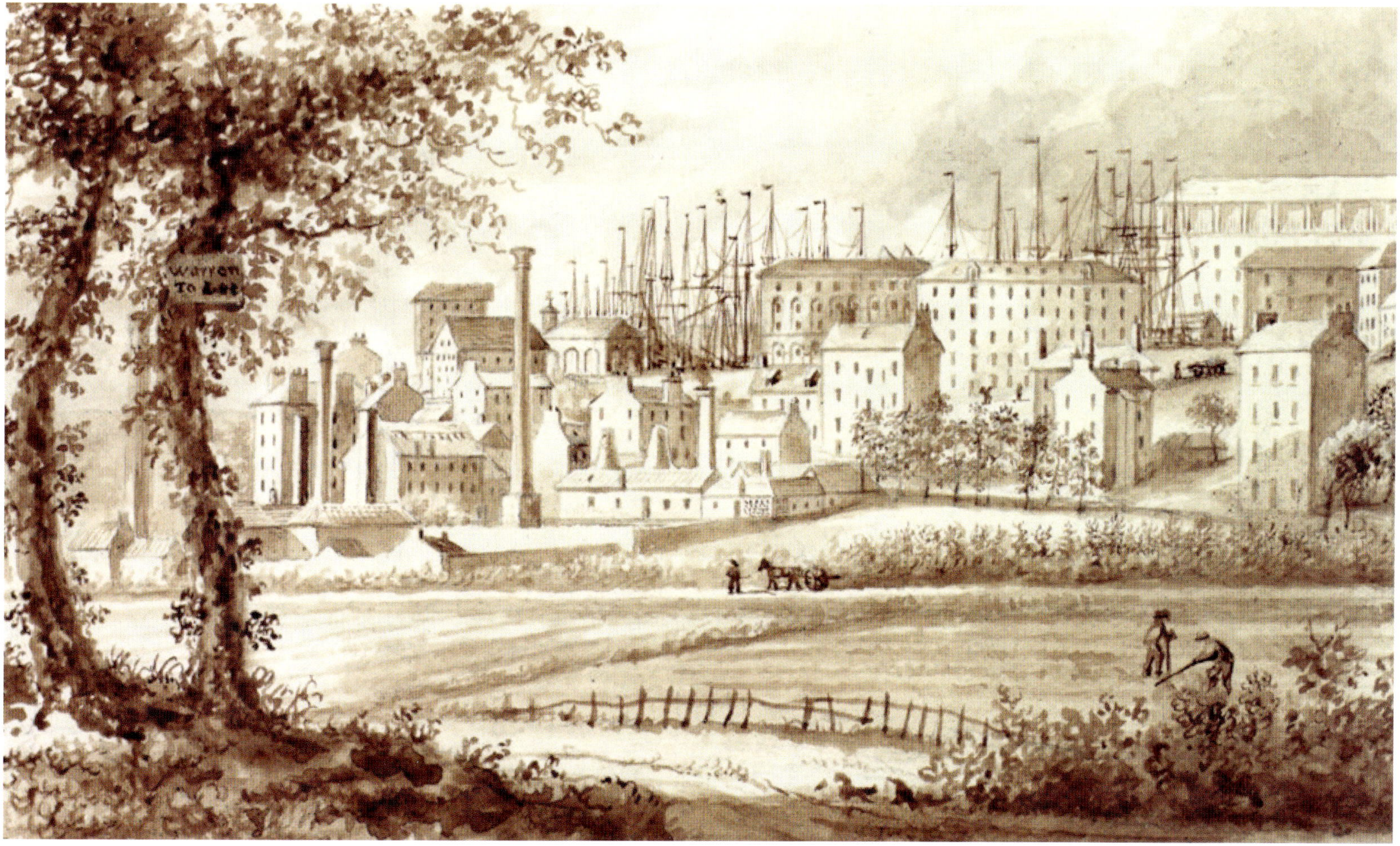

Port Dundas and its ships' masts, stores, sugar refinery, mills, foundries and houses. Drawing for James Hopkins, 1800s.

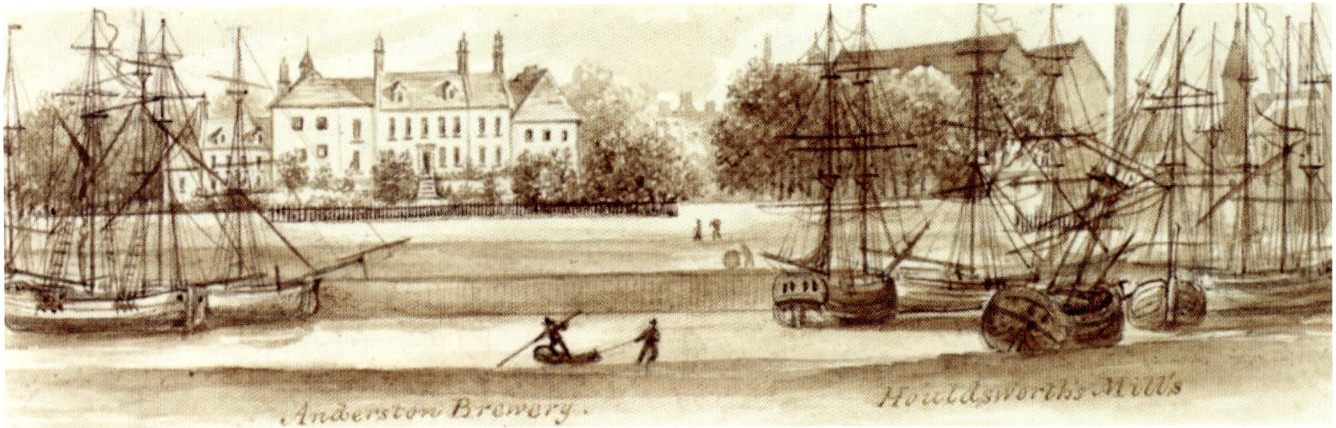

Riverside at Anderston. Drawing for James Hopkins, 1800s.

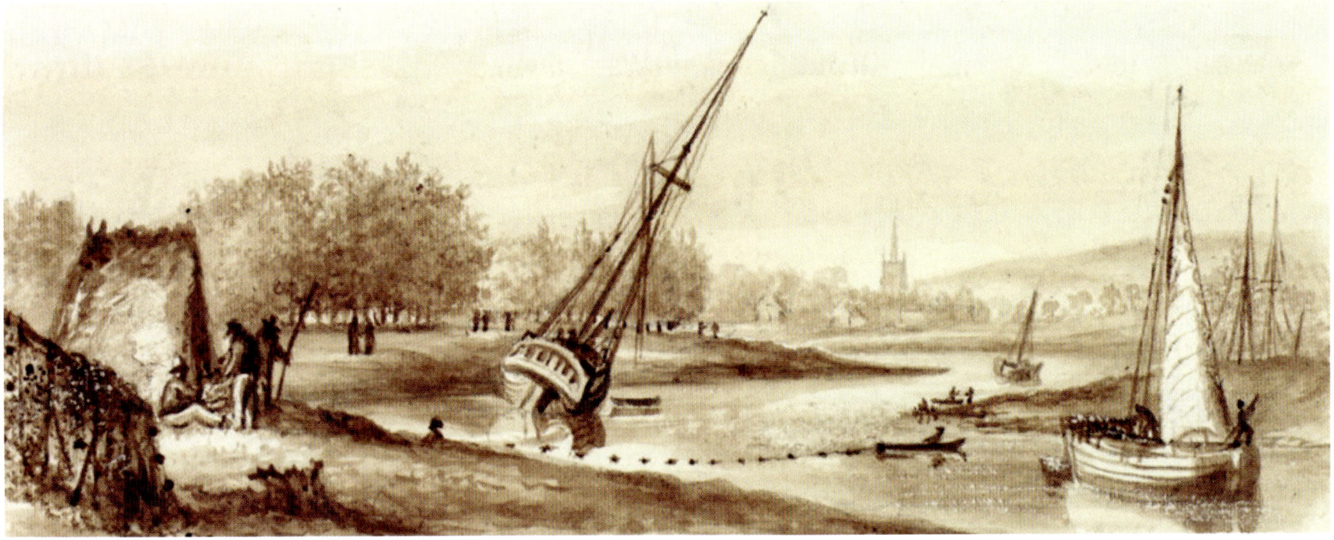

Riverside looking west to Govan. Drawing for James Hopkins, 1800s. Note the salmon net being set out.

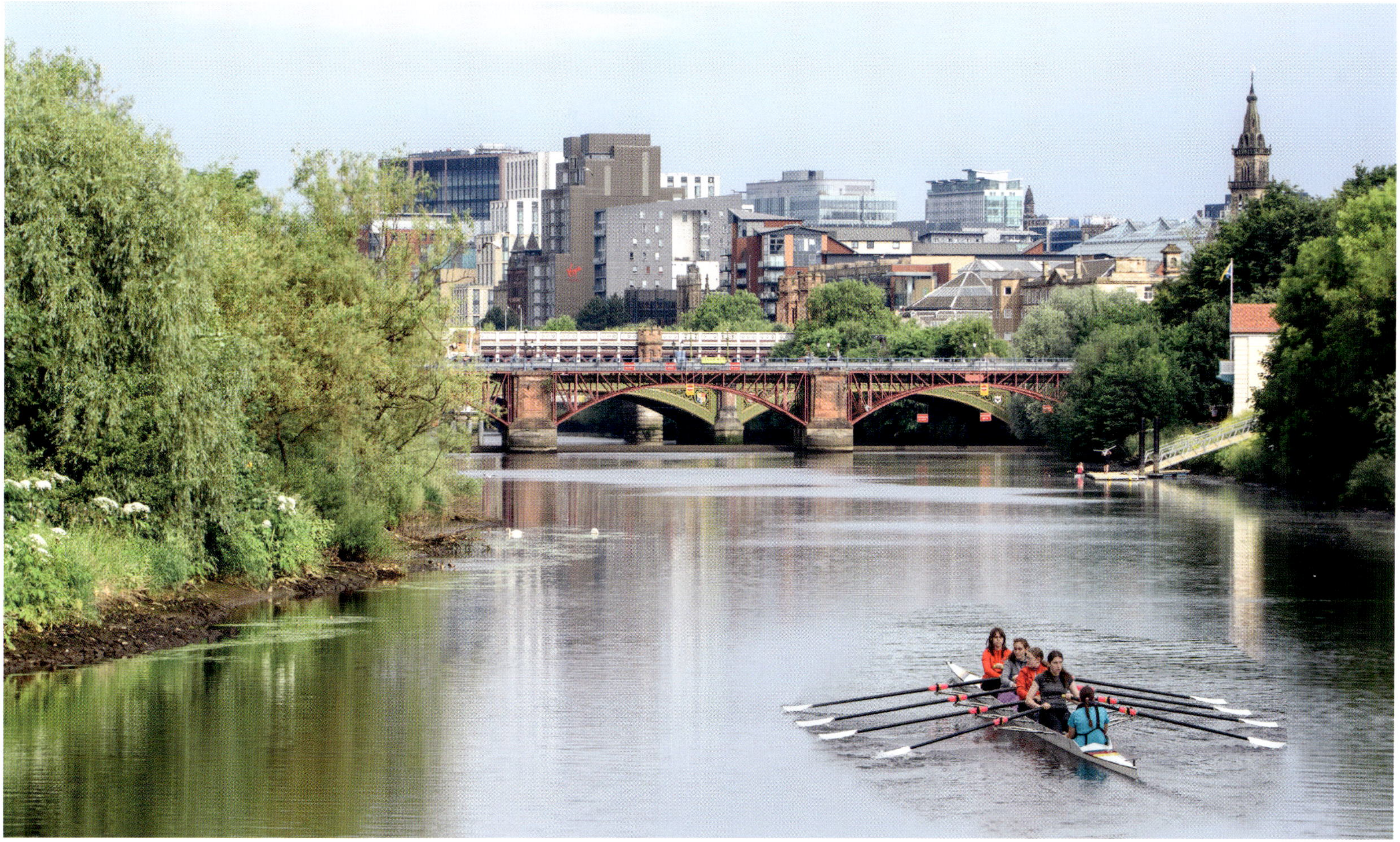

Rowing on the Clyde at Glasgow Green.

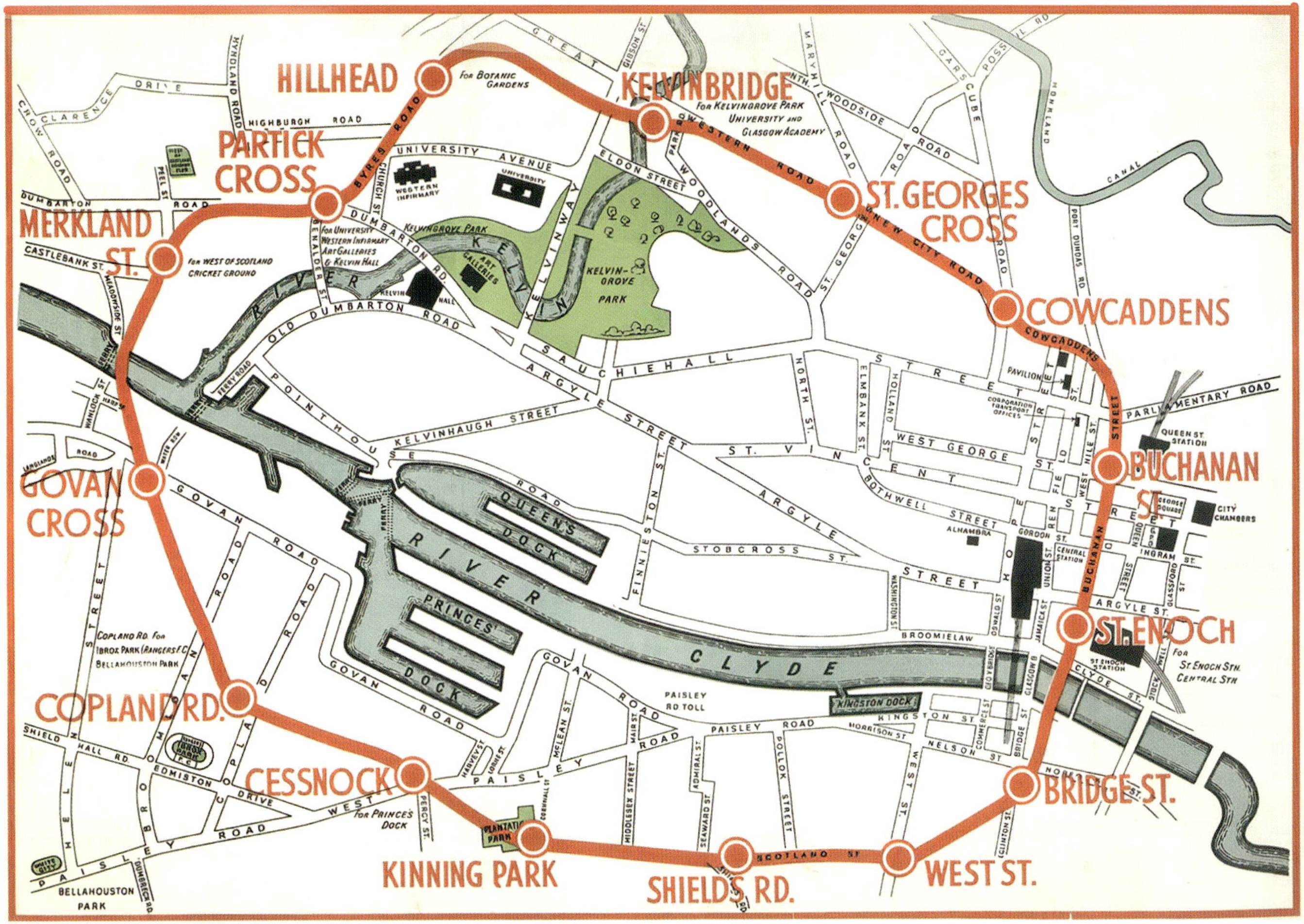

Glasgow District Subway connecting the city and the harbour.

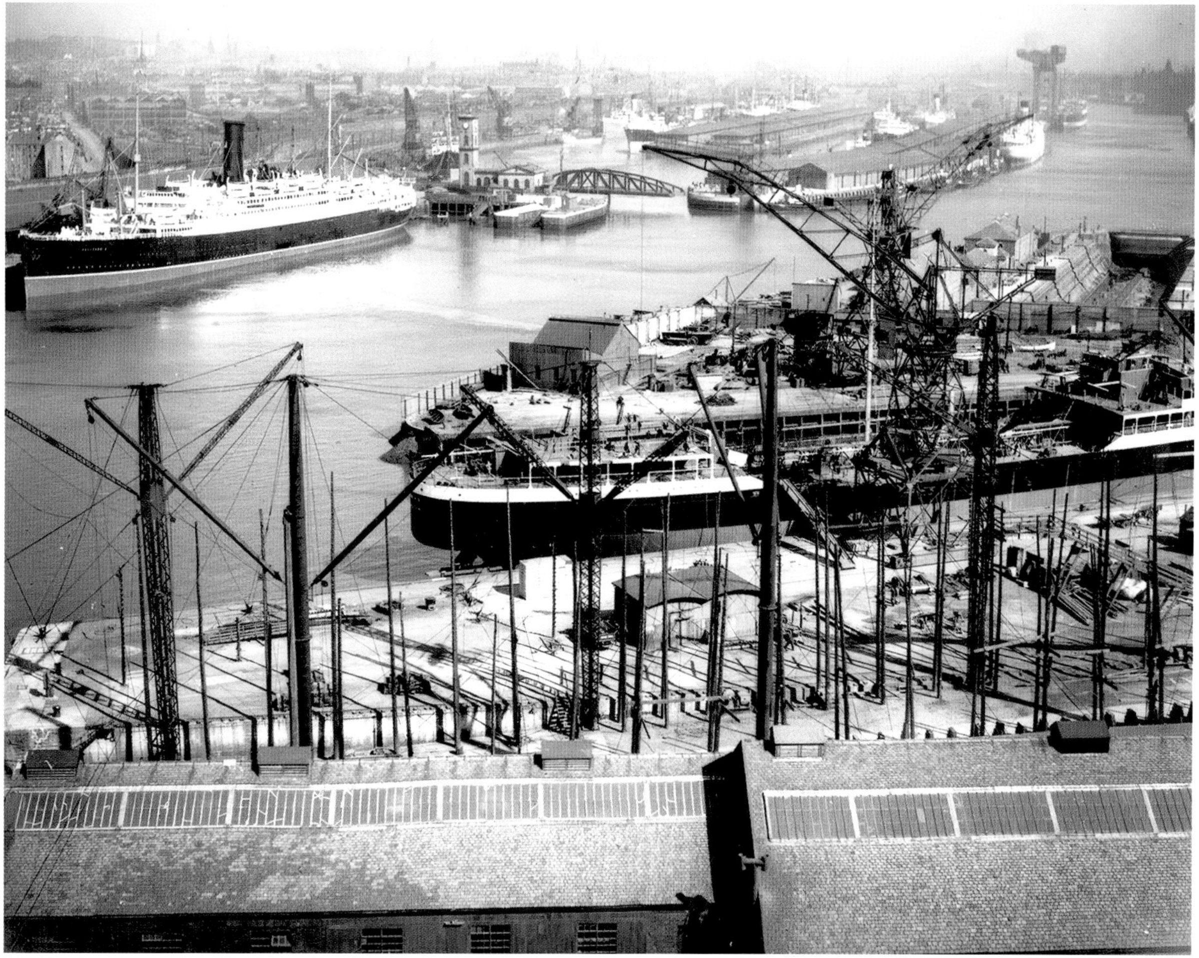

The view to Yorkhill Quay and Queen's Dock from Harland & Wolff's shipyard, Govan.

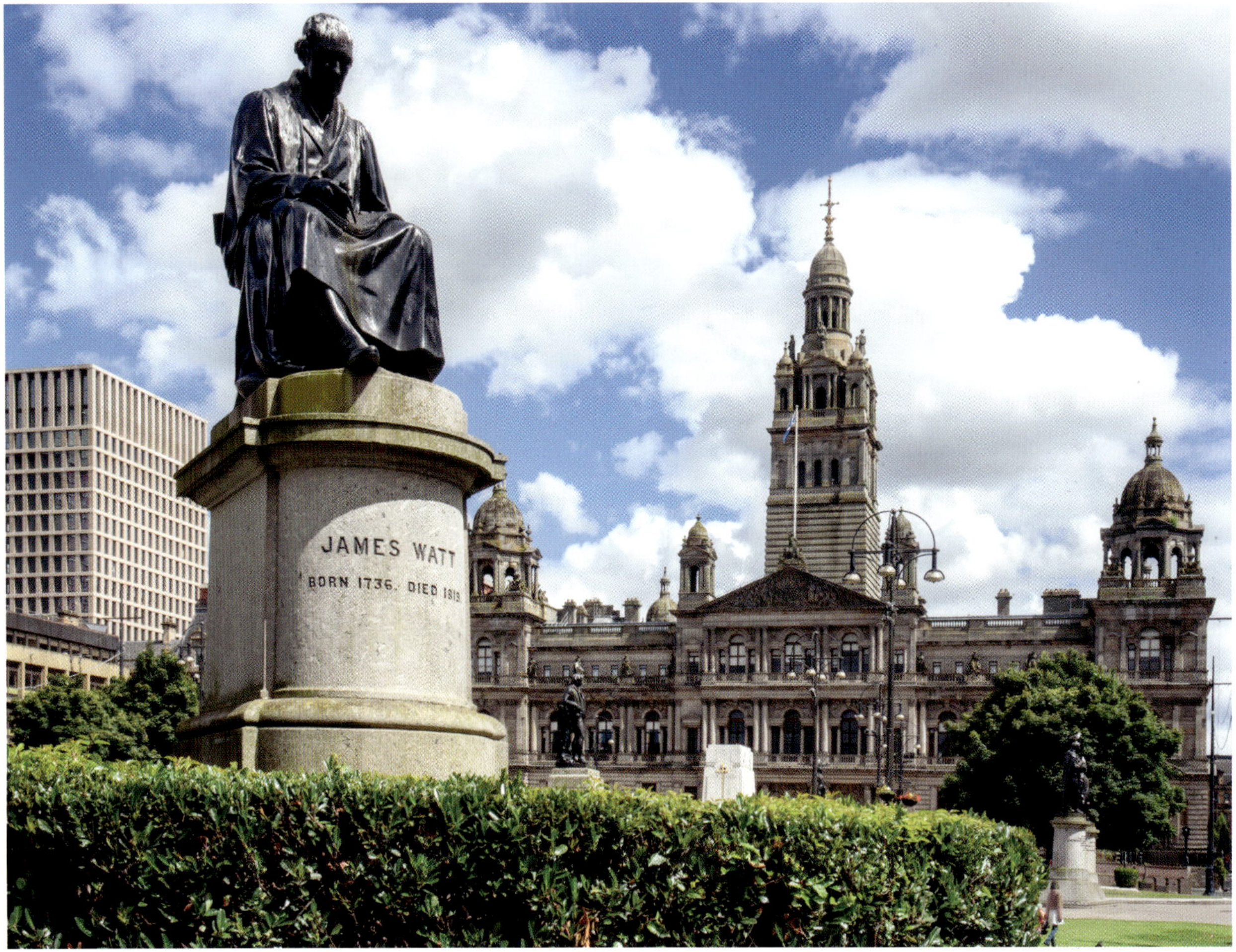

James Watt's statue in George Square, Glasgow, sculpted by Chantrey, 1832.

INVENTION AND INNOVATION

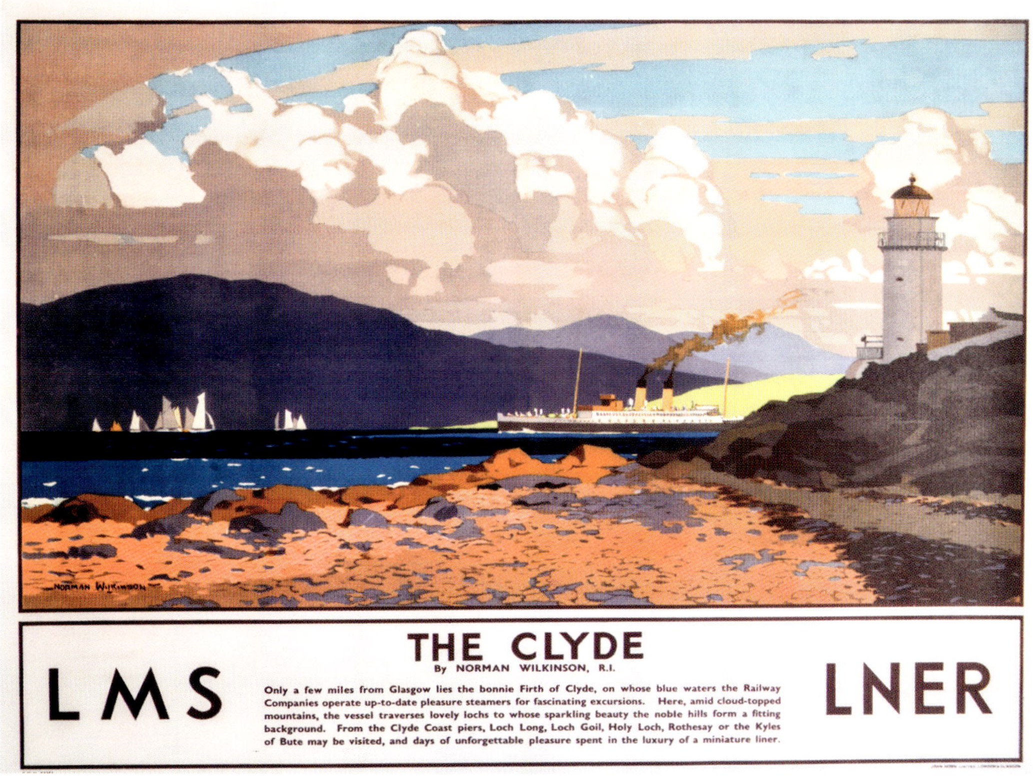

The Clyde, with Cloch Lighthouse in foreground, poster by Sir Norman Wilkinson.

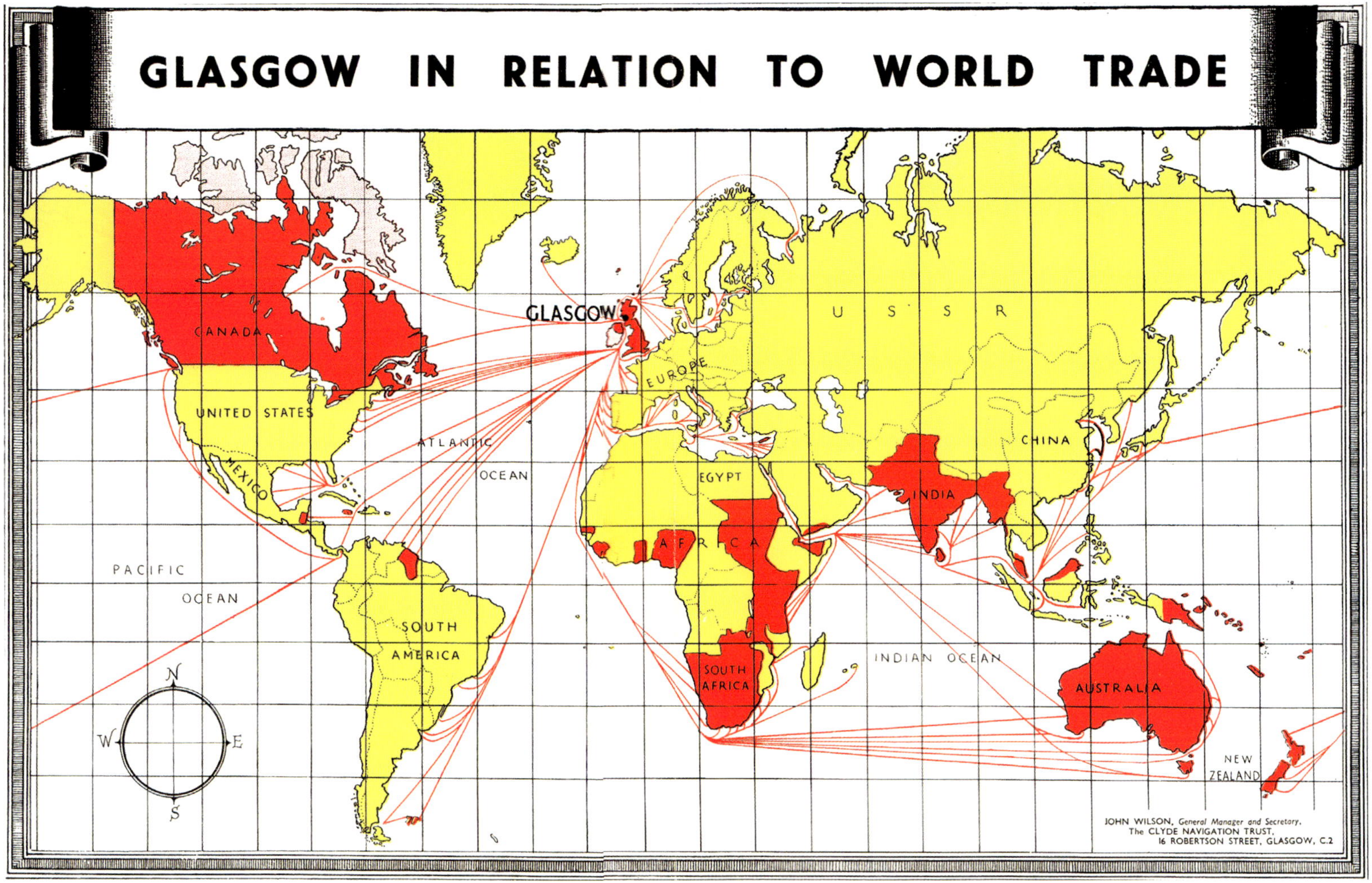
GLASGOW IN RELATION TO WORLD TRADE
GLASGOW
CANADA
UNITED STATES
MEXICO
ATLANTIC
OCEAN
PACIFIC
OCEAN
SOUTH
AMERICA
EUROPE
U S S R
EGYPT
AFRICA
SOUTH
AFRICA
INDIA
CHINA
INDIAN OCEAN
AUSTRALIA
NEW
ZEALAND
N
S
E
W
JOHN WILSON, General Manager and Secretary,
The CLYDE NAVIGATION TRUST,
16 ROBERTSON STREET, GLASGOW, C.2

The leading shipbuilder on the Clyde today is BAE Systems. It has two major sites: the modern production yard on the southside at Govan (formerly Fairfield's), and design and fitting out on the northside at Scotstoun (formerly Yarrow's). It also has the three Elderslie dry docks and a new Applied Shipbuilding Academy.

The main operational shipping dock in Glasgow today is the King George V Dock at Shieldhall, which opened in 1931, the first of three such angled docks planned at the time towards Braehead. This was the busiest and most important dock in Britain during the Second World War.

Economic Powerhouse

Vast seams of black-band ironstone were discovered under Glasgow and its eastern flanks by David Mushet in 1801. With rich and deep coal mining providing fuel for all and powering new engines, in 1828 J. B. Neilson invented his pre-heated 'hot-blast' furnaces and the city became a centre of iron manufacturing – the precursor of steel-making – and the leading centre building ships, making steam locomotives, wagons, carriages and railways. Its pig iron was also sold elsewhere in Britain and overseas. Of the new steamships from 1812, firstly using engines adapted from other uses, it was James Cook who invented and made the first marine engines specifically for ships from 1814 onwards. His works in Commerce Street became known as 'The College', where aspiring engineers learned the new sciences and then set up new businesses. The Napier family added more inventions.

In place of drawing iron rakes across the river by hand-capstans, or small hand- or horse-worked bucket dredgers, the necessary dredging of the Clyde now used steamships, mechanising conveyor buckets to depths and volumes of silt previously incapable of being reached; punts and hopper barges took the material away for use in-filling banks and creeks. Much later the material was deposited in the depths of the Firth. Manufacturing and trade expanded with each decade and the city's river became depths of 25–30 feet at low tide, to 44 feet at high water and greater when and where required.

In 1811 the tonnage of shipping owned or registered in Glasgow was 2,620 tons. By the end of that century it had increased to over 1.6 million tons. Of this, the top eight steamship firms owned 220 ships totalling around 395,000 tons. The city's top four sailing-ship firms had sixty-two ships totalling around 97,000 tons. Glasgow was a birthplace of global shipping companies including Cunard, Allan, British India, Union-Castle, City Line, Clan Line and many others.

The River Trust

The magistrates and city council acted as trustees for improving the 'Navigation of the River Clyde and Harbour of Glasgow'. Known as the River Trust, they had great vision, buying substantial lands on each side, encouraging developments and planning ahead for the increasing railway connections.

The Clyde Navigation Trust, formed in 1858 as its prosperous successor, continued to develop and expand the harbour and to make space for more shipping companies, shipbuilders and marine engineering firms. Its membership representing the city council, adjoining councils, shipping and port users, shipbuilders, the Merchants' House and the Trades House. Total imports and exports of freight reached 1.5 million tons a year in the mid-1860s and would increase to 10 million tons a year. The Trust headquarters building remains in Robertson Street at the Broomielaw.

In 1966, recognising the advent of containerisation – invented by Malcolm McLean of North Carolina, USA – and the much larger vessels requiring deeper water, the Trust became the Clydeport Authority, embracing Greenock Harbour Board and the Clyde Lighthouses Trust. Responsible now (and continuing) for 450 square miles of the sheltered waterways of the Firth of Clyde from Arran to Loch Long and Glasgow. It created the Hunterston deep-water facility. In the early 1990s the Authority was privatised, with a management and employee bid successfully acquiring it. In 2003 Peel Ports Ltd bought the shareholdings trading on the Stock Exchange. Peel Ports still has offices in Robertson Street, and in Greenock and Hunterston. The group bought Manchester Ship Canal in 1993 and Mersey Docks and Harbour in 2005.

Commerce and Innovation

The city and its neighbouring burghs of Govan and Partick led the way in shipbuilding and marine engineering including innovations in construction, propulsion, engine power, fuel efficiencies, metallurgy, navigation, communication, refrigeration – and modern air-conditioning for the benefit of people and freight. New firms emerged and grew, providing banking, legal services, insurance and shipbroking services; chandlery; victualling; coal and oil bunkering; stevedoring and master porterage employing teams of dockers; rail transport and road haulage.

Employees of the shippers, shipbuilders, engineering works, steel works and service suppliers were encouraged to learn and develop skills by apprenticeships in design, production, commerce, trade and navigation and by attending night school, mechanics' institutes and colleges. From these arose the Royal Technical College, the first of its type anywhere, which is today's Strathclyde University, the first technological university in Britain.

Engineering and Naval Architecture

In 1840 Glasgow University was the first in Britain to create a Chair of Civil Engineering, endowed by Queen Victoria (and later enhanced by Mrs Isabella Elder of Fairfield's). From 1855 its second holder, Professor William Macquorn Rankine, mathematician and scientist, also excelled in mechanical engineering, modern thermodynamics and metallurgy. He inspired and advised shipbuilders of the latest research and advances, helping them to conquer international markets. He made naval architecture into an engineering science. The doyen of scientists, Lord Kelvin, set out the laws of thermodynamics, invented the transatlantic telegraph cable and his Kelvin mariner's compass was adopted universally. The Institution of Engineers and Shipbuilders in Scotland was formed in 1857, with Rankine as founding president, and continues today. (Its splendid home in Elmbank Crescent was built in 1907 and became the home of Scottish Opera some sixty years later.)

In 1883, thanks to the further generosity of Mrs Isabella Elder, a Chair of Naval Architecture – the first in the world – was established at Glasgow University, attracting students and professors from far afield and ensuring the pre-eminence of Clyde shipbuilding and engineering.

Today the Chair is a central part of the Naval Architecture, Ocean & Marine Engineering faculty at Strathclyde University and continues to draw students from around the world.

Ship Management

Although Britain's ship-owning companies have given way to global ownerships, the importance of ship management companies has grown. British and international ship management companies in Glasgow have significant reach on behalf of global client companies and their maritime trading. They employ tens of thousands of officers, crew and specialists in the technical management, navigation and services for fleets worldwide involved in shipping, offshore and defence industries.

Glasgow continues its long tradition in educating and training more nautical students than any other city in the United Kingdom. From its advanced Riverside Campus, the City of Glasgow College each year produces almost 40 per cent of all graduate deck officers and marine engineers in Britain, many coming from overseas countries.

Transits and Cranes

Miles and miles of large transit sheds with handling services were added to the quays as the harbour grew. Over half were single storey, and the rest double storey. Once berthed and to meet demand, shipowners required a fast turnround, up to two or three days, to fully discharge cargoes to awaiting railway waggons or into

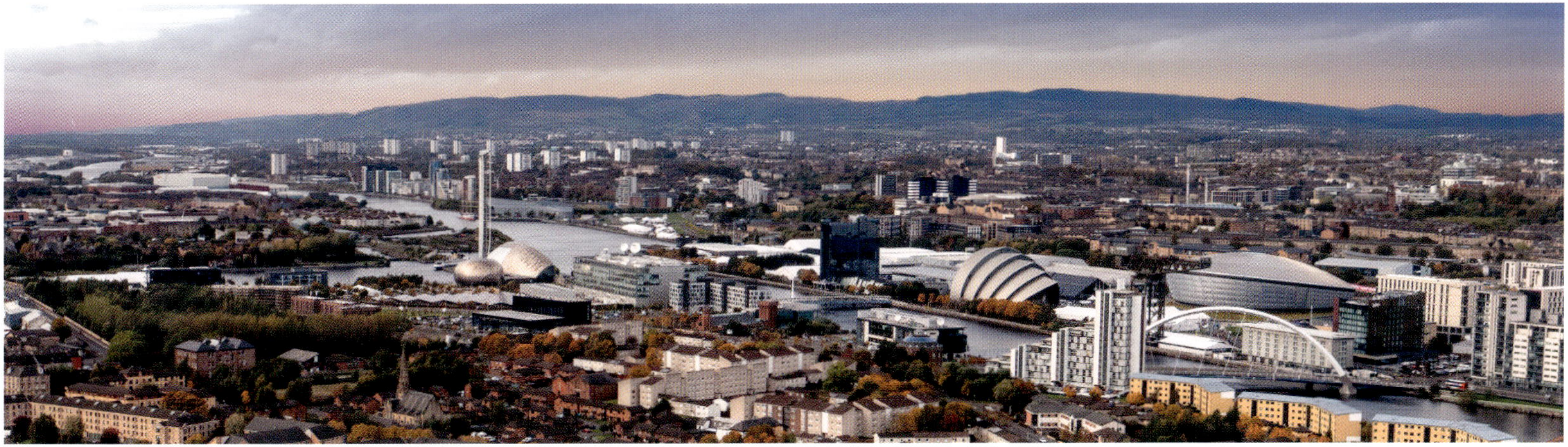

The river panorama today.

the sheds for road hauliers to collect. Likewise, for loading anew. Major transit depots opened at Deanside and Braehead, close to the emerging new Hillington Industrial Estate and the coming M8 motorway.

Cranes to help lifting freight started as shearlegs with pulleys, rising to become powered cantilevers. In due course, the extensive harbour worked with over 170 cranes, including hoists and a major floating crane. Some were hydraulic or steam cranes but most were electrical travelling cranes.

Each of the shipyards had its forest of giant cranes reaching the skies, Fairfield's having the largest in the world at the time. Crane builders used include: Sir William Arrol & Co. of global fame for cranes, bridges and power stations, Babcock & Wilcox, P. & W. McLellan, Butters Bros, George Russell, Sir W. G. Armstrong & Co., Cowans Sheldon, Clyde Cranes, Paterson Hughes and J. H. Carruthers.

Up, Down, Across and Under

For getting to work or visiting, down from Jamaica Bridge (also known as Glasgow Bridge), you could cross the Clyde by rowing-boat ferries, using stairways cut in the quays. From 1865 the Trust introduced engined ferries which directly crossed at seven places. For the growing city, from 1884 the Trust added its fleet of twelve fast and comfortable river ferries, all named 'Clutha', which plied up and down the 3 miles from Victoria Bridge at Stockwell Street to Whiteinch. Each boat accommodated about 200 people and these attracted 3 million passengers a year. Ten landing stages alternatively placed suited the needs of both sides of the river, despite the water odours. The Cluthas (partly competing with the Subway) stopped when Glasgow's tramway services were electrified in around 1900, these serving a much wider metropolis – just slighter smaller than

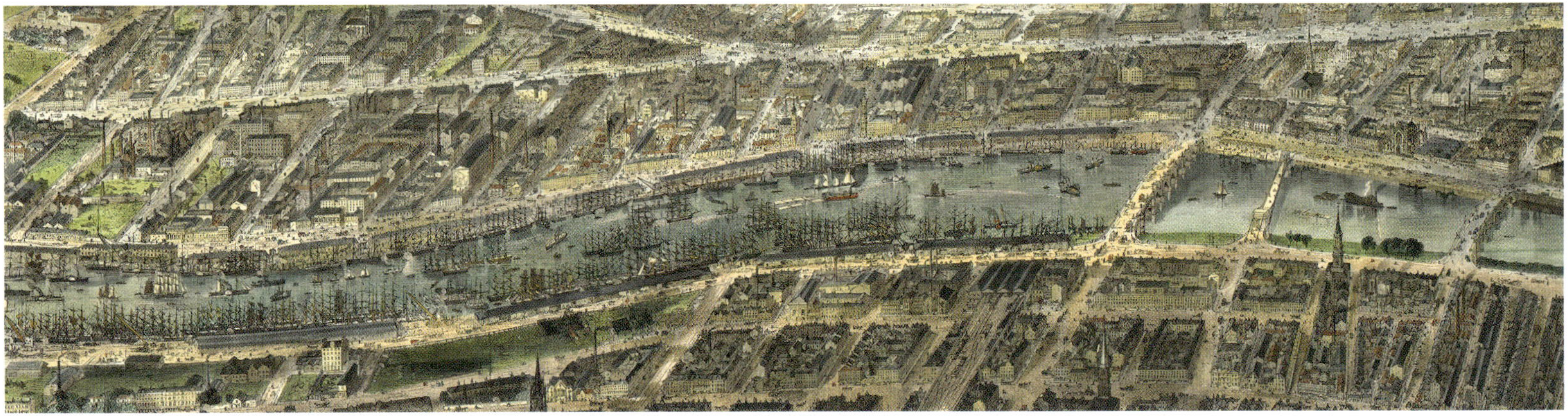

A busy river scene from Sulman's *Bird's-Eye View of Glasgow*, 1864.

London's network. The criss-cross passenger ferries continued night and day and were joined by vehicular ferries with elevating decks that adjusted to the tidal heights.

You could travel under the Clyde, firstly in 1895, thanks to the Glasgow Harbour Tunnel, which was for pedestrians and vehicles. It comprised three tunnels. Its access rotundas on both sides at Finnieston – once holding hydraulic lifts and stairs – are now used as restaurants and offices. Glasgow District Subway opened in 1896 – the third subway after London and Budapest – linking districts on both sides and the city centre, with trains every few minutes and no need for timetables. Much later, in 1964, the deeper Clyde Tunnel at Whiteinch opened for road traffic.

The city centre's King George V bridge was opened in 1927, the same year as the Kelvin Hall. Twenty years later, planning got underway for the M8 motorway with its Kingston Bridge opening in 1970, high above the river to allow shipping underneath. Smaller bridges have been added since.

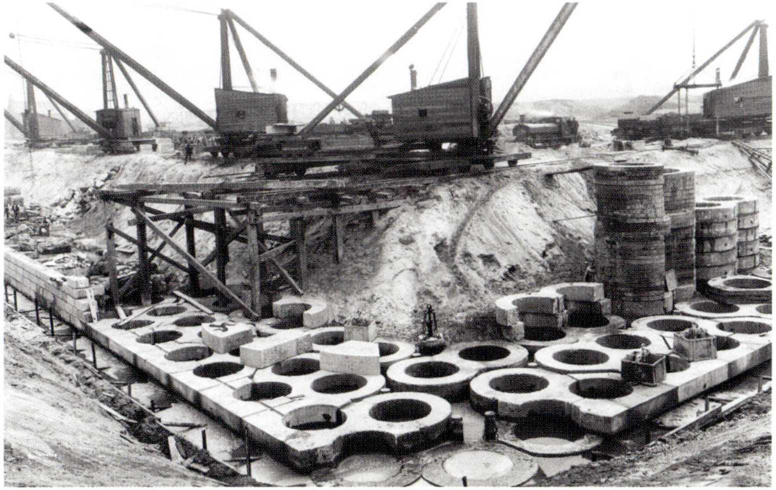

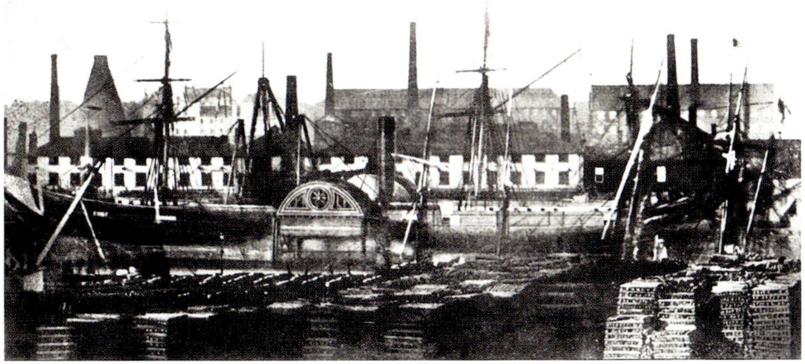

Above: Prince's Dock under construction in the 1890s.

Right: A document stamp of the Glasgow Terminus and Glasgow Harbour Railway Company, 1846.

Left: Napier's fitting-out dock at Lancefield Quay, with the Verreville Pottery beyond, 1853.

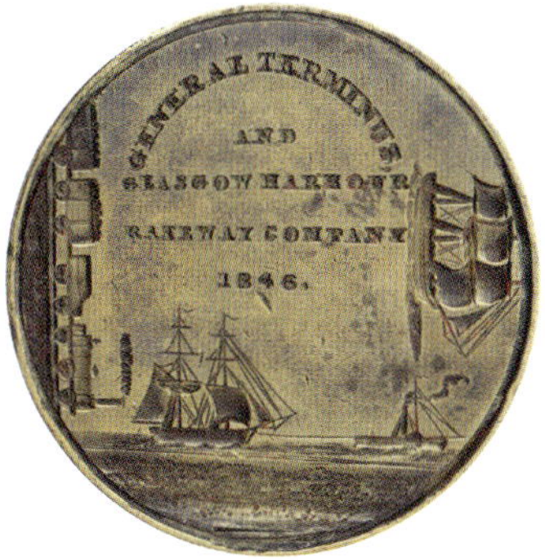

Twelve Miles and More

Eventually the harbour totalled 12 miles of quays and docks, with berthing for some 174 ships, large and small, mercantile and naval. Added to this were forty-five major building berths in the shipyards on the north side and thirty-two major building berths on the south side, making a total of seventy-seven in shipyards.

Northside of the river could berth ninety ships from Custom House Quay, Broomielaw Quay, Anderston Quay, Lancefield Quay, Finnieston Quay, Stobcross Quay; Queen's Dock, completed in 1880; Yorkhill Quay and Basin and Meadowside Granary. The latter comprised four linked buildings, the first by 1913, the second in 1938, the third in 1960 and the fourth added in 1967. In total these could hold 176,000 tons of grain and formed one of the largest facilities in Europe. Each year 600,000 tons of grain from North America and Australia was received for the Scotch whisky industry. Merklands was used for cattle, sheep, horses, pigs later fruit. Rothesay Dock at Clydebank, opening in 1907, completed the northside quays.

Southside of the river could berth eighty-four ships from Clyde Place Quay (to be renamed Bridge Wharf) and Windmillcroft Quay; Kingston Dock, opening in 1867; Springfield Quay and General Terminus Quay; Mavisbank Quay and Plantation Quay; Prince's Dock, opening in 1897, and its Timber Depot; Shieldhall Wharf and Timber Depot; King George V Dock, opening in 1931; Braehead Repair Berths and Renfrew Harbour.

Glasgow created eleven new dry docks, more correctly called graving docks, including its pioneering one in Port Glasgow in 1762. Four were patent slip docks, the first established in 1820. A dry dock and a patent slip were built, in 1858 and 1866 respectively, at Meadowside on the north-west bank where the Kelvin joins the Clyde, known later as D. & W. Henderson's yard. The Hendersons also formed the Anchor Line, and a son, Lieutenant General Sir David Henderson, founded the Royal Flying Corps, the forerunner of the Royal Air Force. Other shipowners, shipbuilding and engineering firms successfully demanded that the Trust build public dry docks. Three were formed in Govan, firstly in 1875, secondly in 1886 and thirdly the largest at 880 feet long in 1898. Three more privately owned dry docks opened between 1904 and 1965 west of Scotstoun, named Elderslie, and continue in use. The Trust planned a dry dock at Braehead/Renfrew, the Admiralty requiring it be 1,000 feet long, which would have made it the largest in the world, but the recession of the 1920s put an end to that plan.

The main contractors building quays and docks include Morrison & Mason Ltd (who also built the City Chambers and more), followed by Sir Robert McAlpine & Sons Ltd and Shanks & McEwan Ltd.

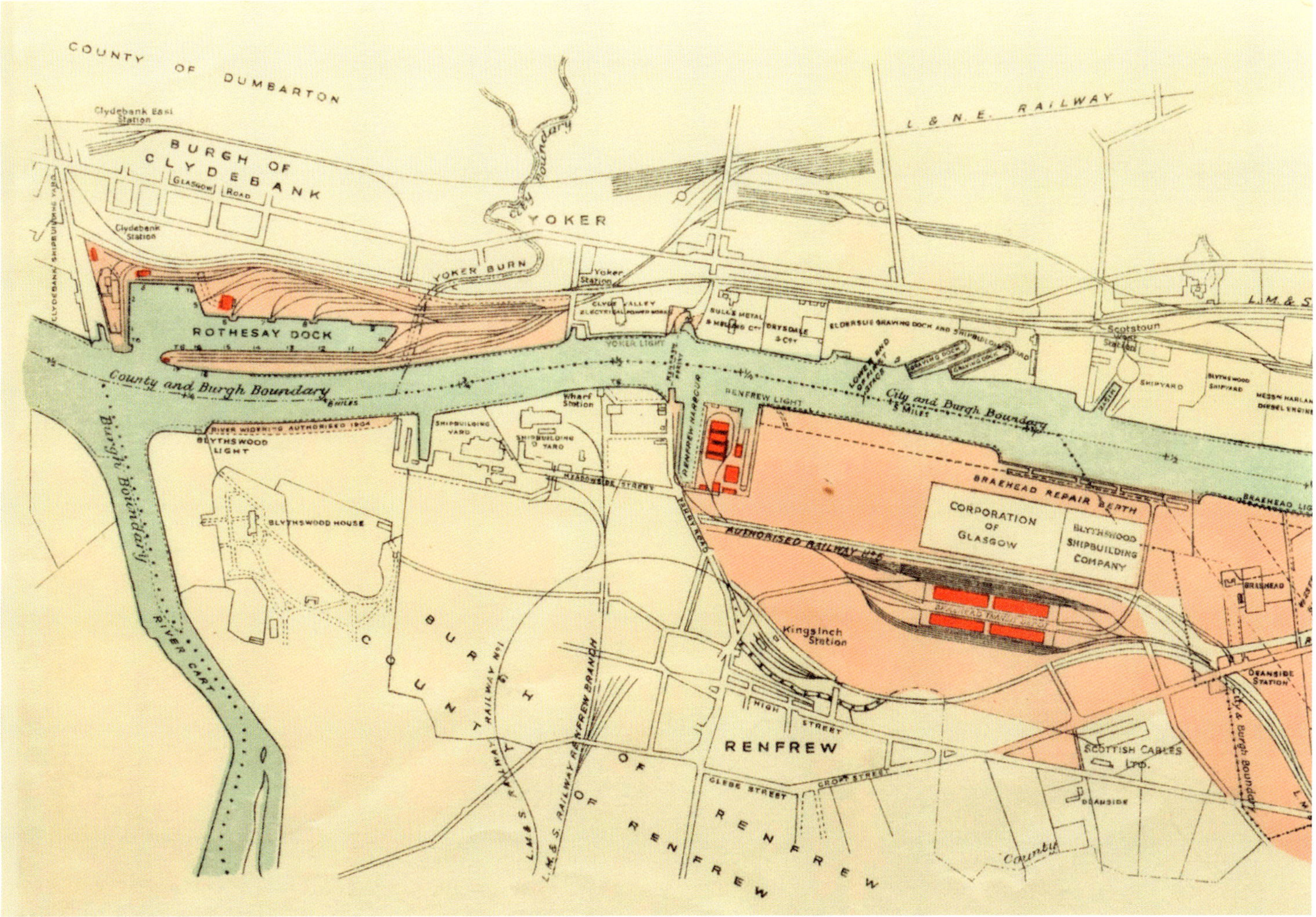

Following pages: details from the map of the River Clyde from Glasgow to Clydebank (above), 1945, published by Clyde Navigation Trust.

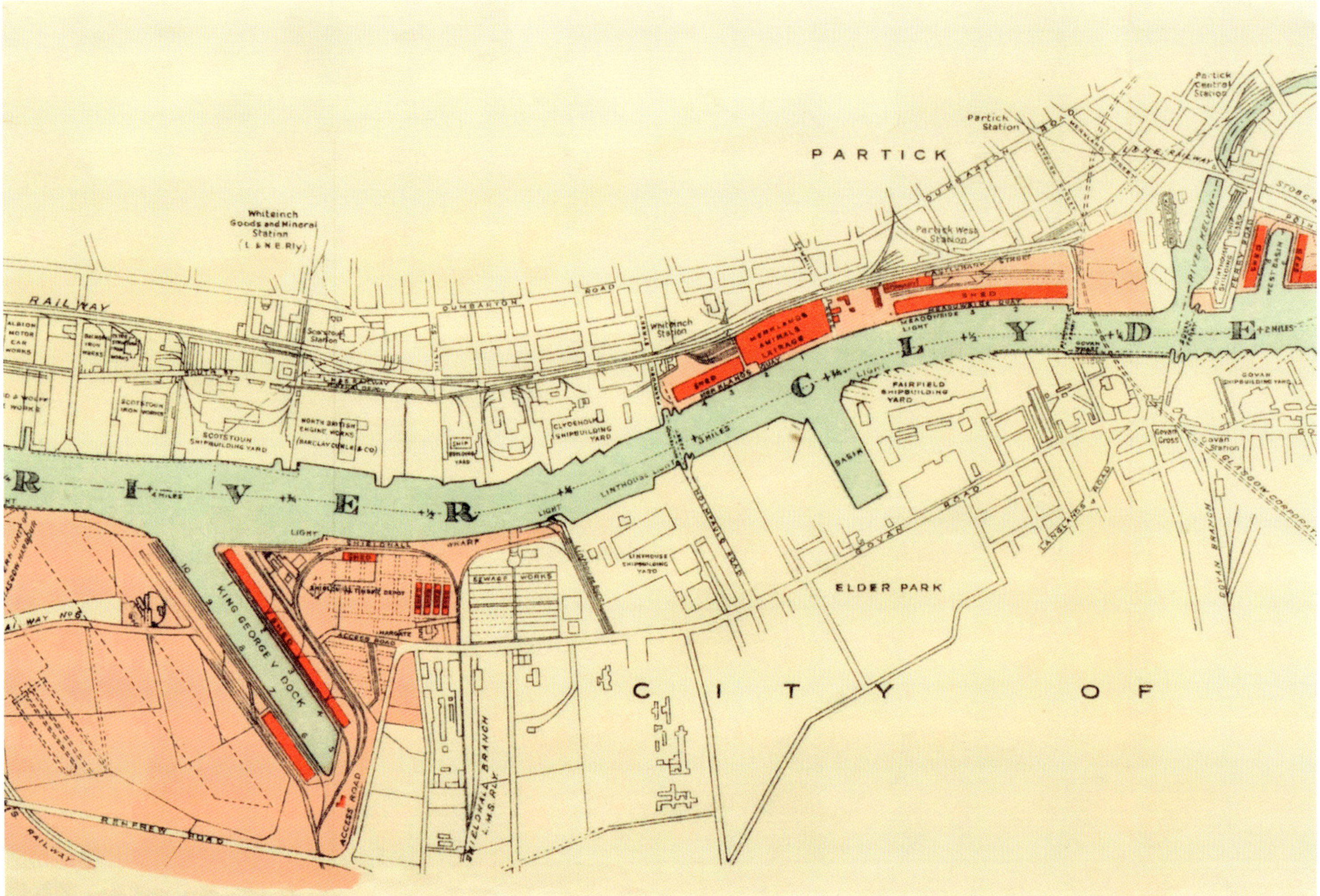
PARTICK
Partick Central Station
Partick Station
Partick West Station
Whiteinch Goods and Mineral Station (L & N E Rly)
Whiteinch Station
Scotstoun Station
DUMBARTON ROAD
RAILWAY
ALBION MOTOR CAR WORKS
SCOTSTOUN IRON WORKS
SCOTSTOUN SHIPBUILDING YARD
NORTH BRITISH ENGINE WORKS (BARCLAY CURLE & CO)
CLYDEHOLM SHIPBUILDING YARD
MEADOWSIDE QUAY
MEIKLEWOOD ANIMALS LAIRAGE
SHED
FAIRFIELD SHIPBUILDING YARD
BASIN
RIVER KELVIN
WEST BASIN
GOVAN SHIPBUILDING YARD
Govan Cross
Govan Station
GLASGOW CORPORATION
GOVAN BRANCH
R I V E R C L Y D E
LIGHT
LINTHOUSE SHIPBUILDING YARD
SEWAGE WORKS
SHIELDHALL WHARF
KING GEORGE V DOCK
ACCESS ROAD
RENFREW ROAD
SHIELDHALL BRANCH L.M.S. RLY
GOVAN ROAD
LANGLANDS ROAD
ELDER PARK
C I T Y O F

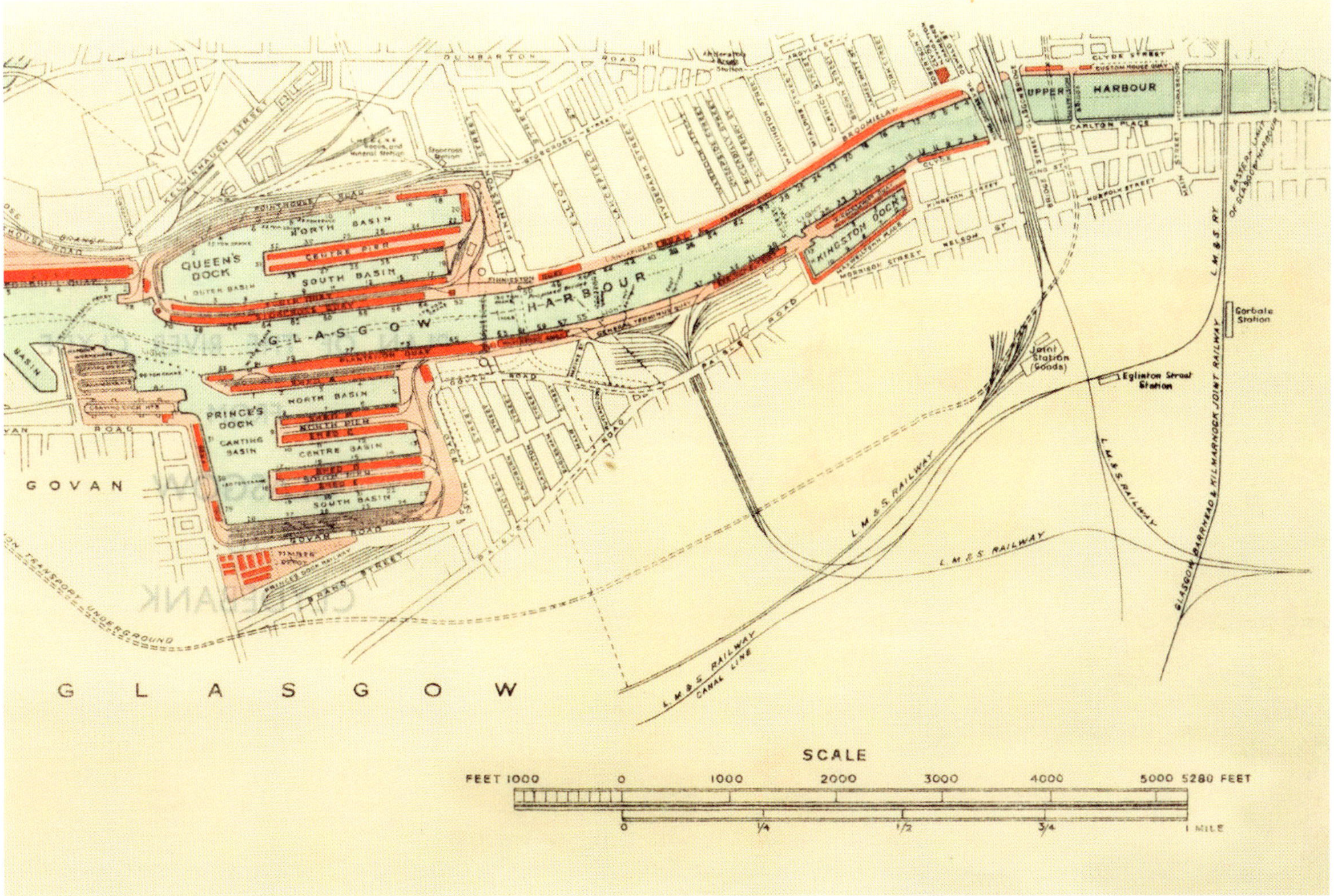
DUMBARTON ROAD
KELVINHAUGH STREET
CLYDE STREET
CUSTOM HOUSE QUAY
UPPER HARBOUR
CARLTON PLACE
BROOMIELAW
QUEEN'S DOCK
NORTH BASIN
CENTRE PIER
SOUTH BASIN
OUTER BASIN
FINNIESTON QUAY
LANCEFIELD QUAY
KINGSTON DOCK
KINGSTON STREET
NELSON ST
MORRISON STREET
NORFOLK STREET
G L A S G O W
H A R B O U R
PLANTATION QUAY
GOVAN ROAD
PAISLEY ROAD
PRINCE'S DOCK
NORTH BASIN
NORTH PIER
CANTING BASIN
CENTRE BASIN
SOUTH BASIN
GOVAN
TIMBER DEPOT
PRINCES DOCK RAILWAY
BRAND STREET
GLASGOW TRANSPORT UNDERGROUND
Joint Station (Goods)
Eglinton Street Station
Gorbals Station
L.M.&S. RY
EASTERN LIMIT OF GLASGOW HARBOUR
GLASGOW BARRHEAD & KILMARNOCK JOINT RAILWAY
L.M.&S. RAILWAY
CANAL LINE
G L A S G O W
SCALE
FEET 1000
0
1000
2000
3000
4000
5000 5280 FEET
0
1/4
1/2
3/4
1 MILE

TO ALL DOCKS

DIRECTIONAL ROUTEING OF ROAD TRANSPORT WITHIN THE CITY OF GLASGOW TO THE DOCKS

In order to assist road transport drivers proceeding to Glasgow Docks, coloured arrow signs have been erected on selected routes starting from the perimeter of the city.

The Docks have been divided into four areas, each served by a separate colour.

Direction to the various Quays and Berths can be obtained from notice-boards at the entrance to the principal Docks.

It is most important that documents carried by drivers should show clearly the Ship's Name, Berth Number, Name of the Dock or Quay, and the appropriate coloured arrow to follow within the city.

Queen's Dock Area

For	*Berths*
Anderston Quay - -	30 - 34
Broomielaw Quay - -	4 - 28
Finnieston Quay - - -	46 - 52
Finnieston Fitting-out Crane	
Lancefield Quay - - -	36 - 44
Queen's Dock - - -	1 - 32
Stobcross Quay - - -	32 - 76
Stobcross 175-ton Crane	
Yorkhill Quay - - -	1 - 9

Meadowside Quay and Merklands Quay Area

For	*Berths*
Meadowside Quay - -	1 - 3
Meadowside Granary	
Merklands Quay - - -	1 - 4
Merklands Lairage and Slaughter House	

Prince's Dock Area

For	*Berths*
Clyde Place Quay - -	5 - 15
General Terminus Quay -	37 - 51
Govan Dry Docks - -	1 - 3
Kingston Dock - - -	1 - 12
Mavisbank Quay - - -	55 - 63
Plantation Quay - - -	65 - 83
Prince's Dock - - -	1 - 25
Prince's Dock (Whitefield Rd.)	26 - 31
Springfield Quay - -	29 - 39
Windmillcroft Quay - -	17 - 27
Whitefield Rd. 120-tons Crane	

King George V Dock Area

For	*Berths*
Braehead Transit Depot	
Braehead Repair Berthage	
Deanside Transit Depot	
King George V Dock - -	1 - 10
Shieldhall Timber Wharf	

Directional Routeing of Road Transport within the City of Glasgow to the Docks.

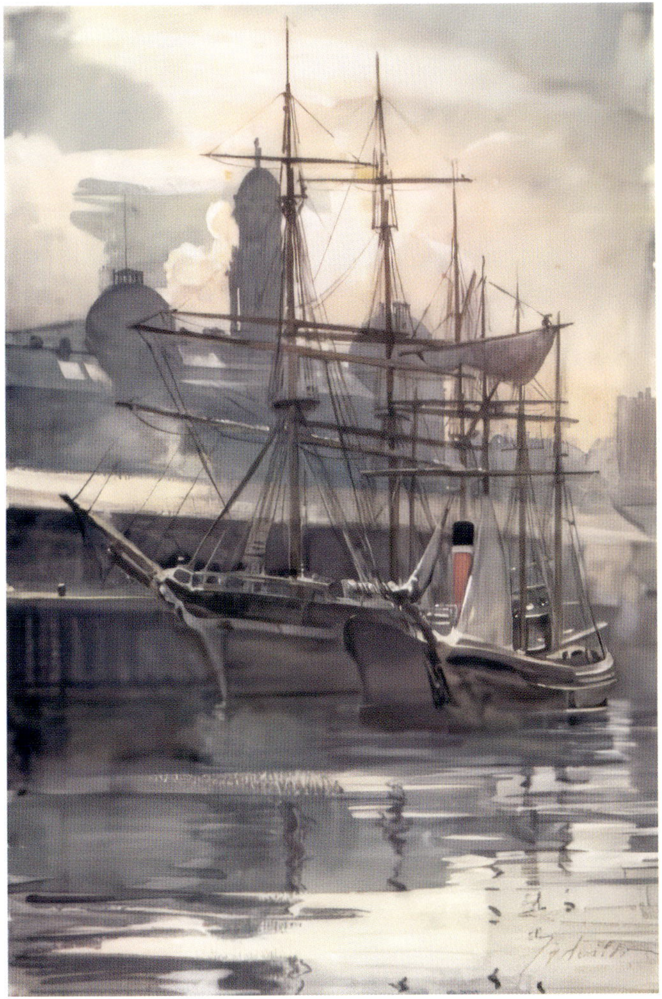

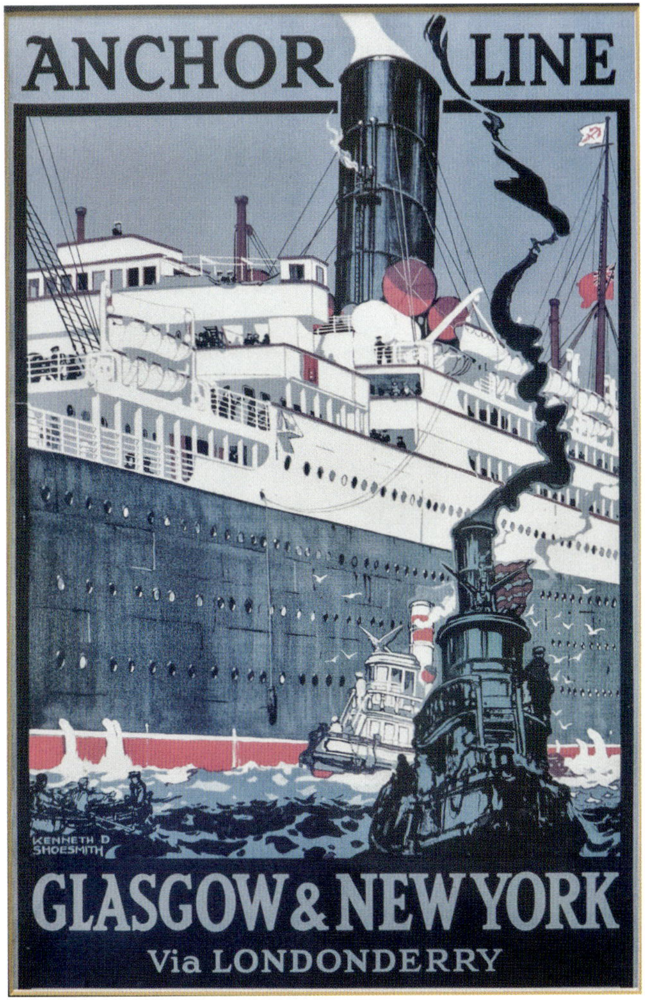

Left: Kingston Dock, with the Scottish Co-operative Wholesale Society building beyond, painting by John Young Hunter, 1900s.

Right: An Anchor Line poster, by Kenneth D. Shoesmith.

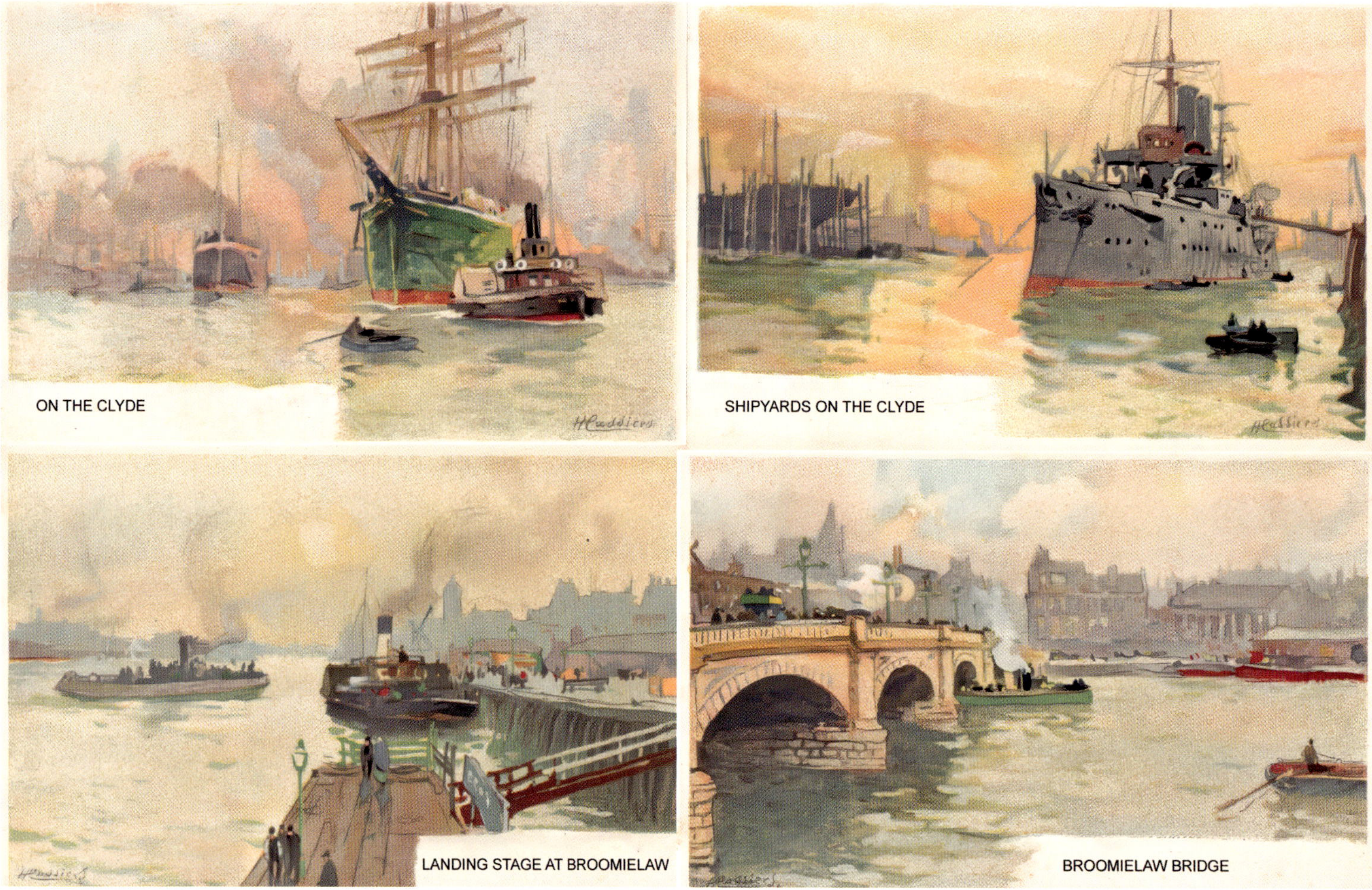

A montage of postcards featuring scenes painted by Henri Cassiers.

Conveying Art

Numerous pictorial artists created works conveying the skills and art of ship design, day-to-day construction and sailing, such as stateroom decoration, furnishings and externally in paintings, engravings, postcards, posters, murals, industrial photography and films. Stanley Spencer's canvas murals depicting Lithgow's Yard, Port Glasgow, in the Second World War epitomise shipbuilding: *The Burners*, *Riggers*, *Welders*, *Riveters*, *The Template*, *Bending the Keel Plate*, *Plumbers* and *The Furnaces*.

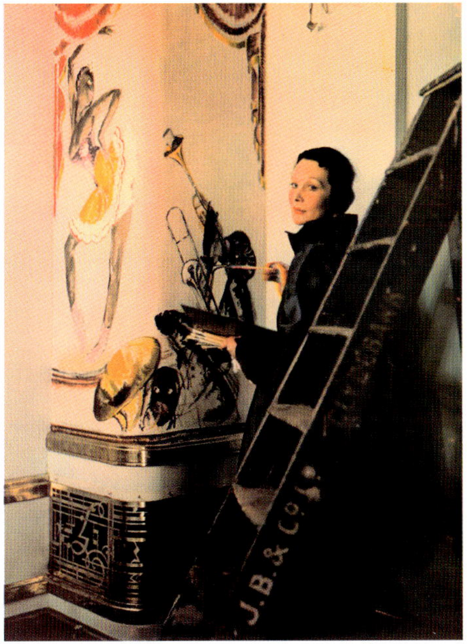

Doris Zinkeisen at work on murals for Cunard's *Queen Mary*.

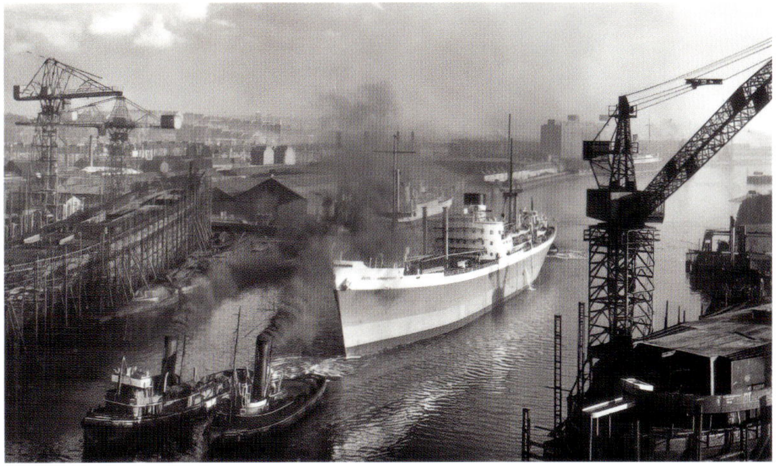

Above and below: Postcards from Wm Ralston Ltd, marine and industrial photographers.

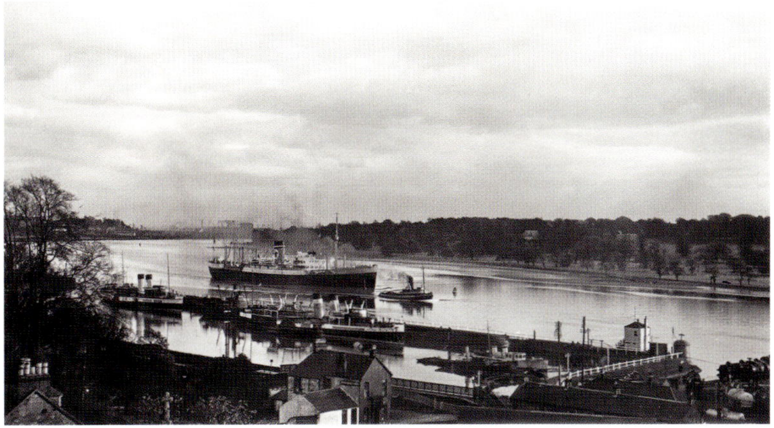

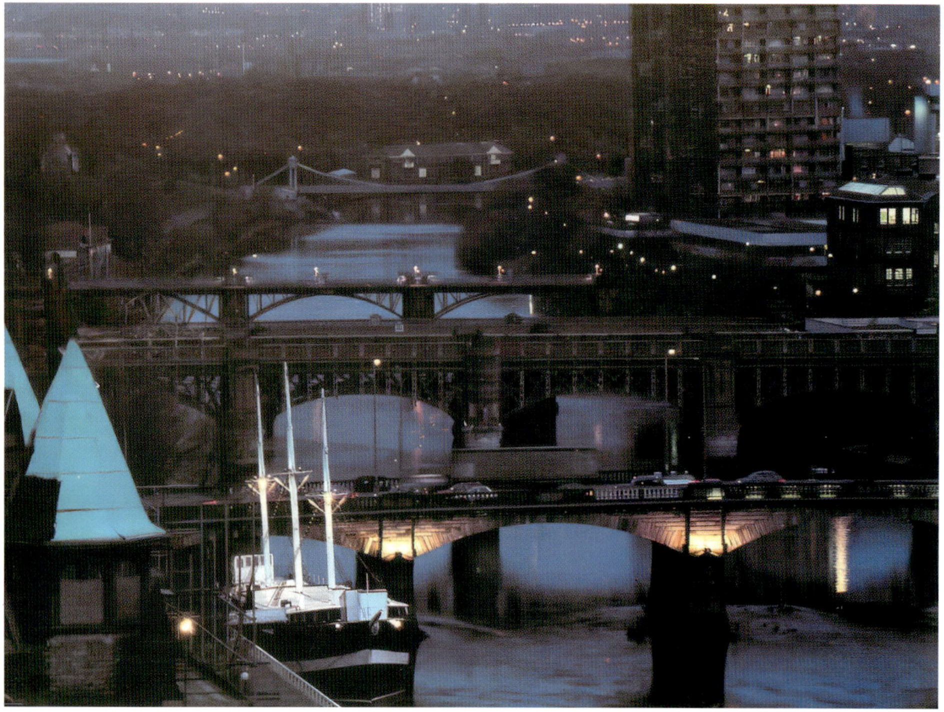

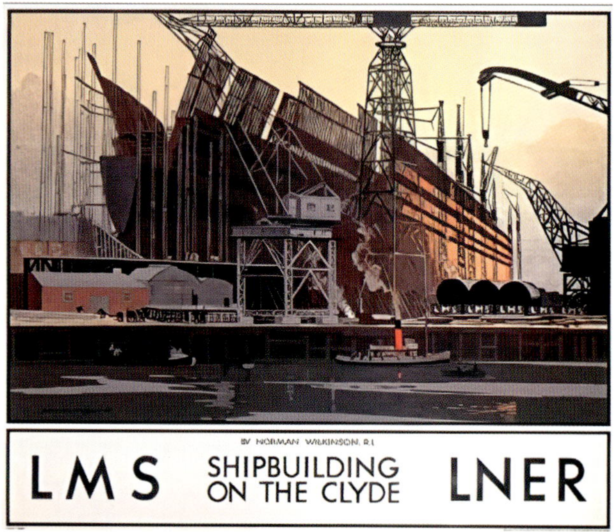

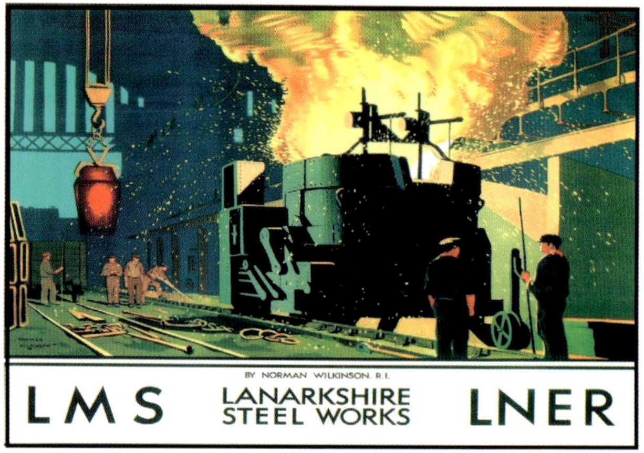

Above: High above Custom House Quay, Clyde Street, looking east to Glasgow Green. RNVR club ship *Carrick* is floodlit.

Above right: Shipbuilding on the Clyde, poster by Sir Norman Wilkinson.

Right: Lanarkshire Steel Works, poster by Sir Norman Wilkinson.

Flags and Funnels of Shipping Companies at Glasgow

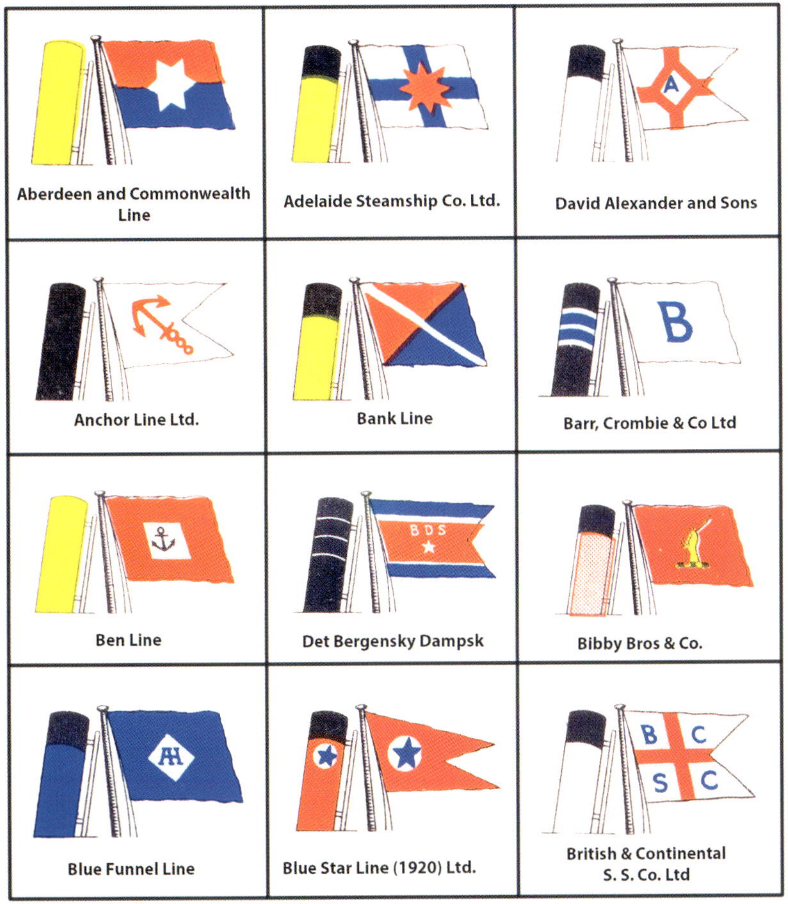

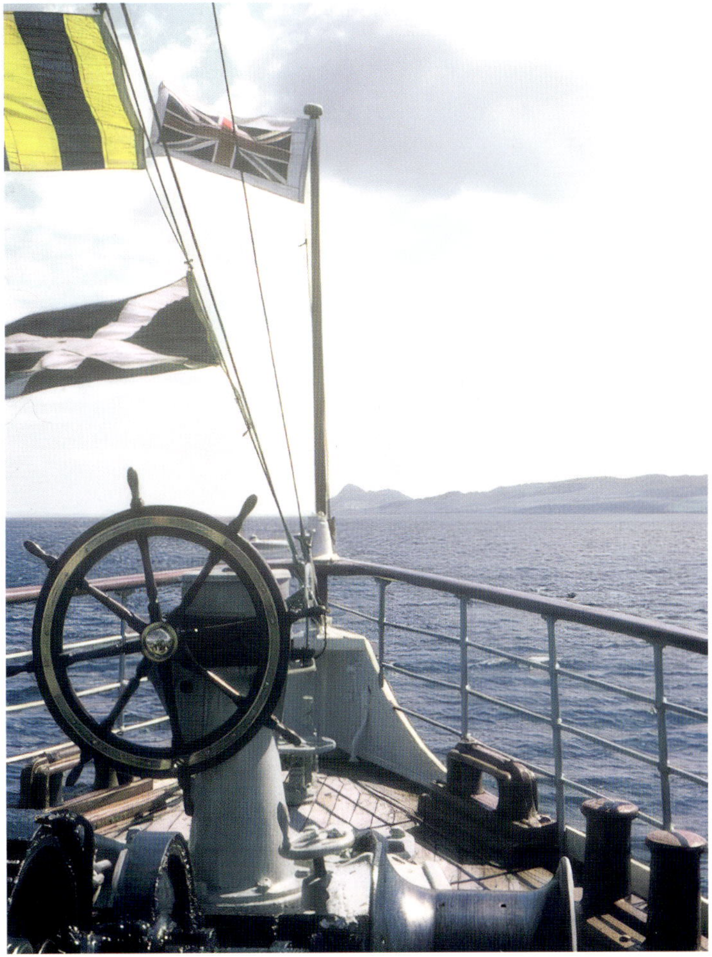

Sailing down the Clyde.

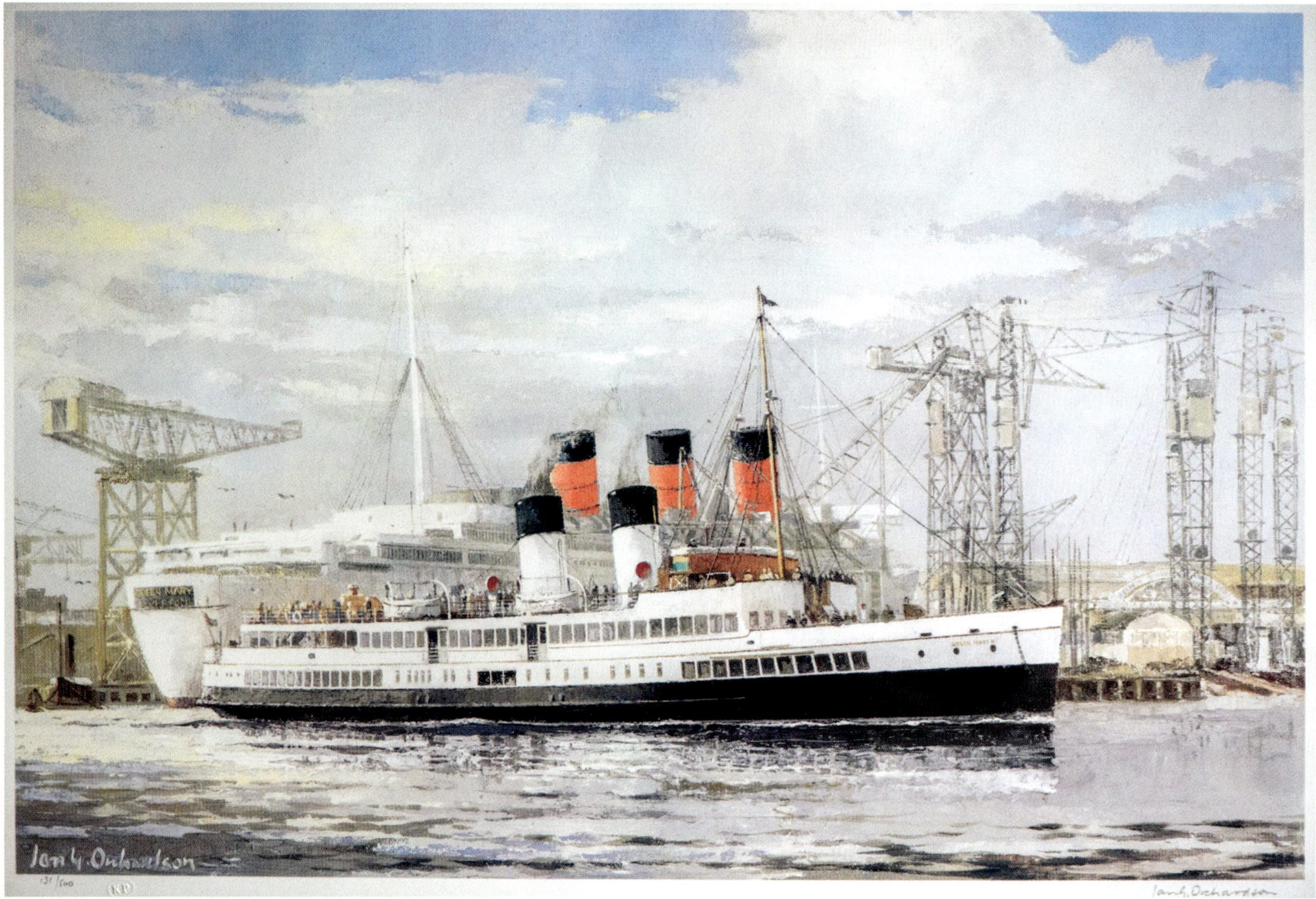

Cunard's *Queen Mary* fitting out at John Brown's Clydebank and Clyde steamer *Queen Mary II* passing upstream, painting by Ian Orchardson.

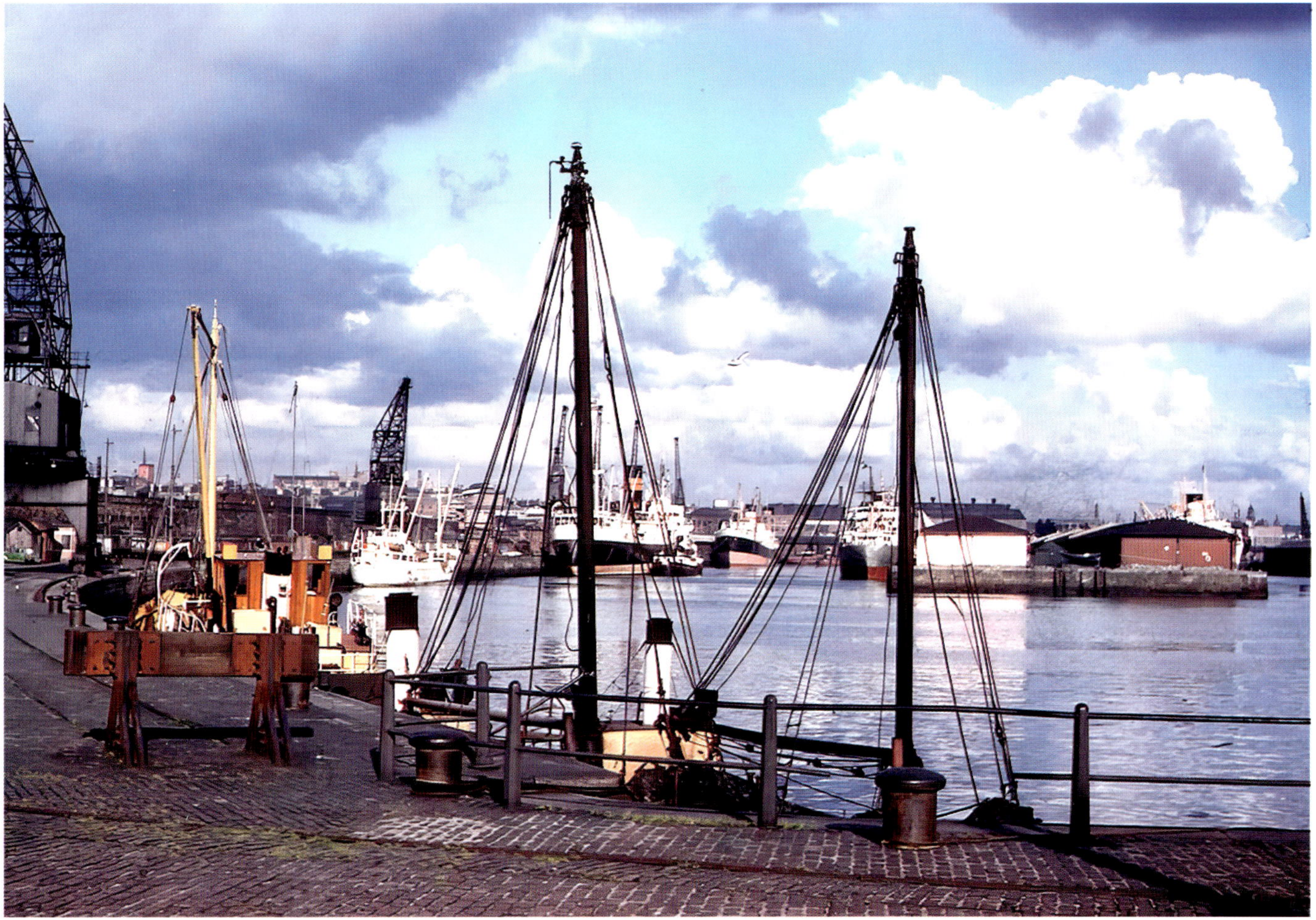

North Basin and Central Pier of Queen's Dock, viewing towards Finnieston Street.

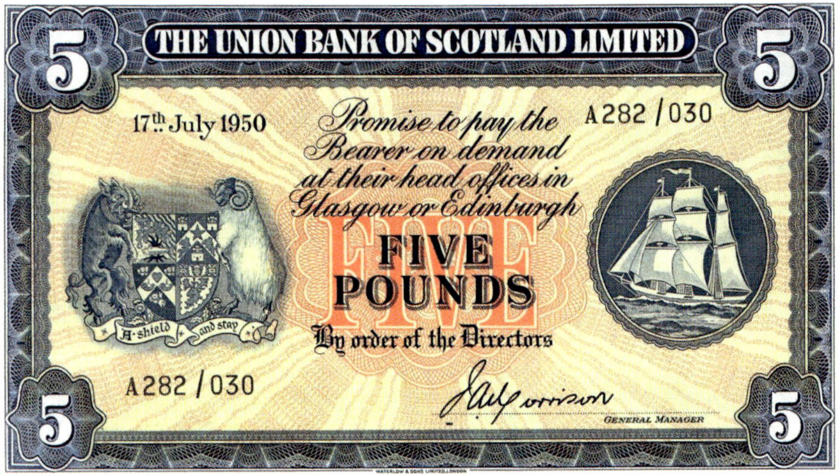

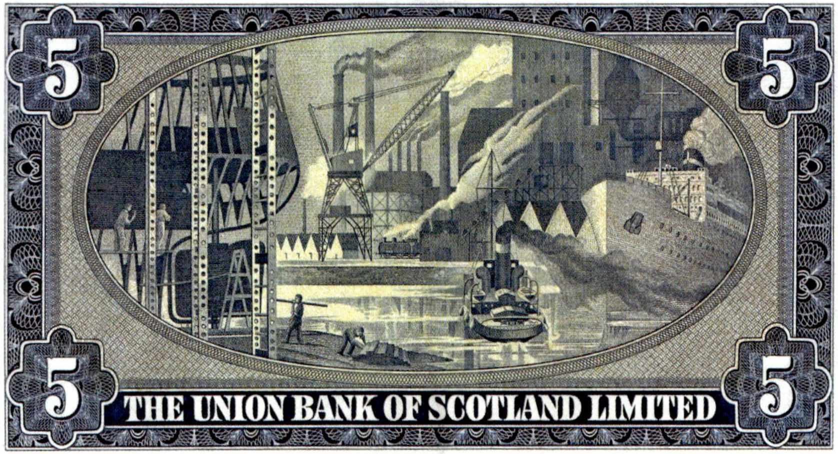

The banking sector expanded alongside the growing shipping and shipbuilding industry, including the Bank of Scotland, Royal Bank of Scotland, Clydesdale Bank and Union Bank of Scotland.

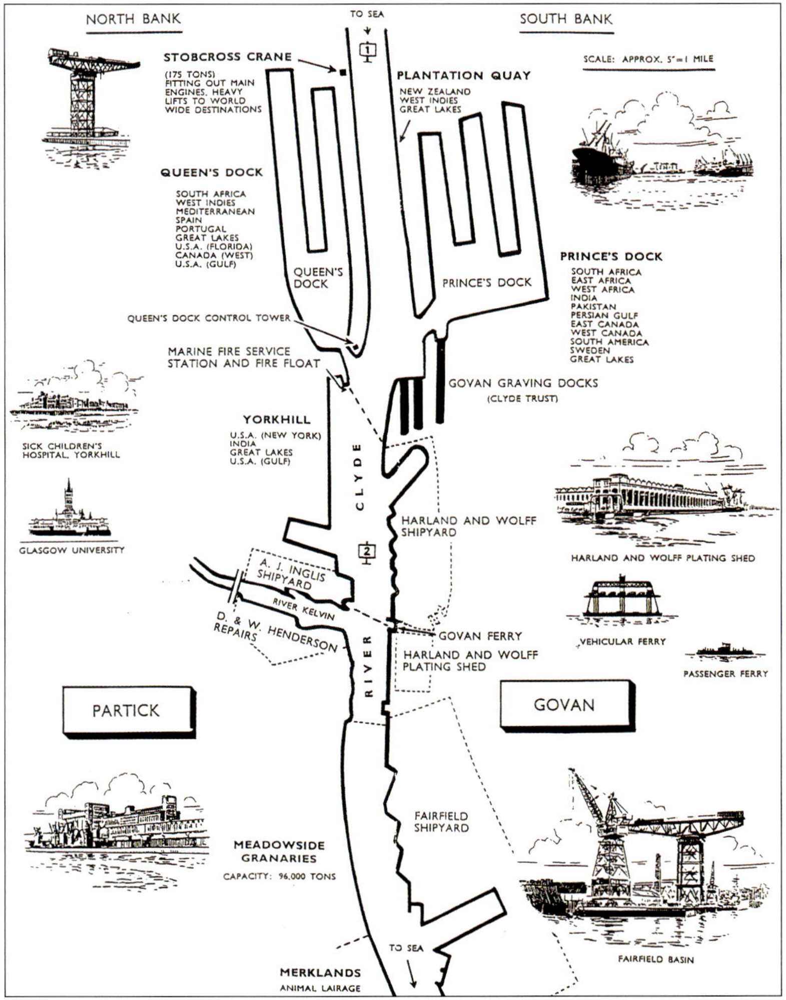

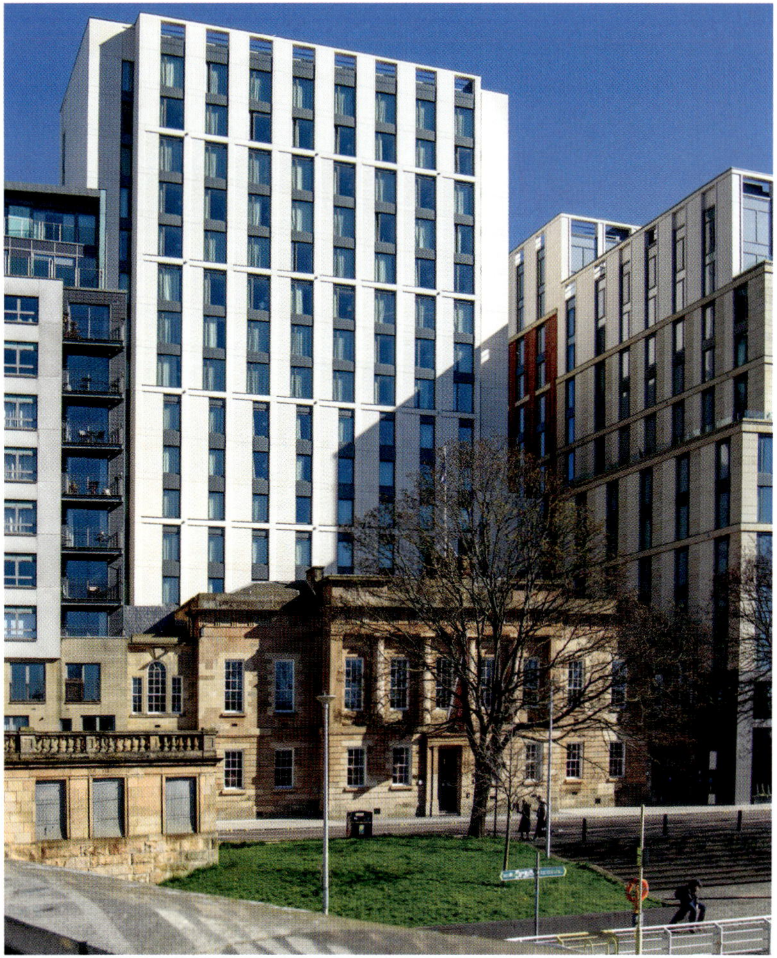

The historic Customs & Excise building in Clyde Street today.

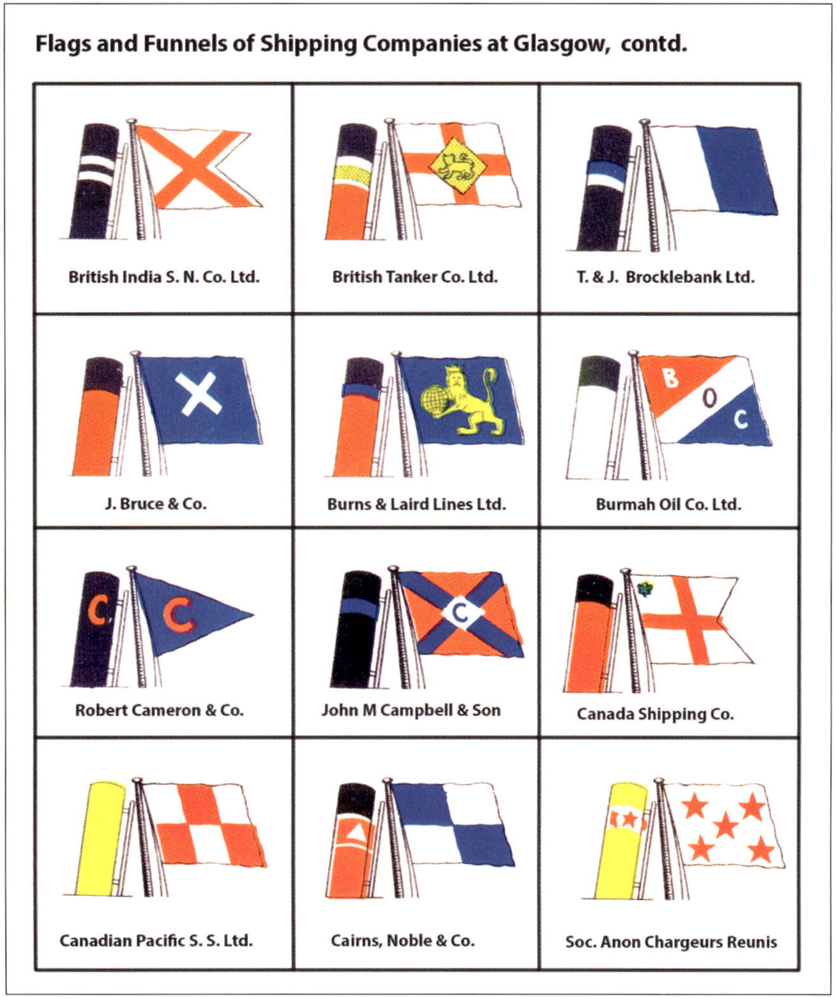
Flags and Funnels of Shipping Companies at Glasgow, contd.
British India S. N. Co. Ltd.
British Tanker Co. Ltd.
T. & J. Brocklebank Ltd.
J. Bruce & Co.
Burns & Laird Lines Ltd.
Burmah Oil Co. Ltd.
Robert Cameron & Co.
John M Campbell & Son
Canada Shipping Co.
Canadian Pacific S. S. Ltd.
Cairns, Noble & Co.
Soc. Anon Chargeurs Reunis

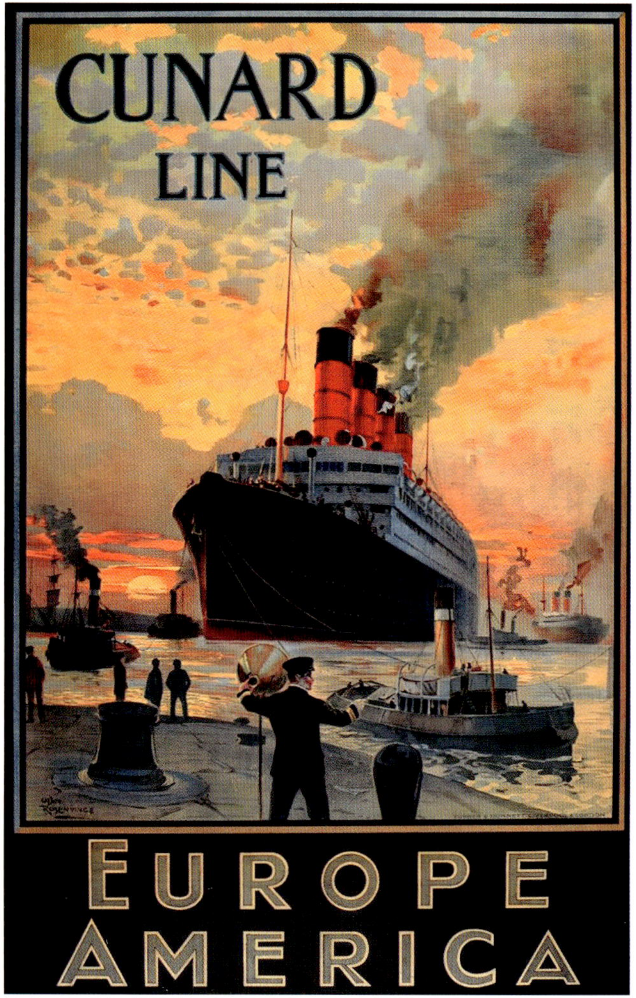
CUNARD
LINE
EUROPE
AMERICA

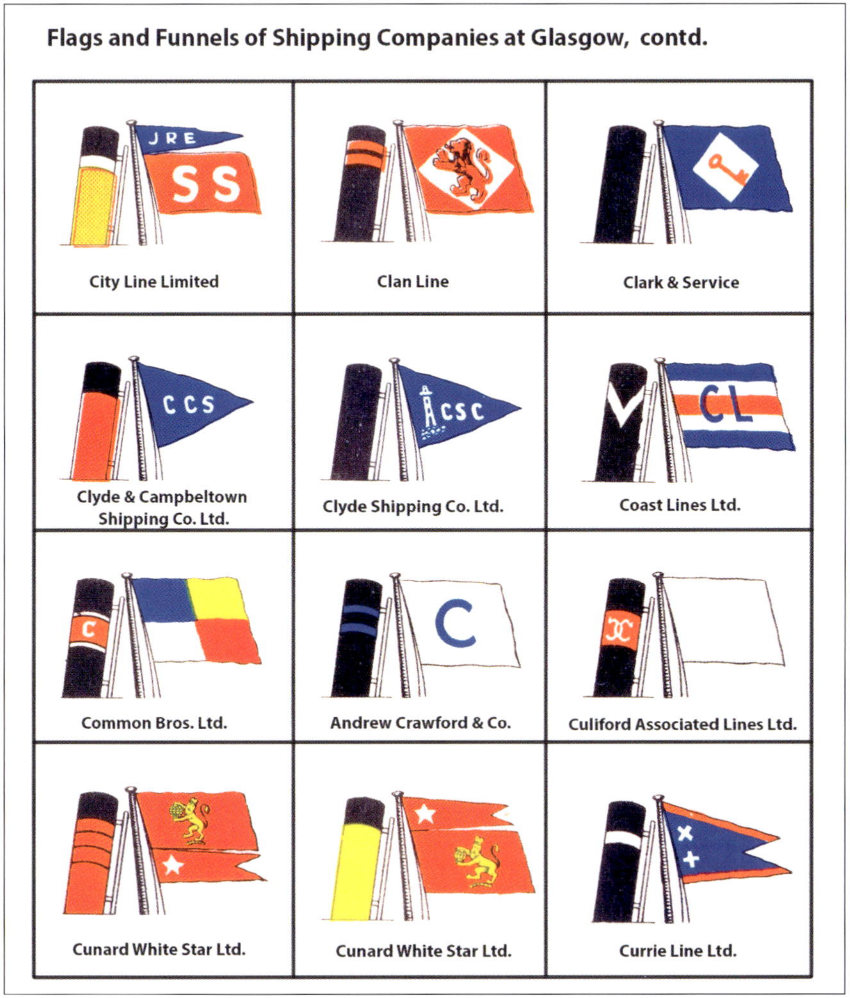
Flags and Funnels of Shipping Companies at Glasgow, contd.
City Line Limited
Clan Line
Clark & Service
Clyde & Campbeltown Shipping Co. Ltd.
Clyde Shipping Co. Ltd.
Coast Lines Ltd.
Common Bros. Ltd.
Andrew Crawford & Co.
Culiford Associated Lines Ltd.
Cunard White Star Ltd.
Cunard White Star Ltd.
Currie Line Ltd.

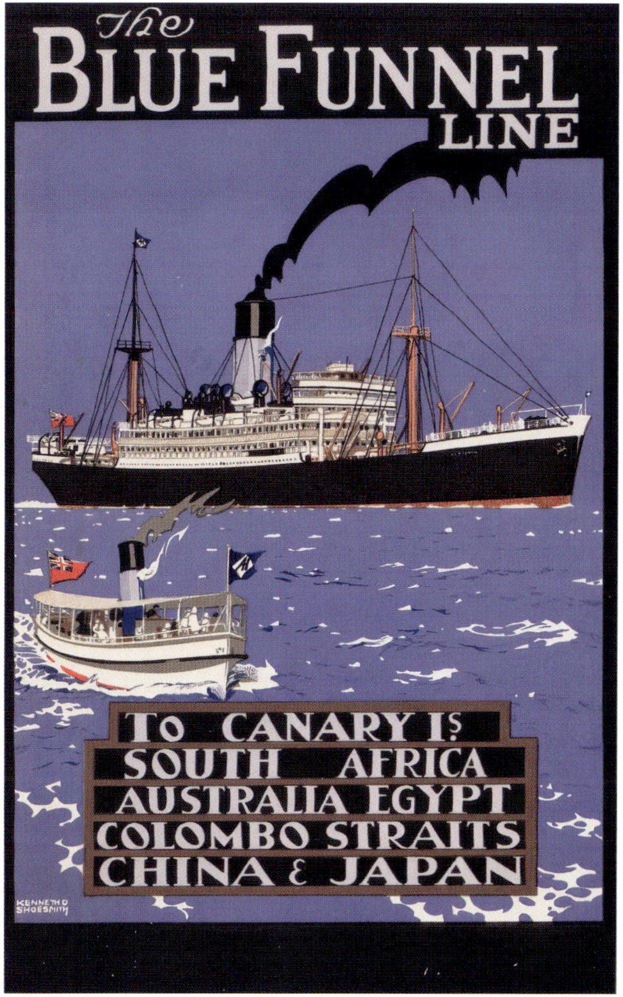
The BLUE FUNNEL LINE
TO CANARY IS
SOUTH AFRICA
AUSTRALIA EGYPT
COLOMBO STRAITS
CHINA & JAPAN
KENNETH D SHOESMITH

Flags and Funnels of Shipping Companies at Glasgow, contd.

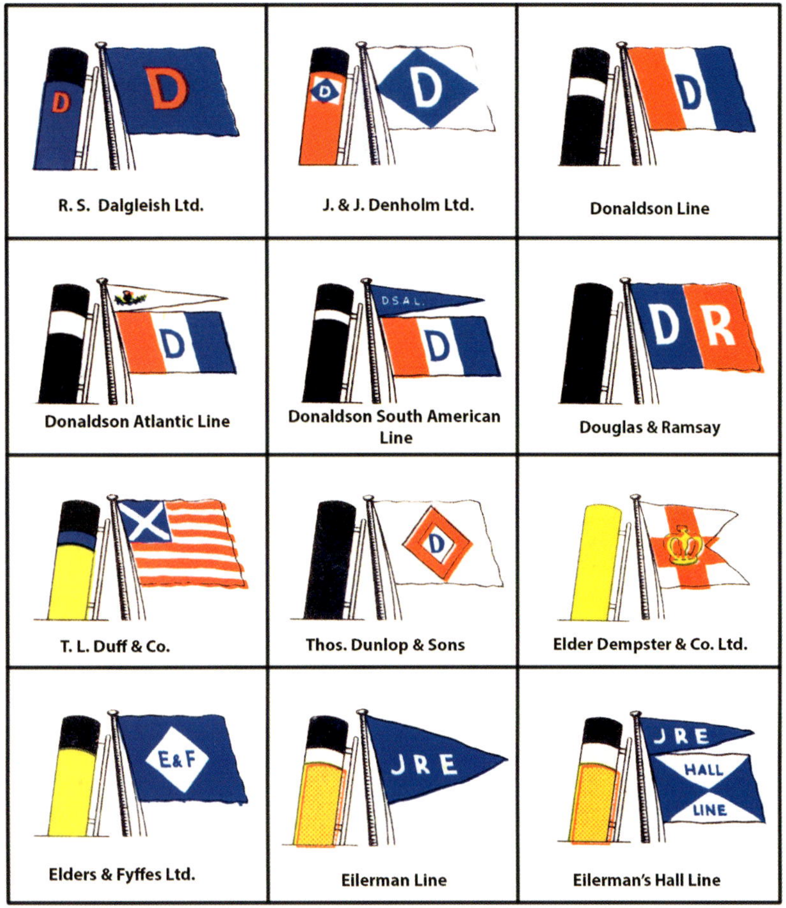

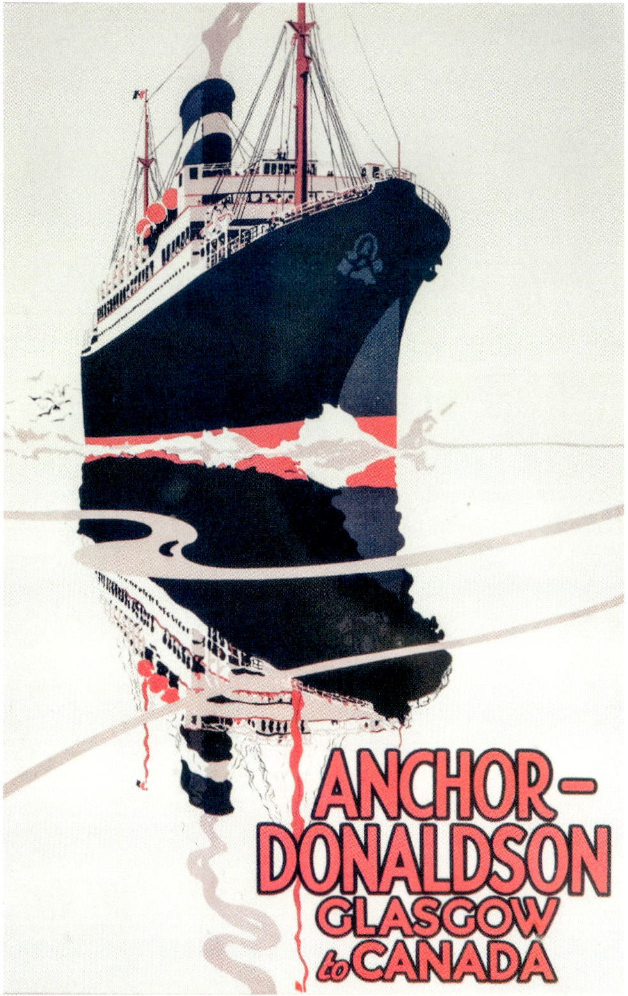

Flags and Funnels of Shipping Companies at Glasgow, contd.

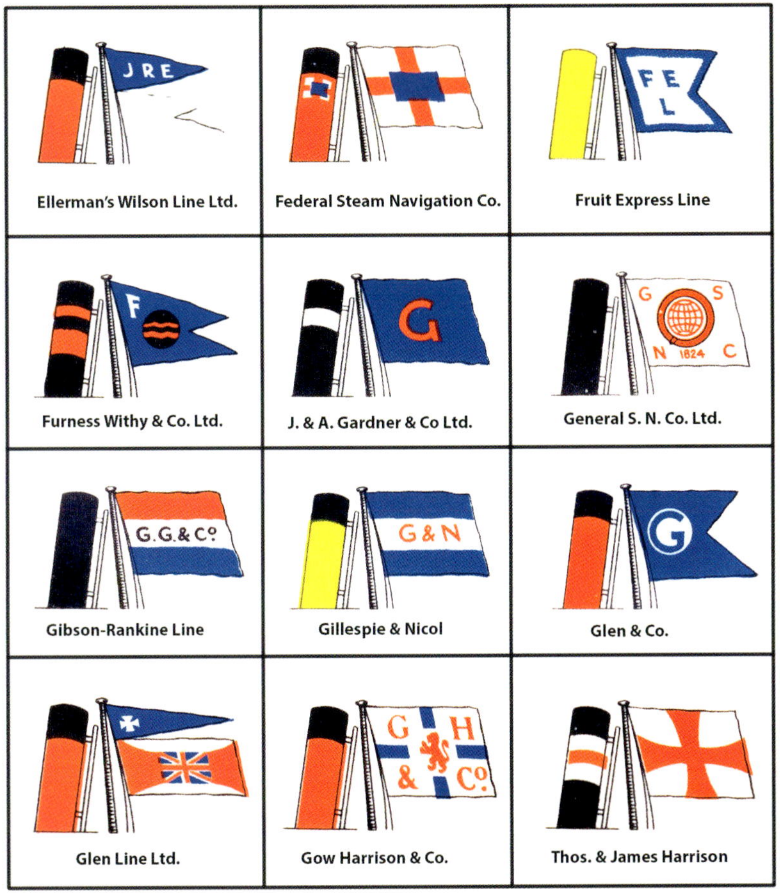

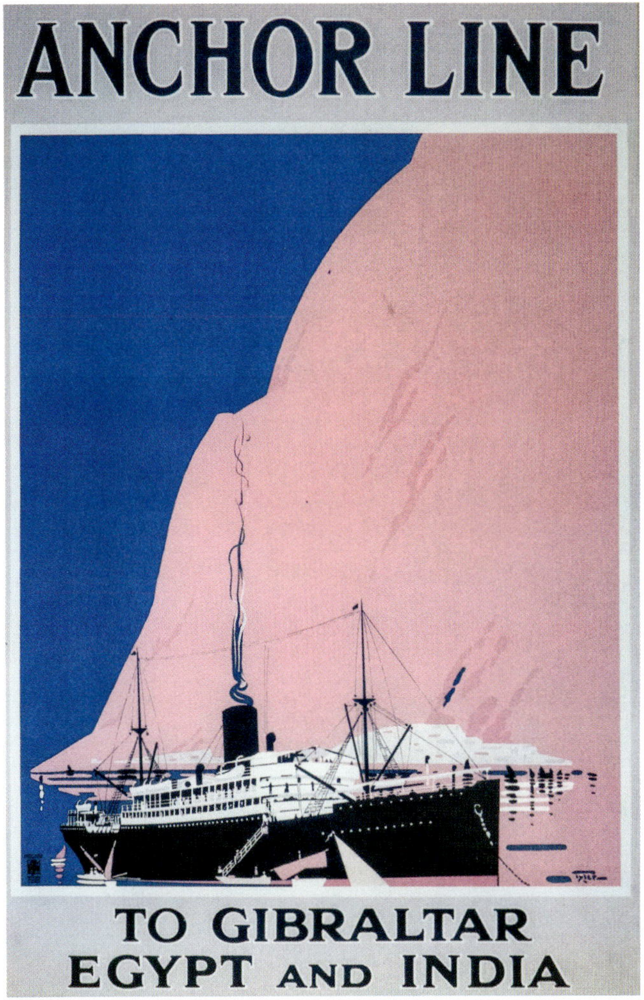

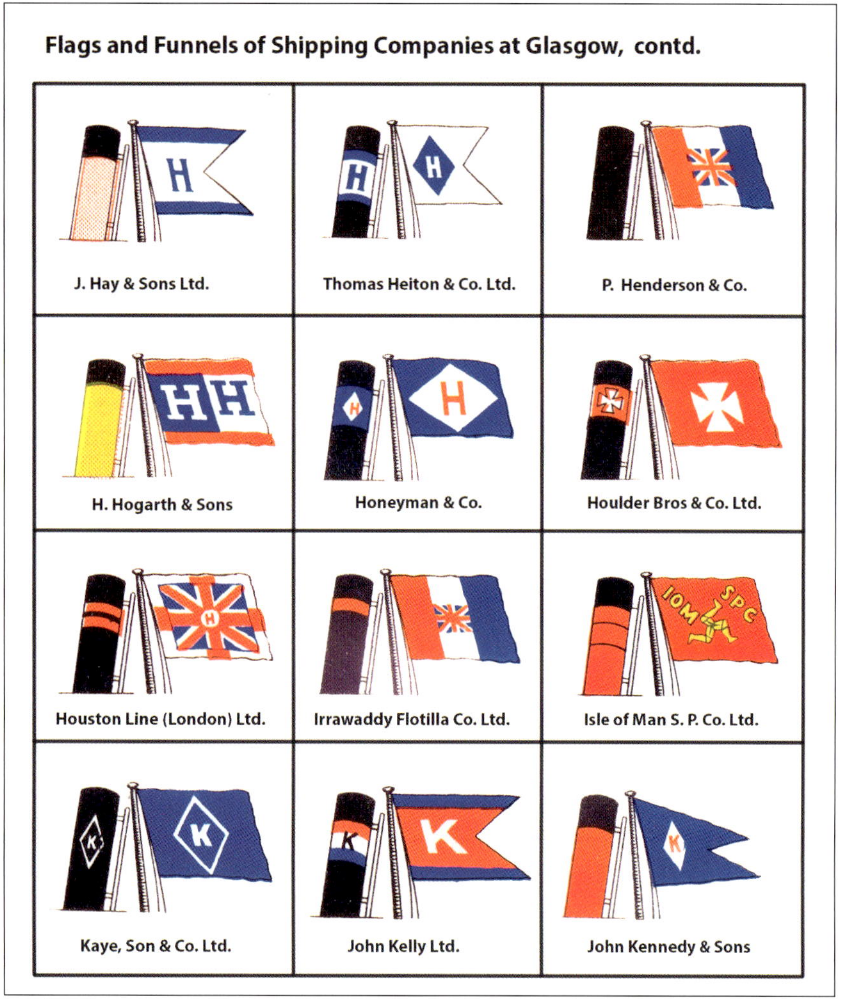
Flags and Funnels of Shipping Companies at Glasgow, contd.
J. Hay & Sons Ltd.
Thomas Heiton & Co. Ltd.
P. Henderson & Co.
H. Hogarth & Sons
Honeyman & Co.
Houlder Bros & Co. Ltd.
Houston Line (London) Ltd.
Irrawaddy Flotilla Co. Ltd.
Isle of Man S. P. Co. Ltd.
Kaye, Son & Co. Ltd.
John Kelly Ltd.
John Kennedy & Sons

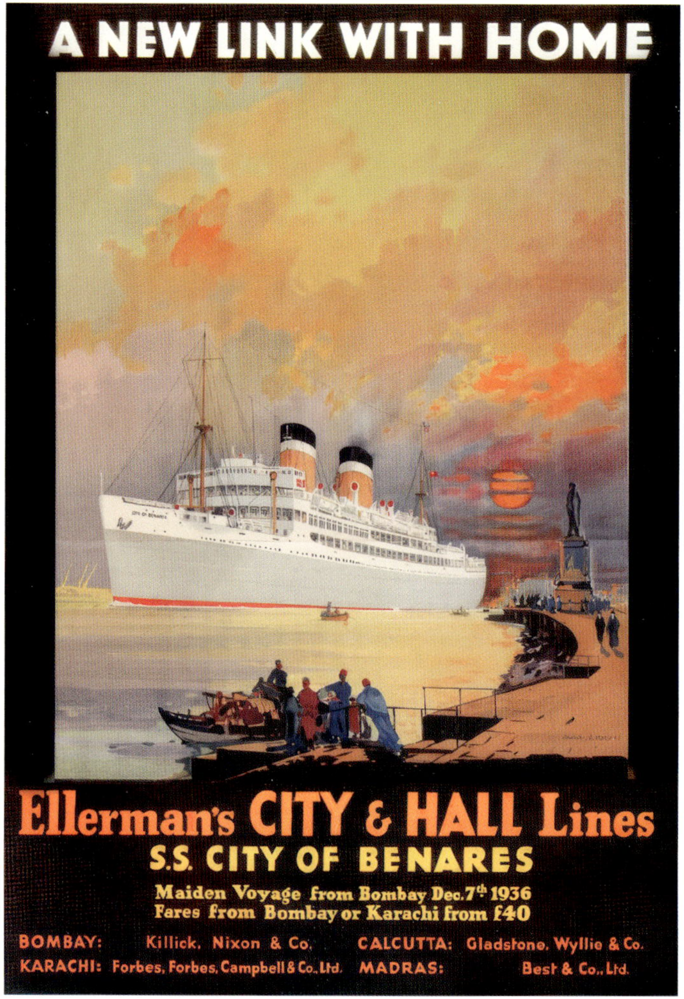
A NEW LINK WITH HOME
Ellerman's CITY & HALL Lines
S.S. CITY OF BENARES
Maiden Voyage from Bombay Dec. 7th 1936
Fares from Bombay or Karachi from £40
BOMBAY: Killick, Nixon & Co.
CALCUTTA: Gladstone, Wyllie & Co.
KARACHI: Forbes, Forbes, Campbell & Co. Ltd.
MADRAS: Best & Co., Ltd.

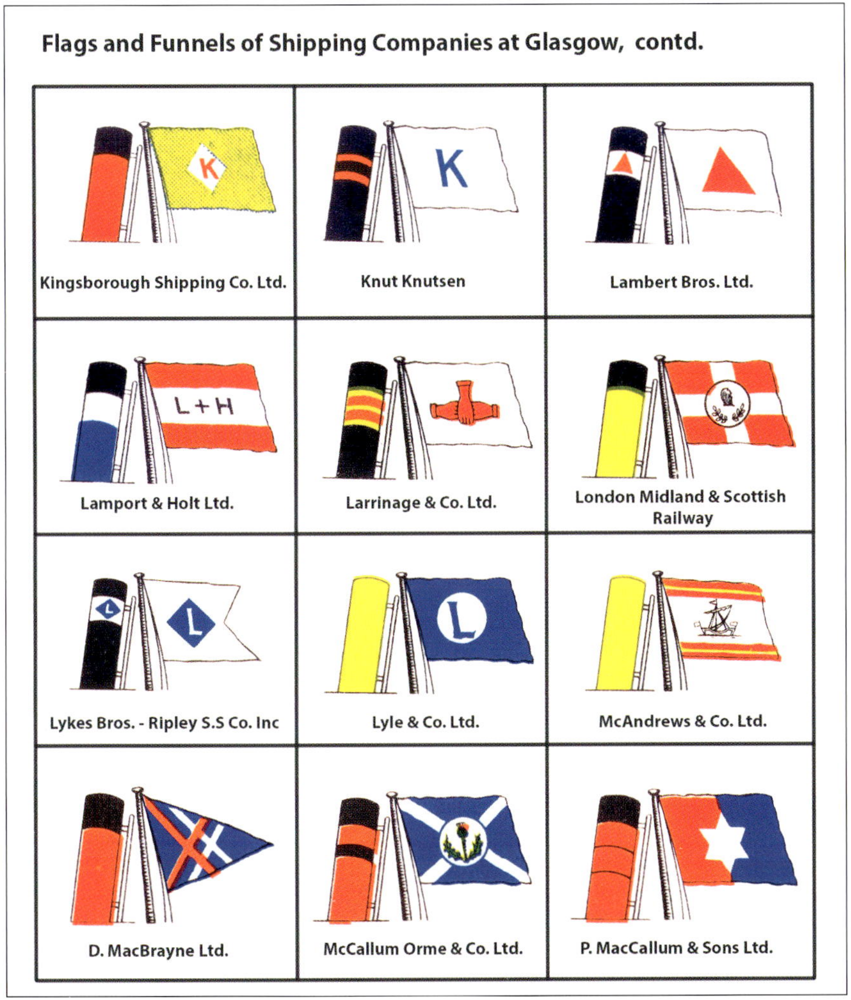
Flags and Funnels of Shipping Companies at Glasgow, contd.
Kingsborough Shipping Co. Ltd.
Knut Knutsen
Lambert Bros. Ltd.
Lamport & Holt Ltd.
Larrinage & Co. Ltd.
London Midland & Scottish Railway
Lykes Bros. - Ripley S.S Co. Inc
Lyle & Co. Ltd.
McAndrews & Co. Ltd.
D. MacBrayne Ltd.
McCallum Orme & Co. Ltd.
P. MacCallum & Sons Ltd.

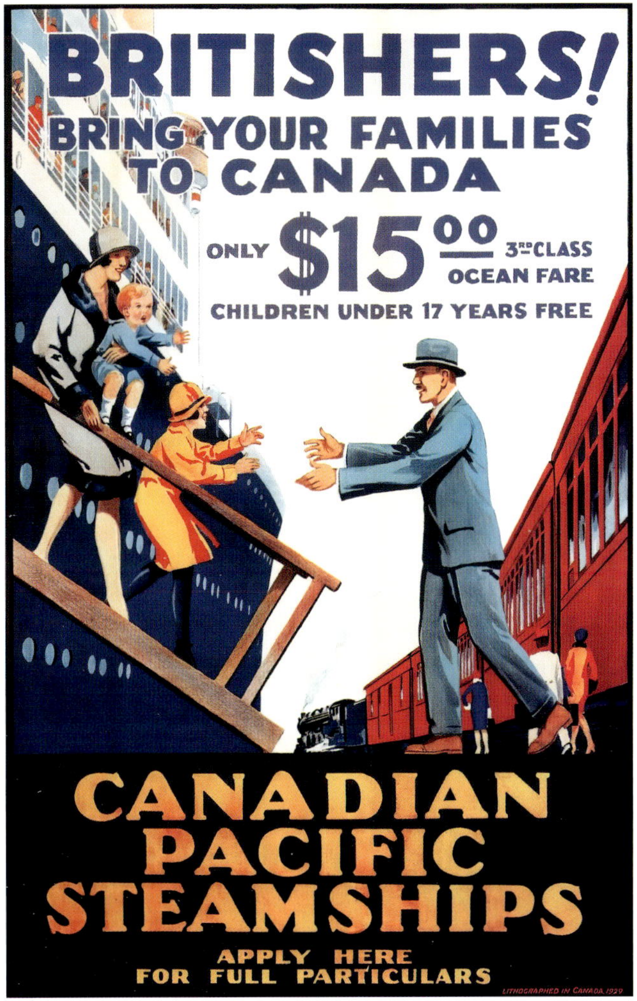
BRITISHERS!
BRING YOUR FAMILIES TO CANADA
ONLY $15.00 3RD CLASS OCEAN FARE
CHILDREN UNDER 17 YEARS FREE
CANADIAN PACIFIC STEAMSHIPS
APPLY HERE FOR FULL PARTICULARS
LITHOGRAPHED IN CANADA 1929

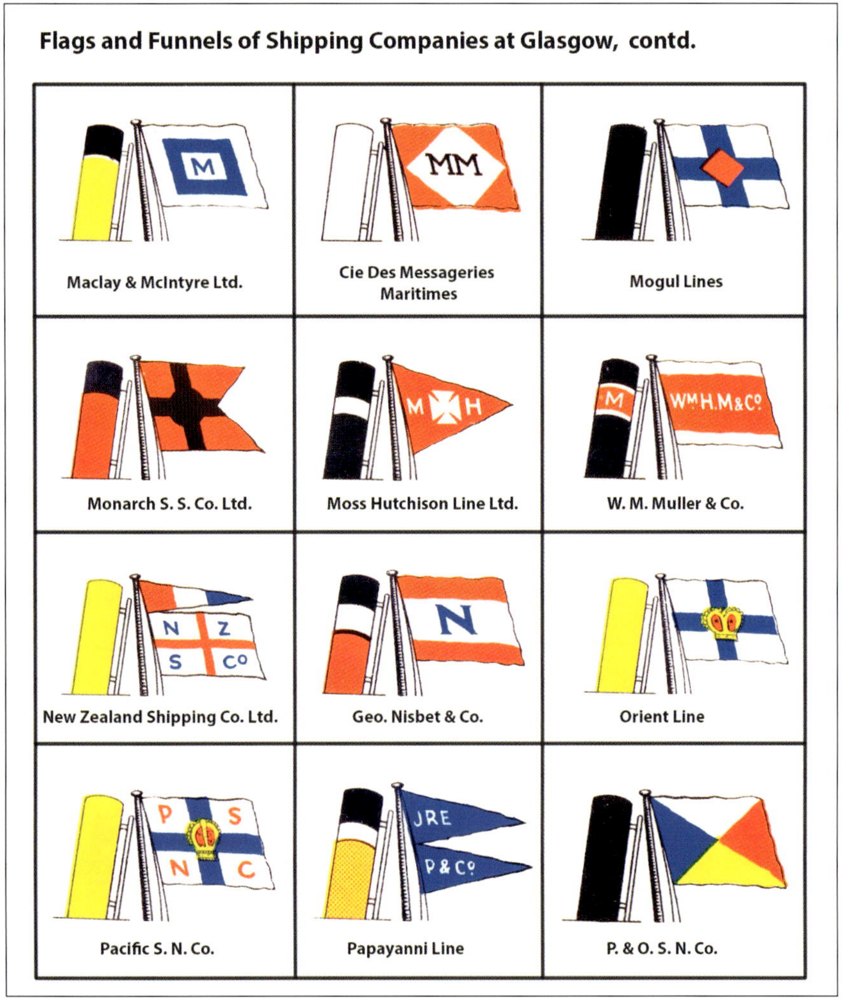
Flags and Funnels of Shipping Companies at Glasgow, contd.
Maclay & McIntyre Ltd.
Cie Des Messageries Maritimes
Mogul Lines
Monarch S. S. Co. Ltd.
Moss Hutchison Line Ltd.
W. M. Muller & Co.
New Zealand Shipping Co. Ltd.
Geo. Nisbet & Co.
Orient Line
Pacific S. N. Co.
Papayanni Line
P. & O. S. N. Co.

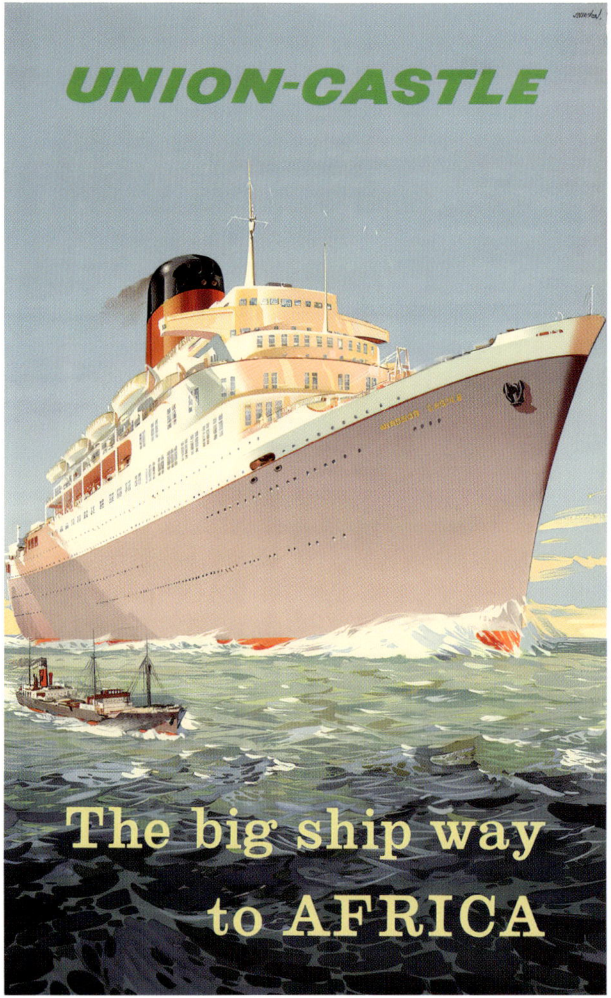
UNION-CASTLE
The big ship way to AFRICA

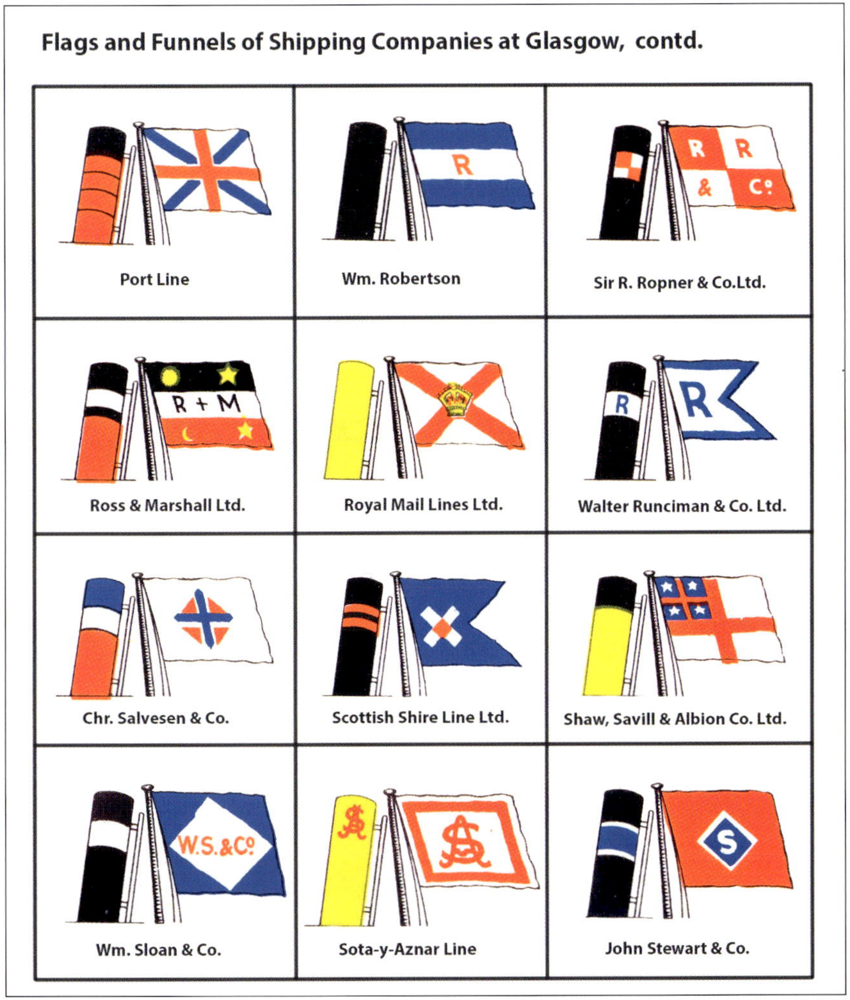
Flags and Funnels of Shipping Companies at Glasgow, contd.
R
R
R
&
Cº
R + M
R
R
W.S.&Cº
S
Port Line
Wm. Robertson
Sir R. Ropner & Co.Ltd.
Ross & Marshall Ltd.
Royal Mail Lines Ltd.
Walter Runciman & Co. Ltd.
Chr. Salvesen & Co.
Scottish Shire Line Ltd.
Shaw, Savill & Albion Co. Ltd.
Wm. Sloan & Co.
Sota-y-Aznar Line
John Stewart & Co.

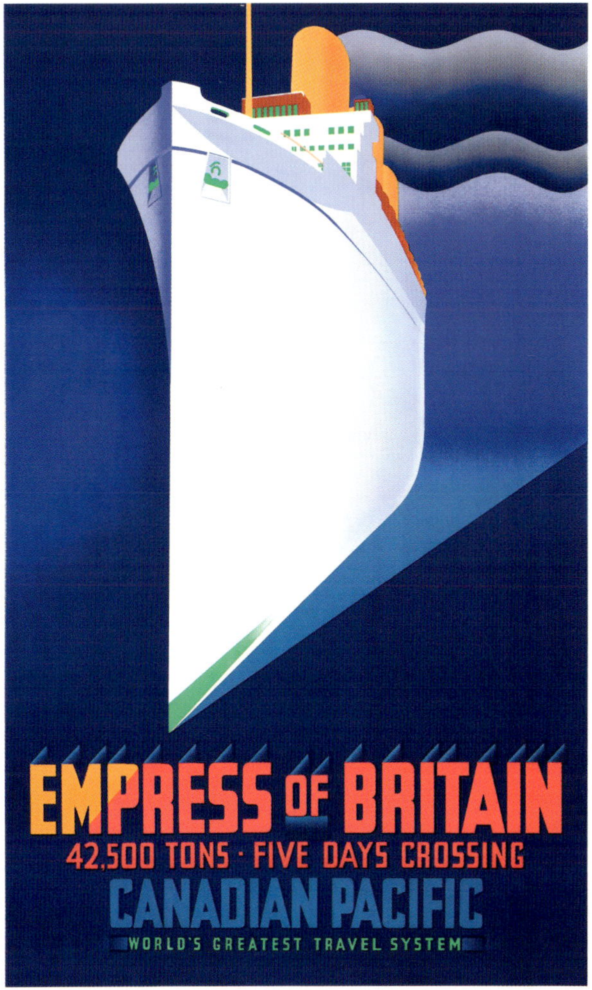
EMPRESS OF BRITAIN
42,500 TONS · FIVE DAYS CROSSING
CANADIAN PACIFIC
WORLD'S GREATEST TRAVEL SYSTEM

Flags and Funnels of Shipping Companies at Glasgow, contd.

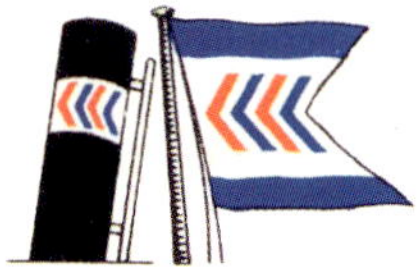

Strick Line Ltd.

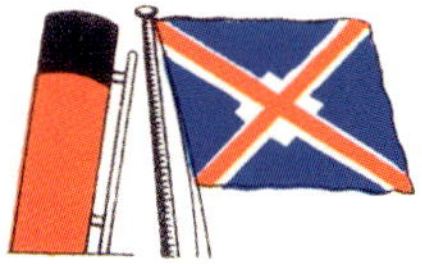

Union Castle Mail S. S. Co. Ltd.

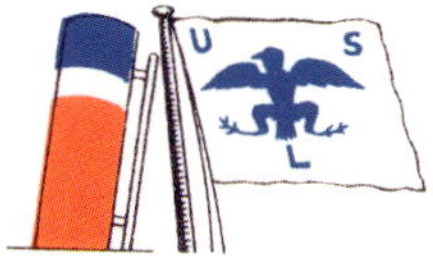

United States Lines

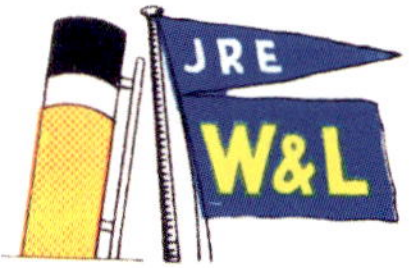

Westcott and Laurence Line Ltd.

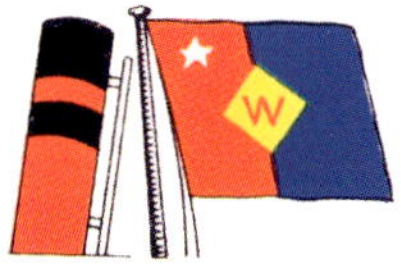

Whimster & Co. Ltd.

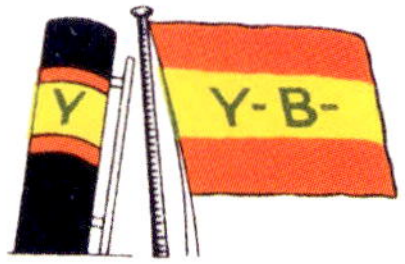

Yeoward Line Ltd.

British Ensigns

Merchant Navy

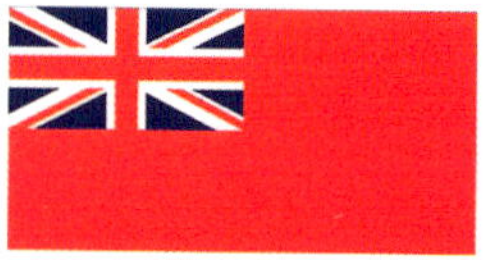

Royal Navy

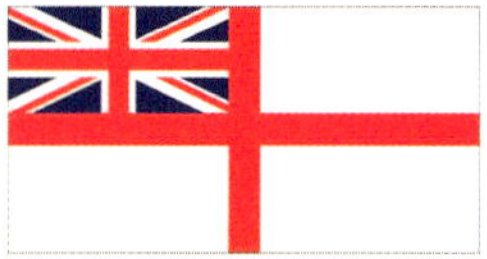

Royal Naval Reserve

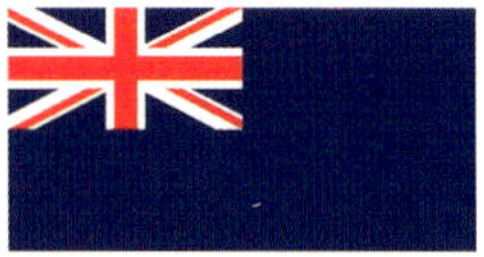

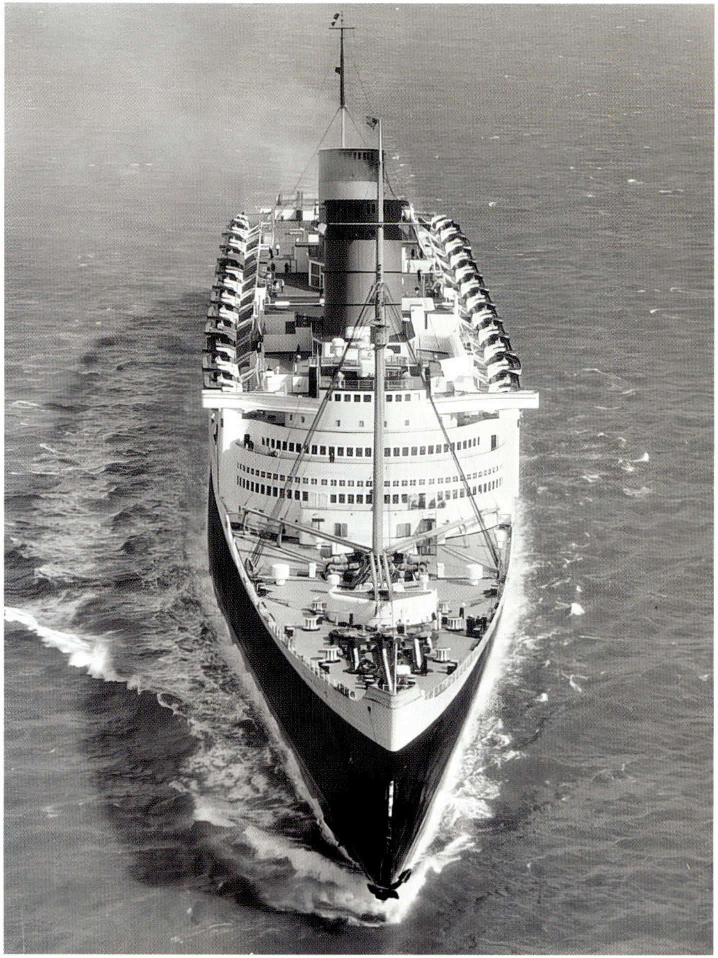

RMS *Queen Elizabeth*.

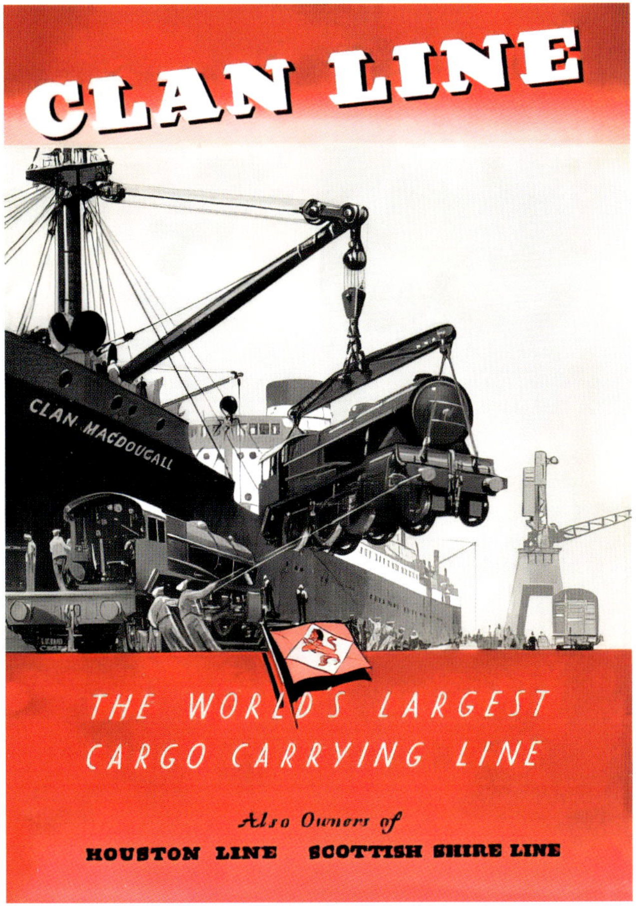

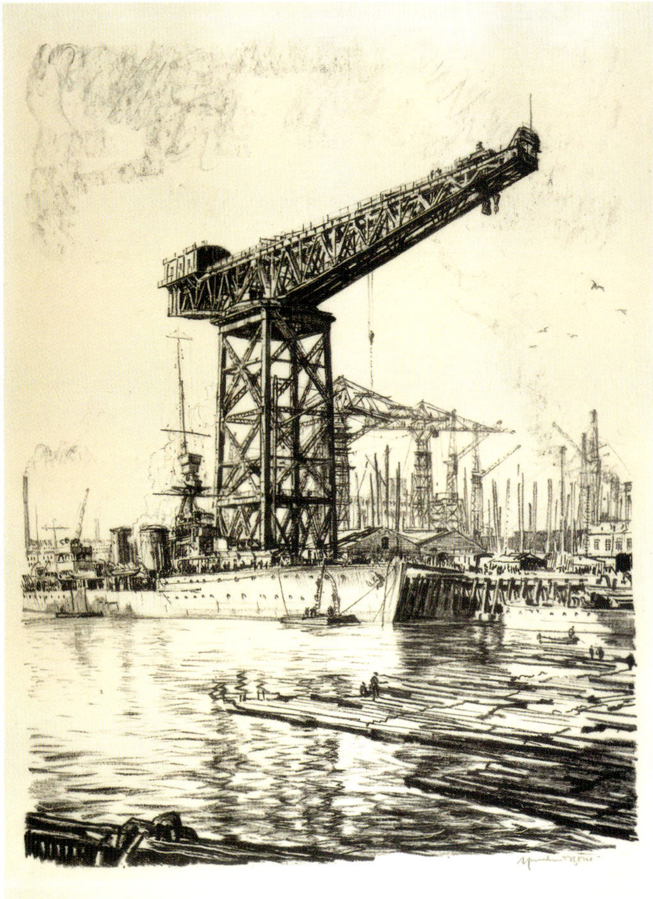

Left: A Clan Line company magazine cover, 1936.

Right: Fairfield's shipyard and hammerhead crane, the largest in the world, drawing by Sir Muirhead Bone.

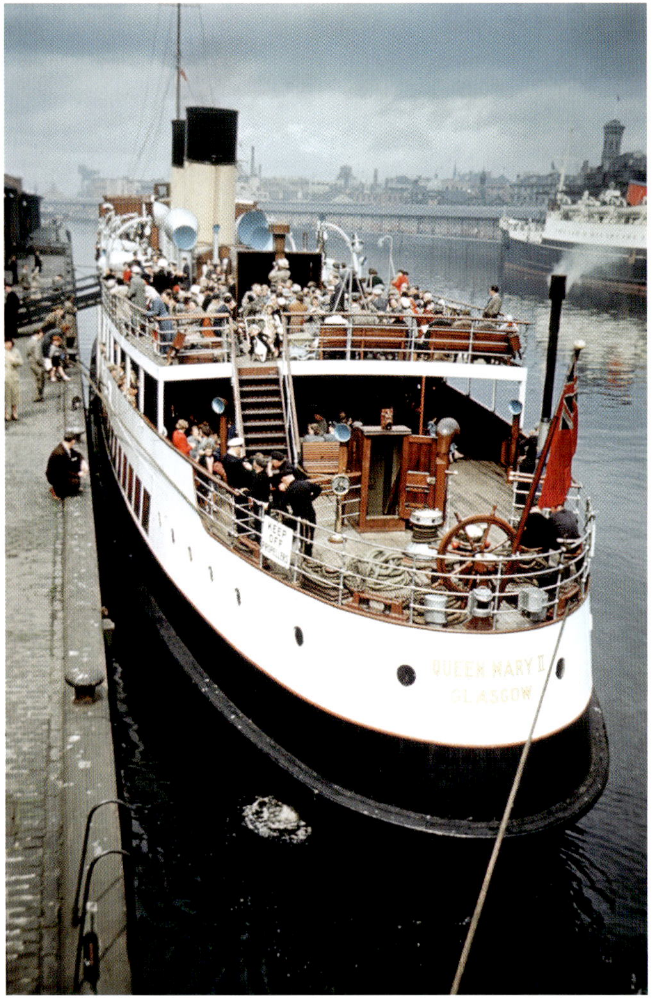

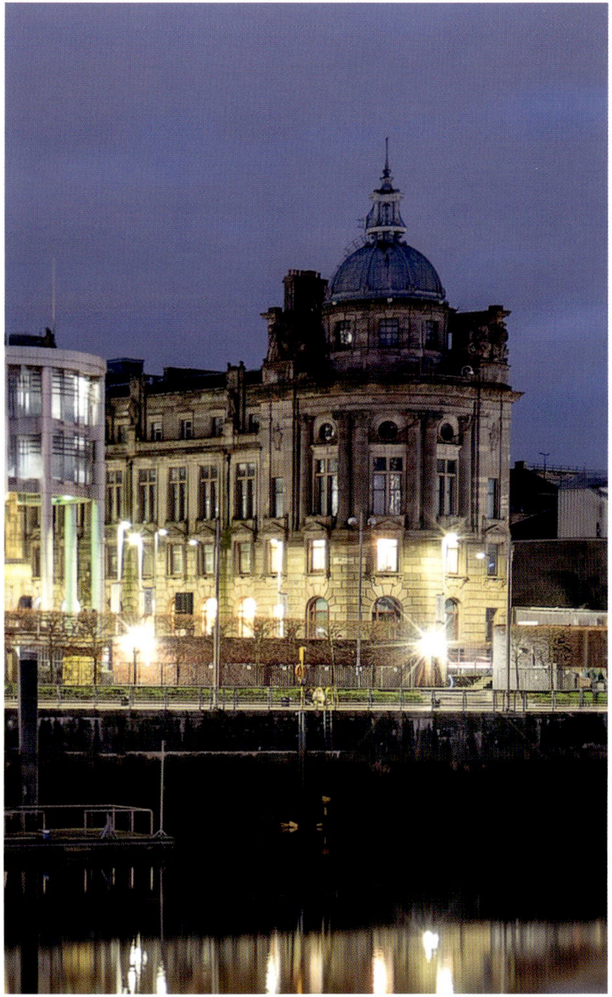

Left: Pleasure steamer *Queen Mary II* awaits her daily departure from Bridge Wharf to Rothesay and the Kyles of Bute.

Right: Clyde Navigation Trust offices, with dome, at Broomielaw and Robertson Street.

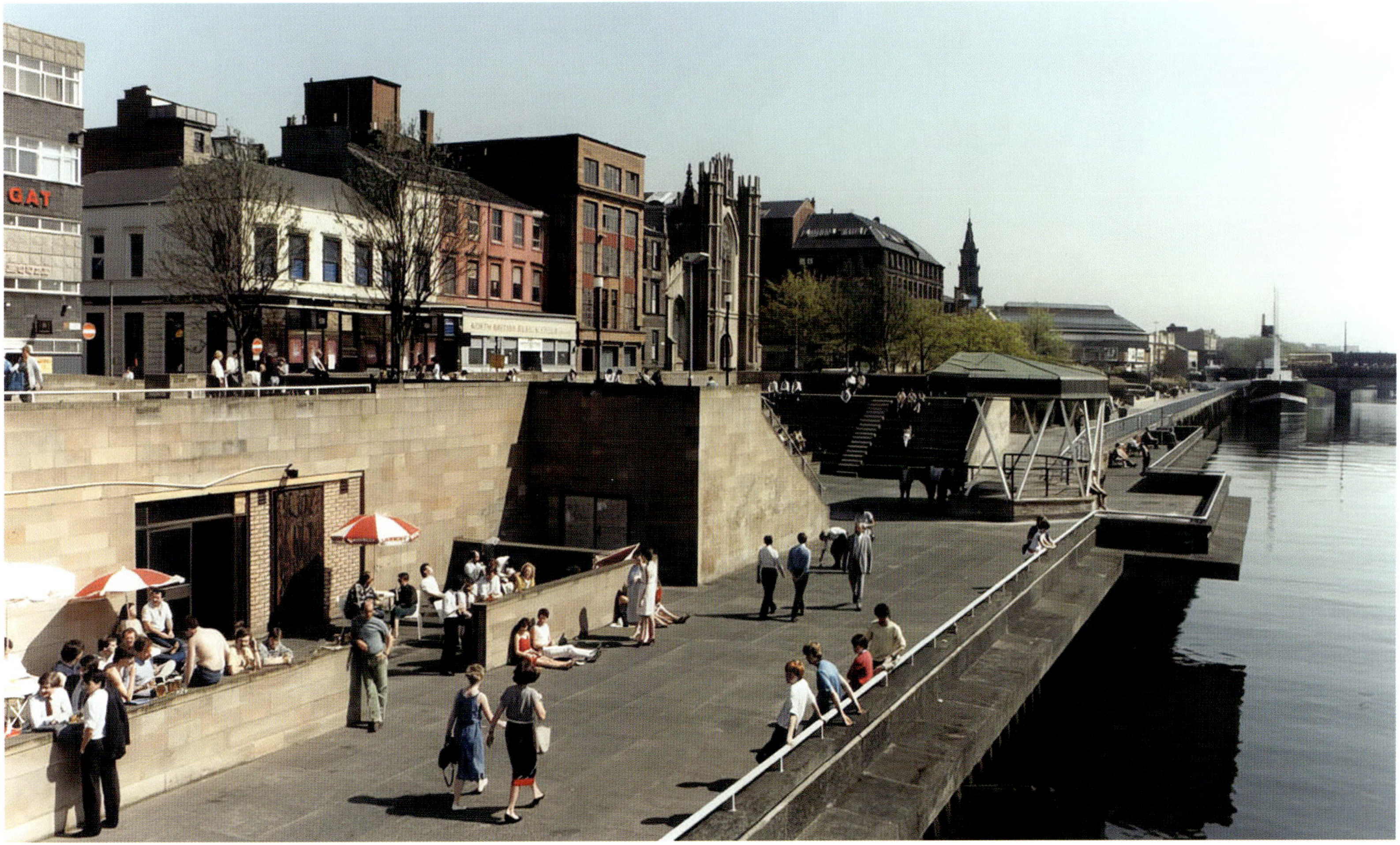

Customhouse Quay, Clyde Street, remodelled in 1973 as Clyde Walkway gardens and venues.

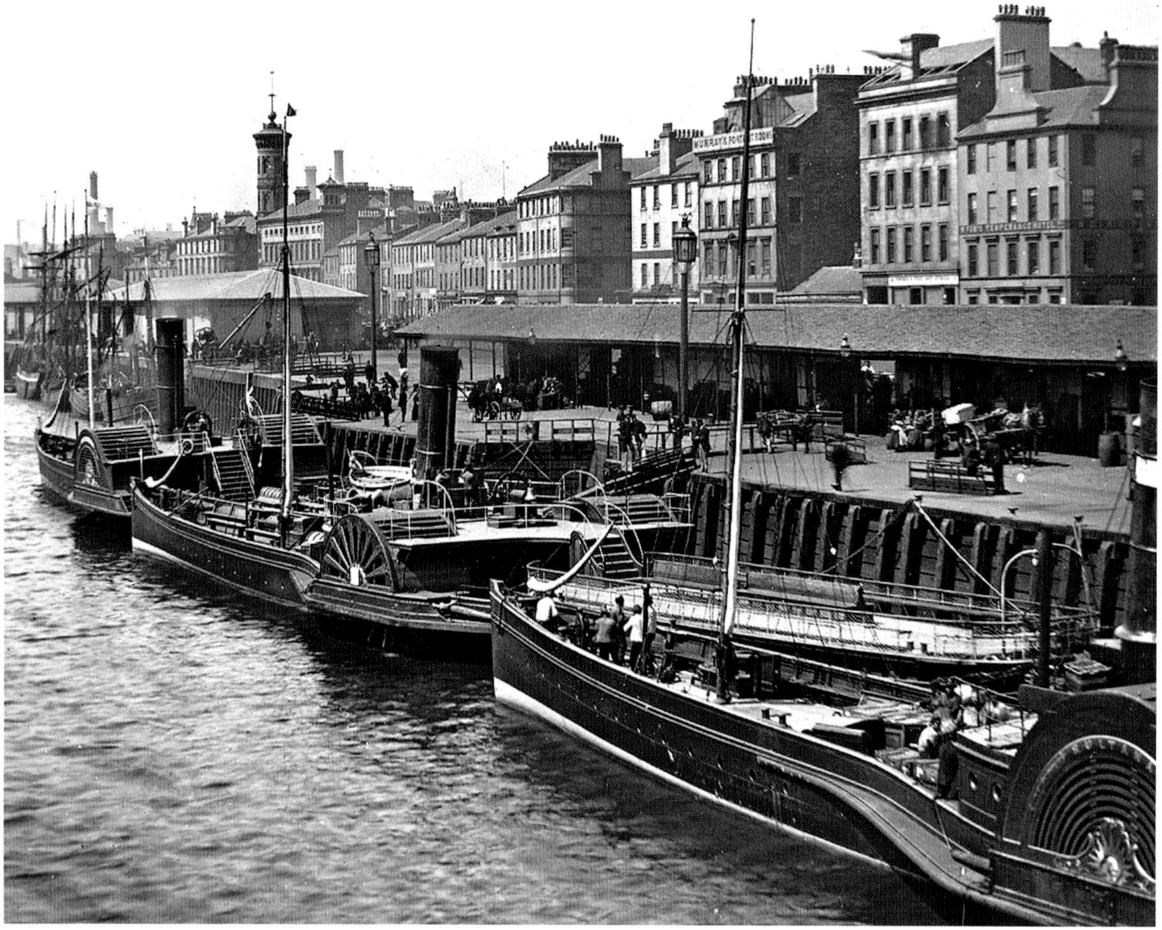

Broomielaw and early Clyde steamers with the Sailors Home tower in background.

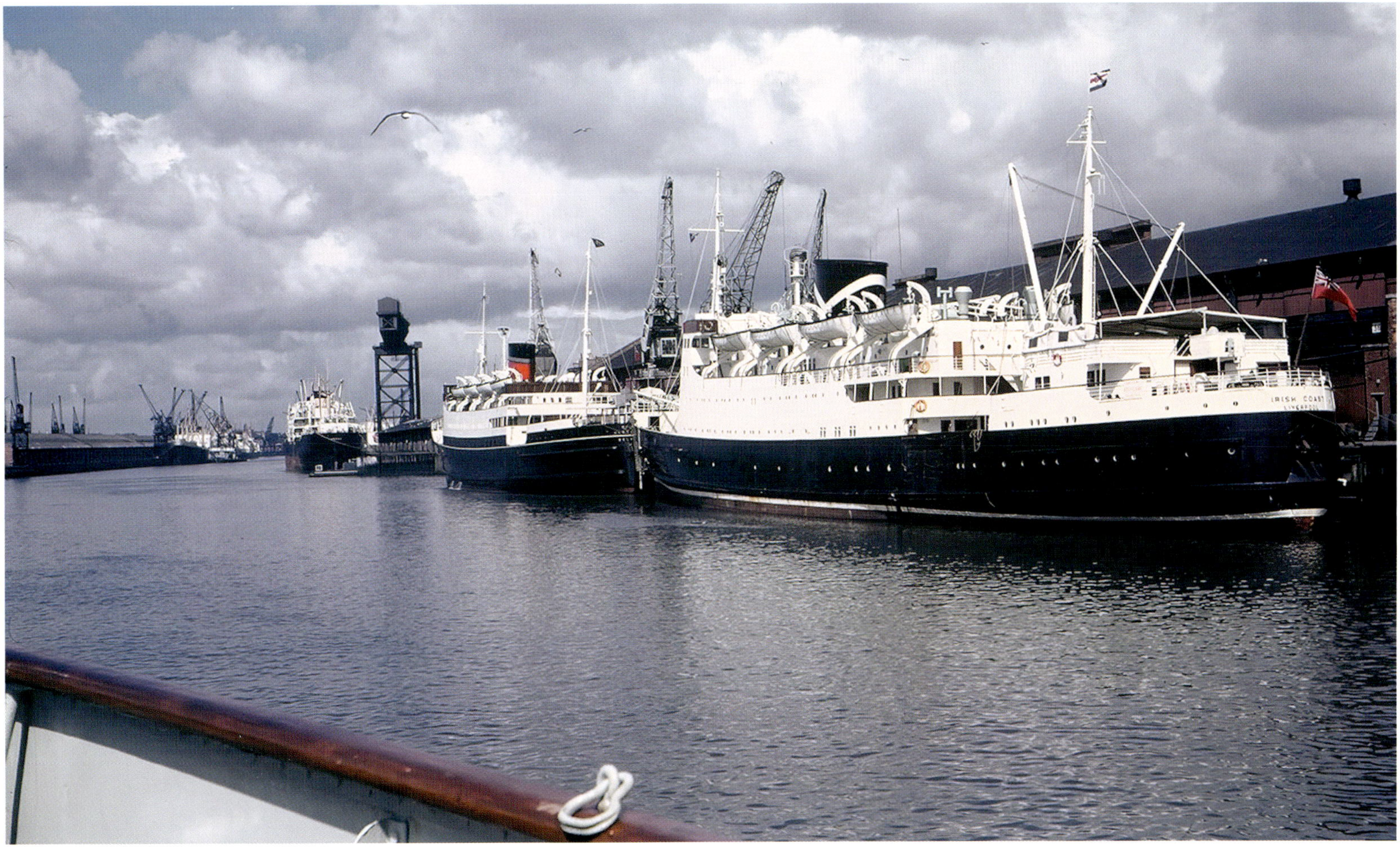

Belfast steamers at Anderston Quay.

All Aboard

With ease, passengers and cargoes sailed to and from regular destinations in Britain and Ireland, Iceland, Scandinavia, the Continent and the Mediterranean, France, Portugal, Spain, Italy, Turkey, Egypt, Canada (East and West), the Great Lakes, USA (East and West), Gulf of Mexico, West Indies, South America, North Africa, West Africa, South Africa, East Africa, Mauritius, Persian Gulf, India, Ceylon, Pakistan, Burma, Philippines, Java, Hong Kong, China, Korea, Japan, Australia and New Zealand.

The city thrived and was home to over thirty foreign consulates. As now, there were commercial diplomatic officers in each trading country. There were Commonwealth trade commissioners throughout the world, and more than twenty-four British Chambers of Commerce overseas. (Glasgow's Chamber was the first major one in the English-speaking world.) HM Customs & Excise were on hand. There was competition and choices of shipping lines. Some larger shipping lines in Glasgow had their own waiting rooms at the docks and their own stowage equipment.

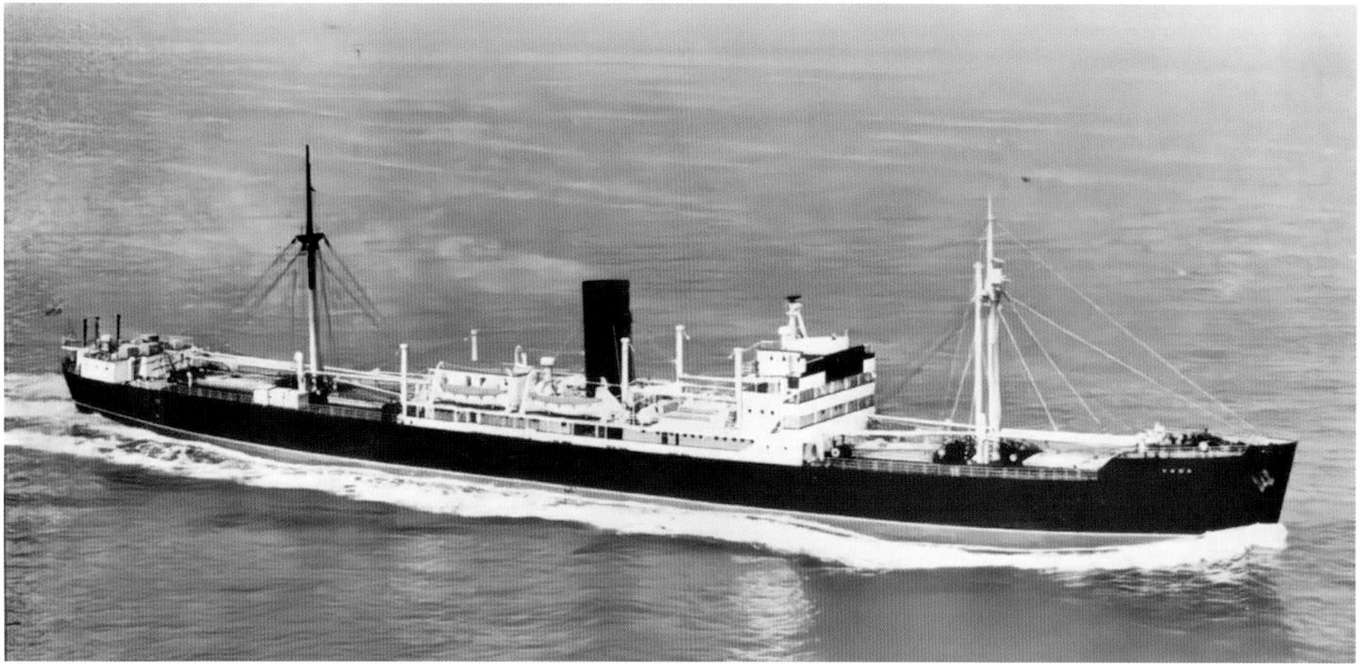

Paddy Henderson passenger cargo liner.

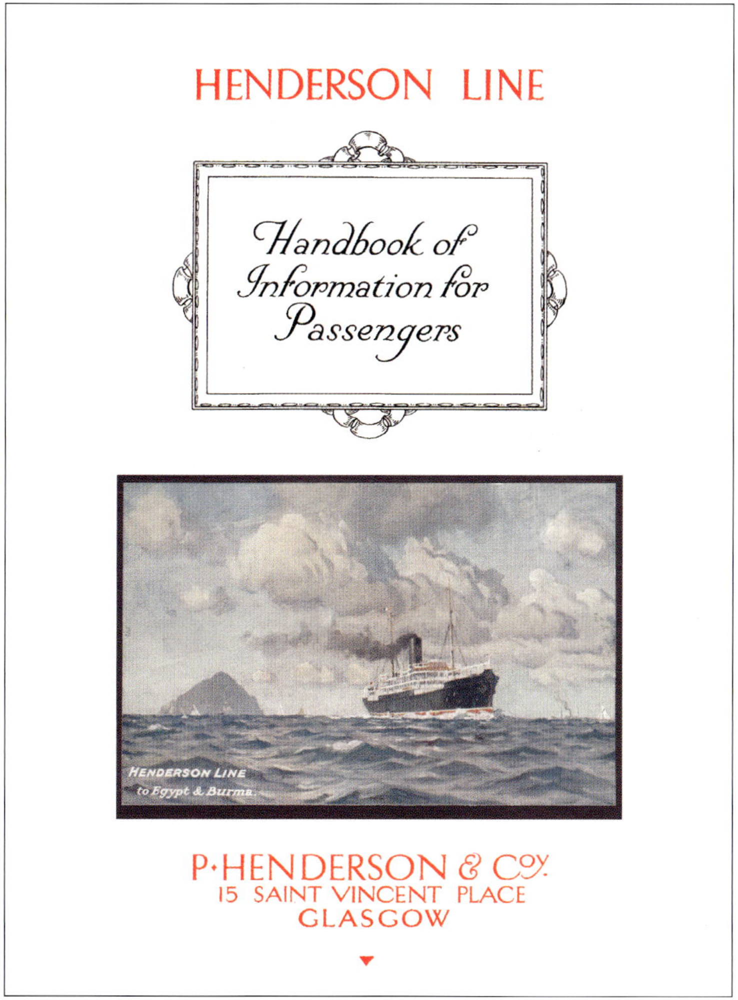
HENDERSON LINE
Handbook of Information for Passengers
HENDERSON LINE
to Egypt & Burma.
P·HENDERSON & Coy.
15 SAINT VINCENT PLACE
GLASGOW

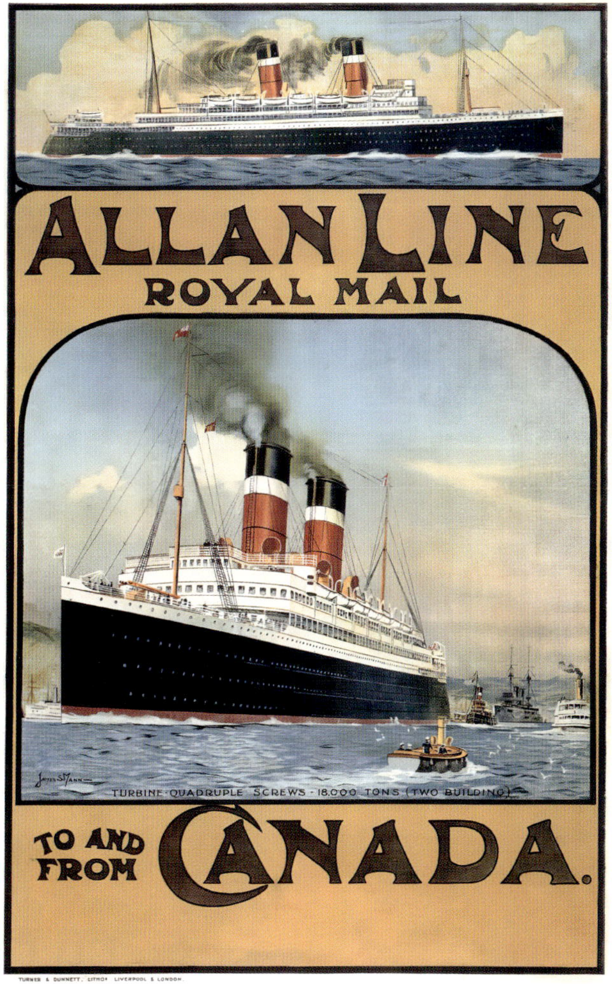
ALLAN LINE
ROYAL MAIL
TURBINE-QUADRUPLE SCREWS - 18,000 TONS (TWO BUILDING)
TO AND FROM CANADA.
TURNER & DUNNETT, LITHO. LIVERPOOL & LONDON.

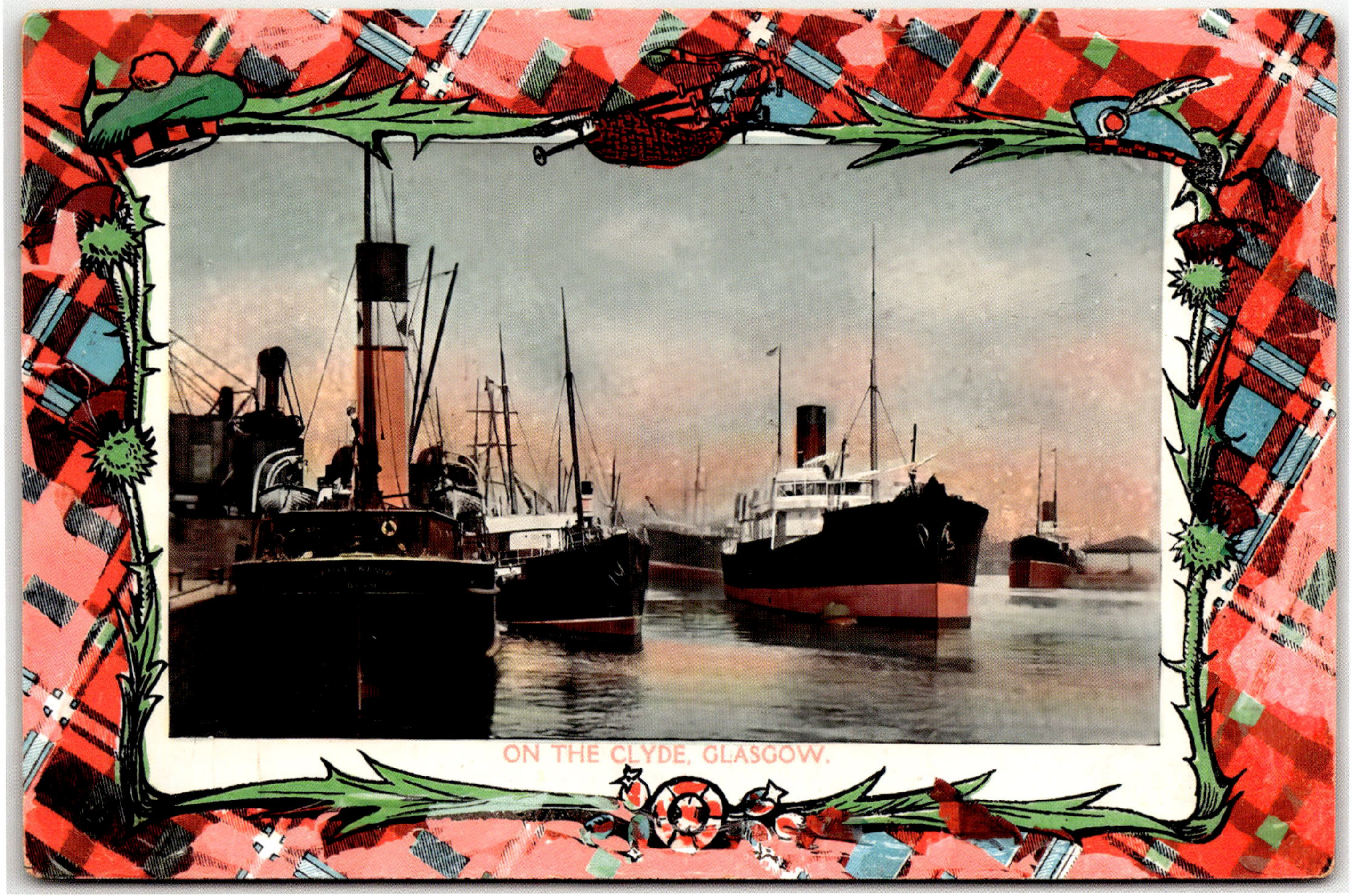

The sender of the postcard writes: 'A Busy Narrow River. Ship Building Trade Very Large.'

For All Seas and Weathers

The Nautical Cookery Book was used worldwide in many editions and over many decades. First published in the 1890s, it came about when ships' cooks, crewmen and pressed volunteers found they were all required to become certificated for catering at sea and in all weathers and seasons and for all types and sizes of ships. Deck officers and marine engineers were already long required to have certificates of competence, progressing from one level to the next according to destinations and size of vessels.

A ship is a floating town that embarks on voyages lasting weeks and even months. Smaller ships and companies had to reorganise to meet the requirements, while larger shipping lines had their own victualling departments and chefs. The book's aim was to enable the unskilled cook to do well and the trained cook to do better, twenty-four hours a day and throughout night watches.

A good cook became as important as a ship's surgeon, who maintained health, and a ship's captain, who maintained discipline. During its ocean voyaging, ships of the Glasgow-registered Hogarth Line were called the 'Hungry Hogarths', until changes were made.

The Nautical Cookery Book became a standard for the Shipping Federation and formed the mainstay of its Nautical Schools of Cookery, which followed the example of Glasgow and Liverpool. The publishers, Brown, Son & Ferguson, continue to produce nautical titles.

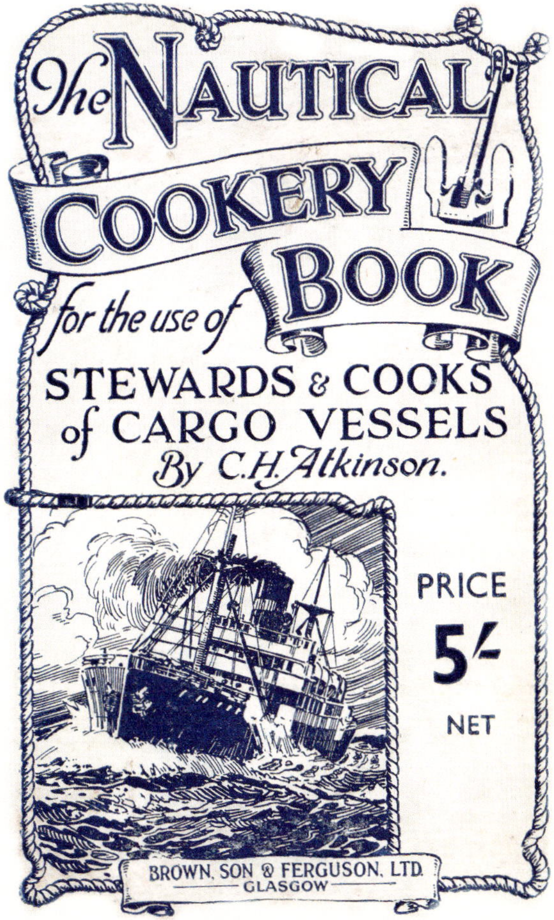

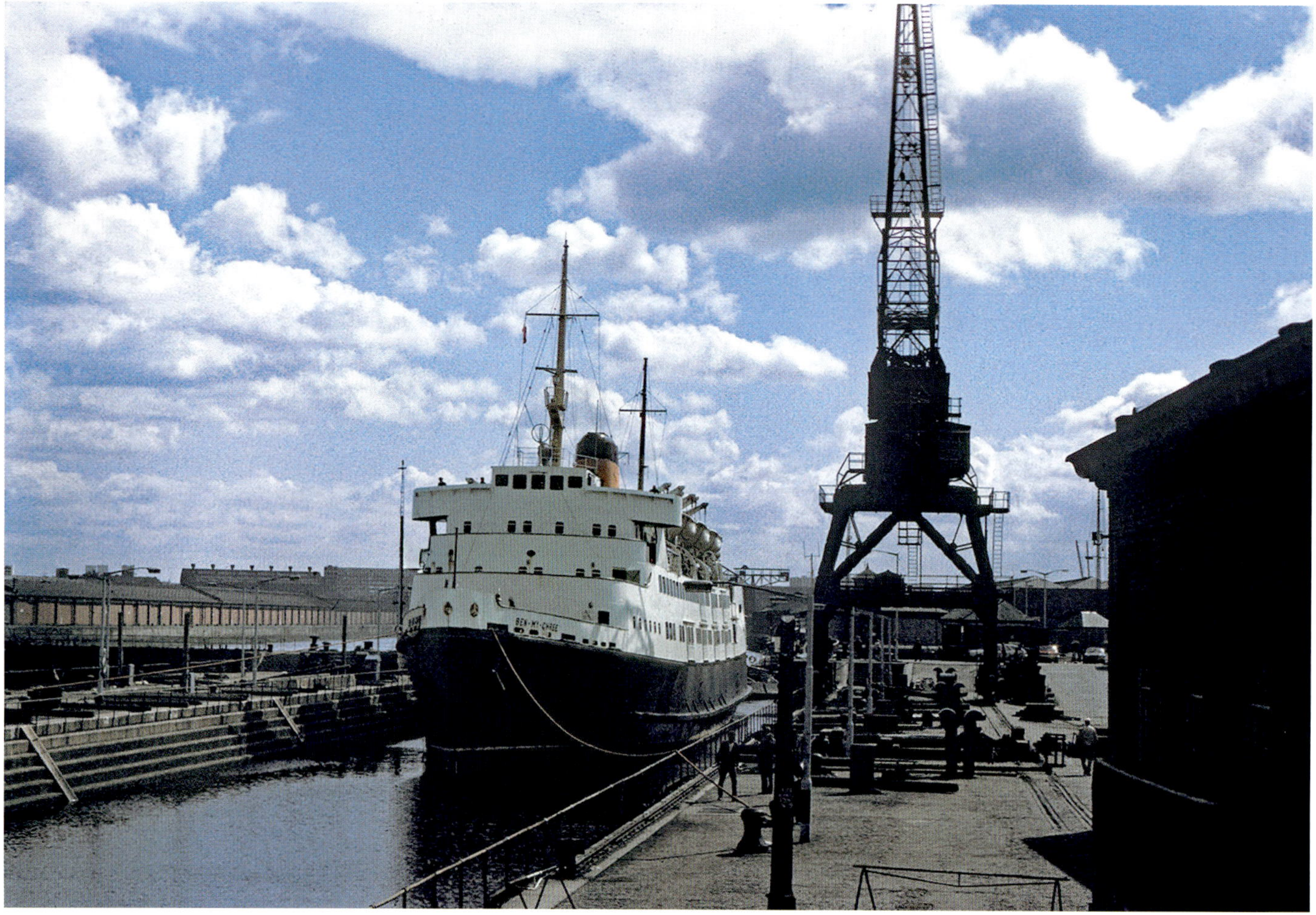

Isle of Man steamer entering dry dock at Govan.

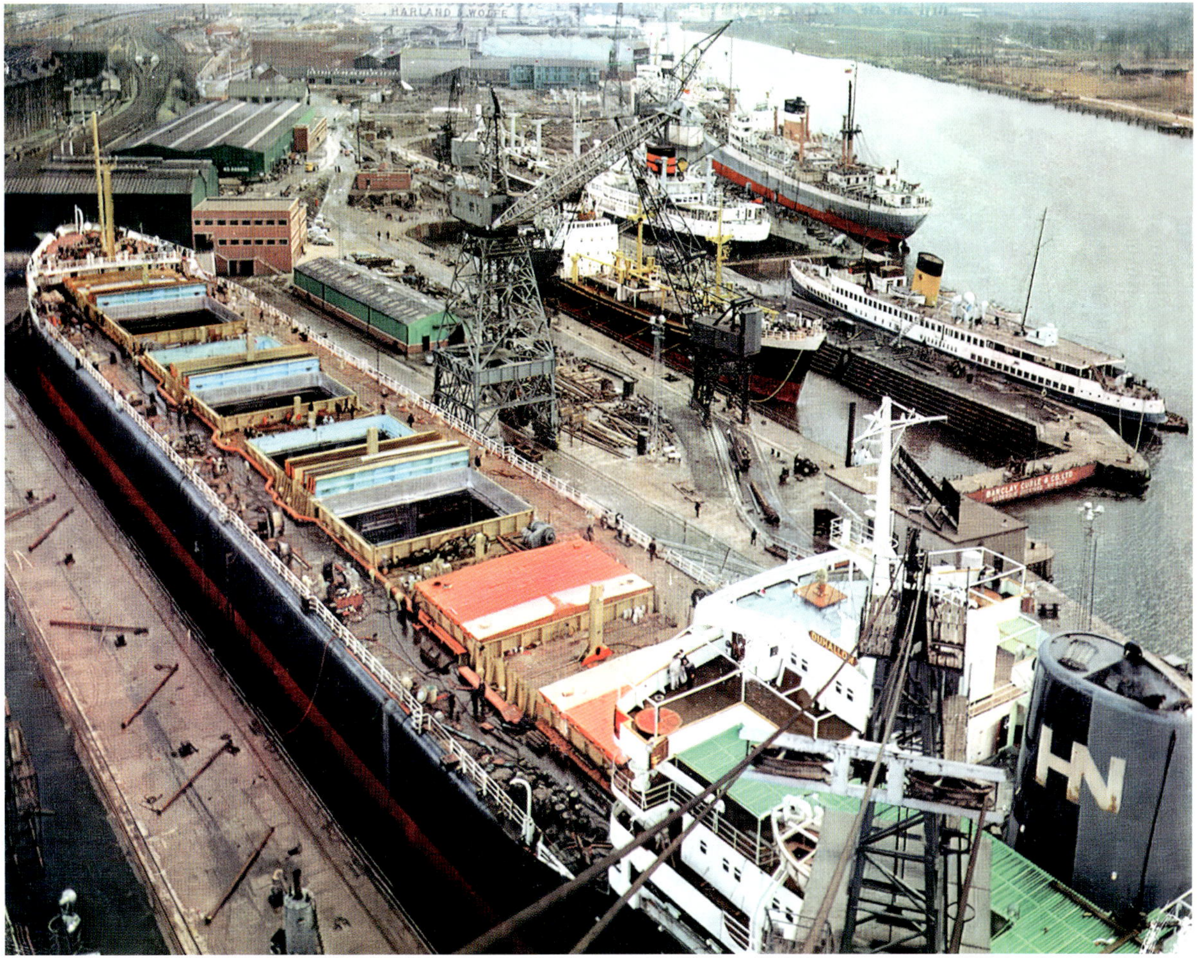

Barclay Curle's Elderslie dry docks at Scotstoun. They continue in use.

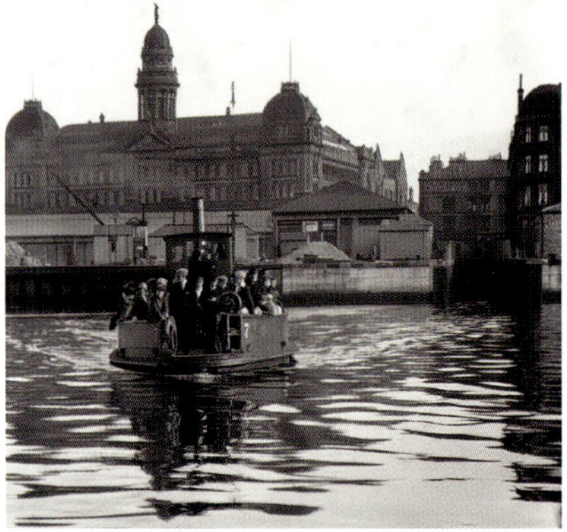

Left: The ferry from Kingston Dock to Anderston.

Right: *Bound for the Front*, painting by James Kay. This depicts a troopship departing from the Clyde, passing Govan.

Below left: *Clyde Street Ferry*, painting by David Small, 1861.

Below right: *Glasgow Docks in Winter*, painting by Robert Eadie, 1920s.

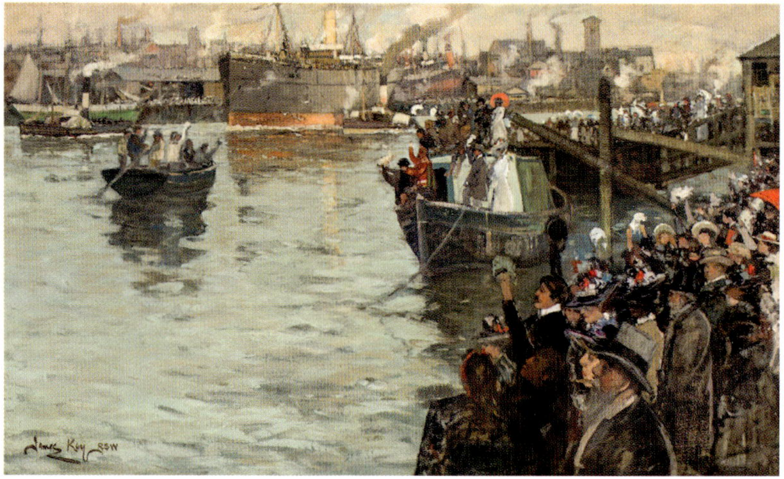

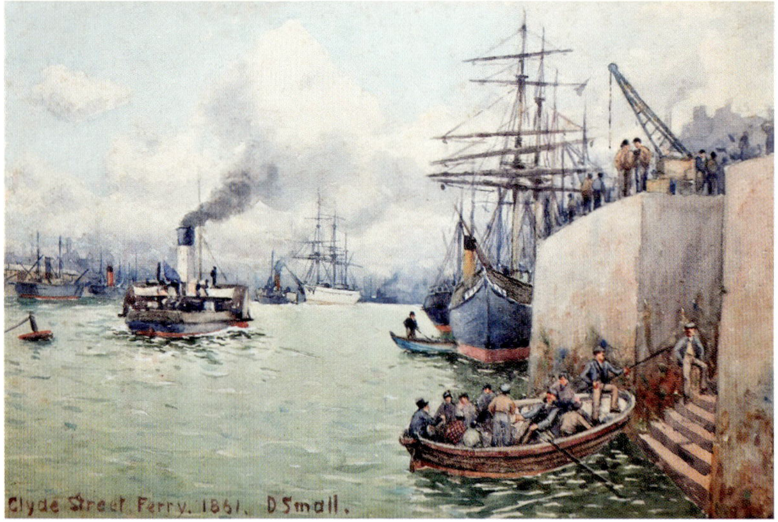

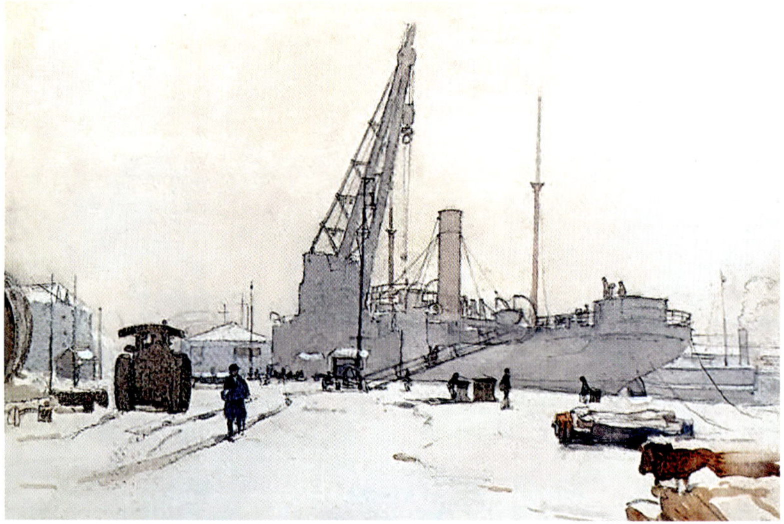

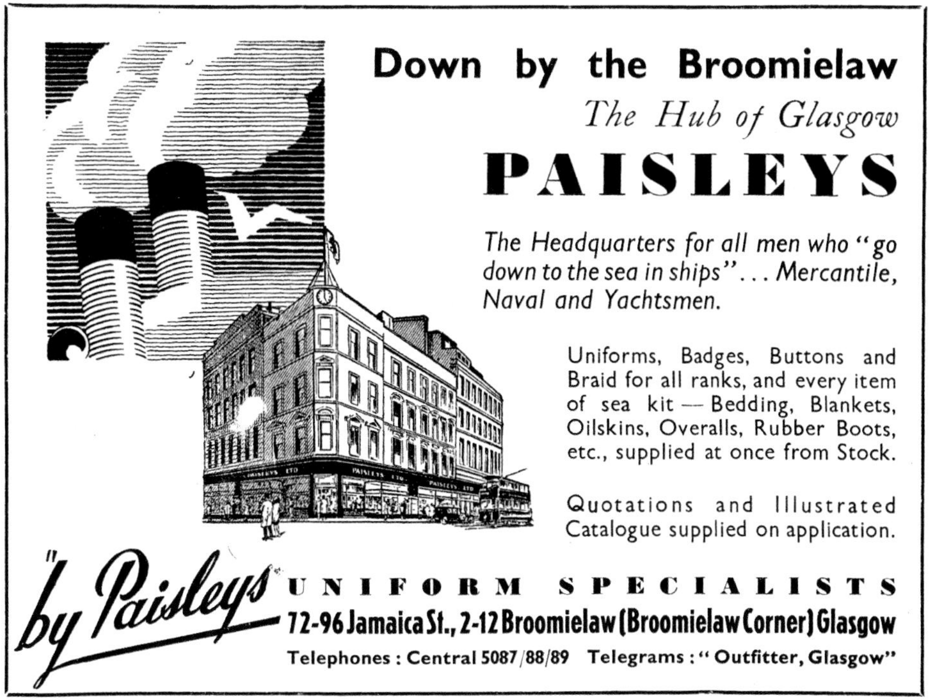

Workwear and Uniforms

Yard and dock workers required dungarees and the warmest of jackets and bunnets. Boiler suits proved their worth in production sheds and engine works. Mariners – mercantile and naval – needed the full range of uniforms, reefer jackets and workwear to accommodate all manner of climates to be available at the shortest notice and worn in all weathers on voyages.

Prominently situated at the foot of Jamaica Street at the Broomielaw, Paisleys became the largest supplier of uniforms for all organisations. Other suppliers to companies and sailors were found around the Broomielaw, including the Clyde Outfitting Company at the corner of James Watt Street and Boyd Bros further up Jamaica Street. Malcolm the Tailors in West Nile Street, near Gordon Street, specialised in tropical suits and uniforms.

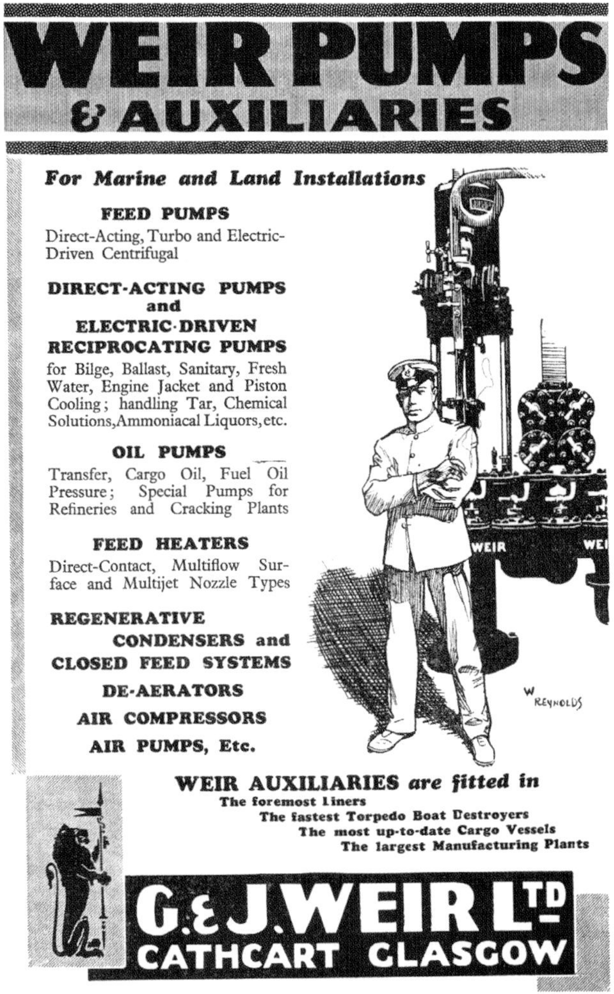
WEIR PUMPS
& AUXILIARIES
For Marine and Land Installations
FEED PUMPS
Direct-Acting, Turbo and Electric-Driven Centrifugal
DIRECT-ACTING PUMPS and ELECTRIC-DRIVEN RECIPROCATING PUMPS
for Bilge, Ballast, Sanitary, Fresh Water, Engine Jacket and Piston Cooling; handling Tar, Chemical Solutions, Ammoniacal Liquors, etc.
OIL PUMPS
Transfer, Cargo Oil, Fuel Oil Pressure; Special Pumps for Refineries and Cracking Plants
FEED HEATERS
Direct-Contact, Multiflow Surface and Multijet Nozzle Types
REGENERATIVE CONDENSERS and CLOSED FEED SYSTEMS
DE-AERATORS
AIR COMPRESSORS
AIR PUMPS, Etc.
WEIR
W REYNOLDS
WEIR AUXILIARIES are fitted in
The foremost Liners
The fastest Torpedo Boat Destroyers
The most up-to-date Cargo Vessels
The largest Manufacturing Plants
G. & J. WEIR LTD
CATHCART GLASGOW

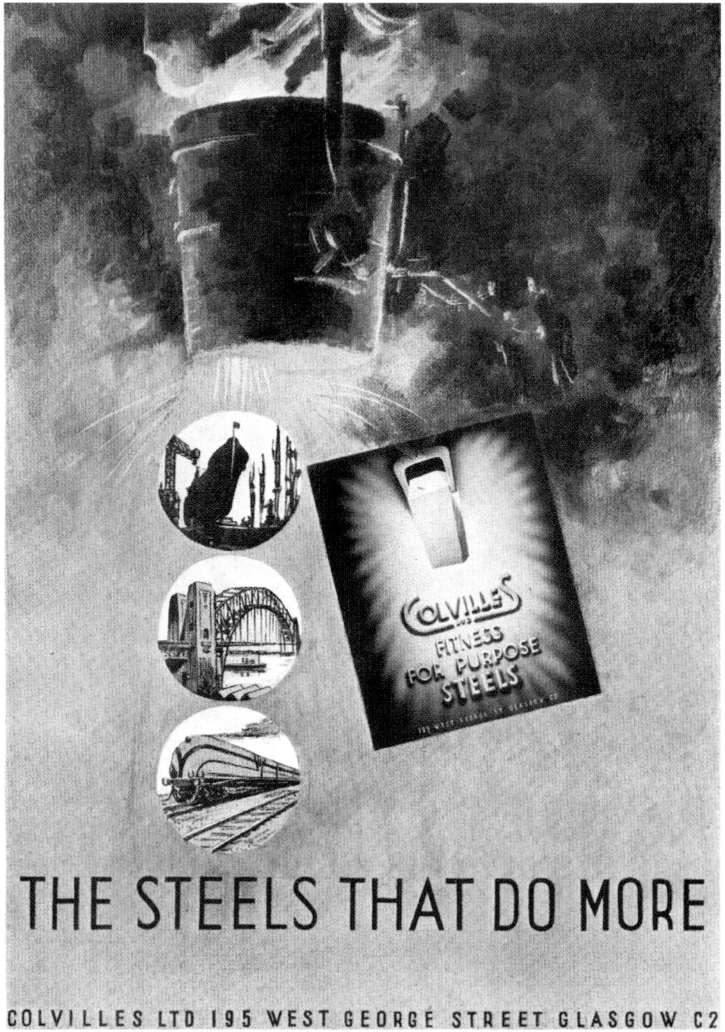
COLVILLES
FITNESS FOR PURPOSE STEELS
THE STEELS THAT DO MORE
COLVILLES LTD 195 WEST GEORGE STREET GLASGOW C2

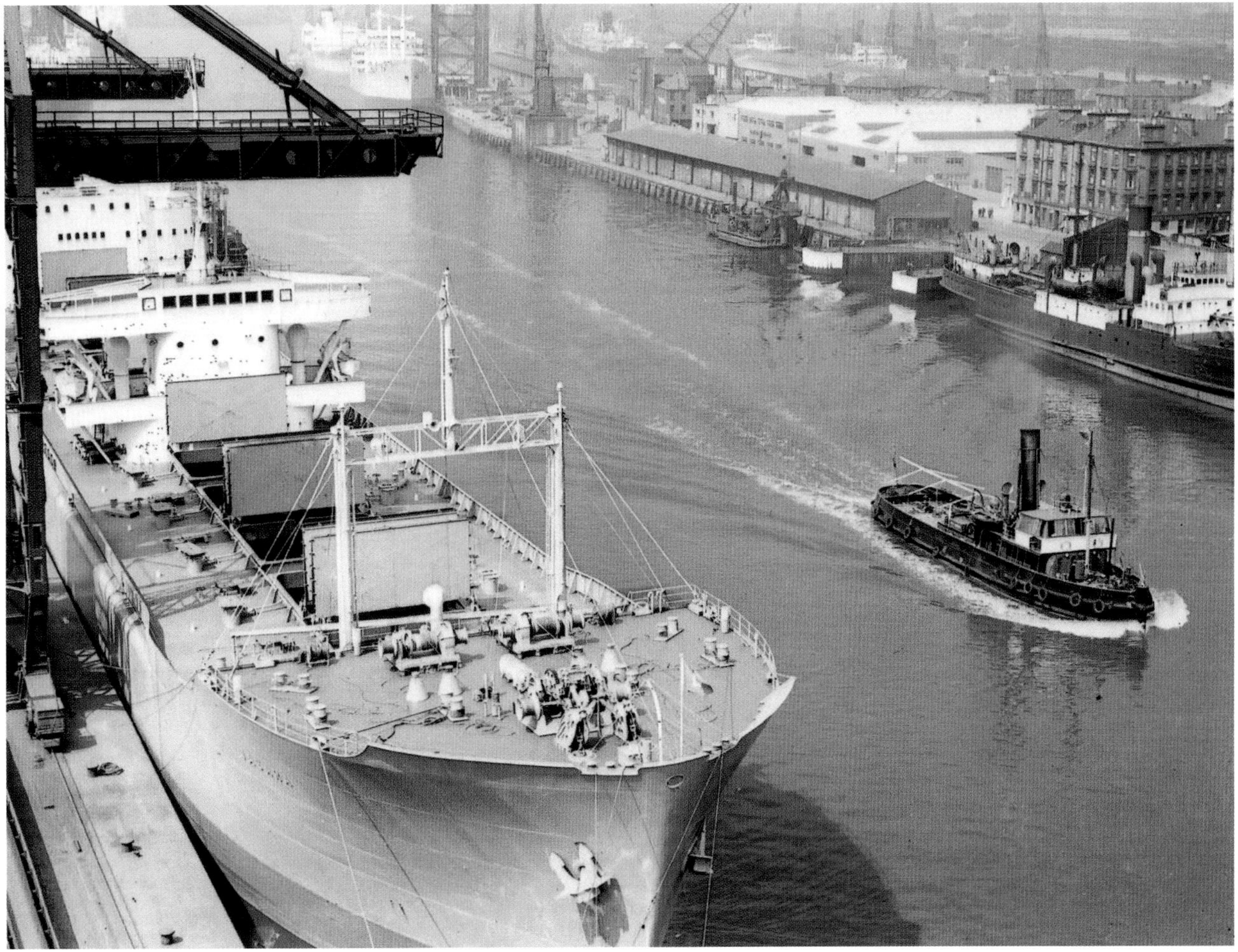

An iron-ore carrier is unloaded at General Terminus Quay, looking towards Finnieston and Queen's Dock.

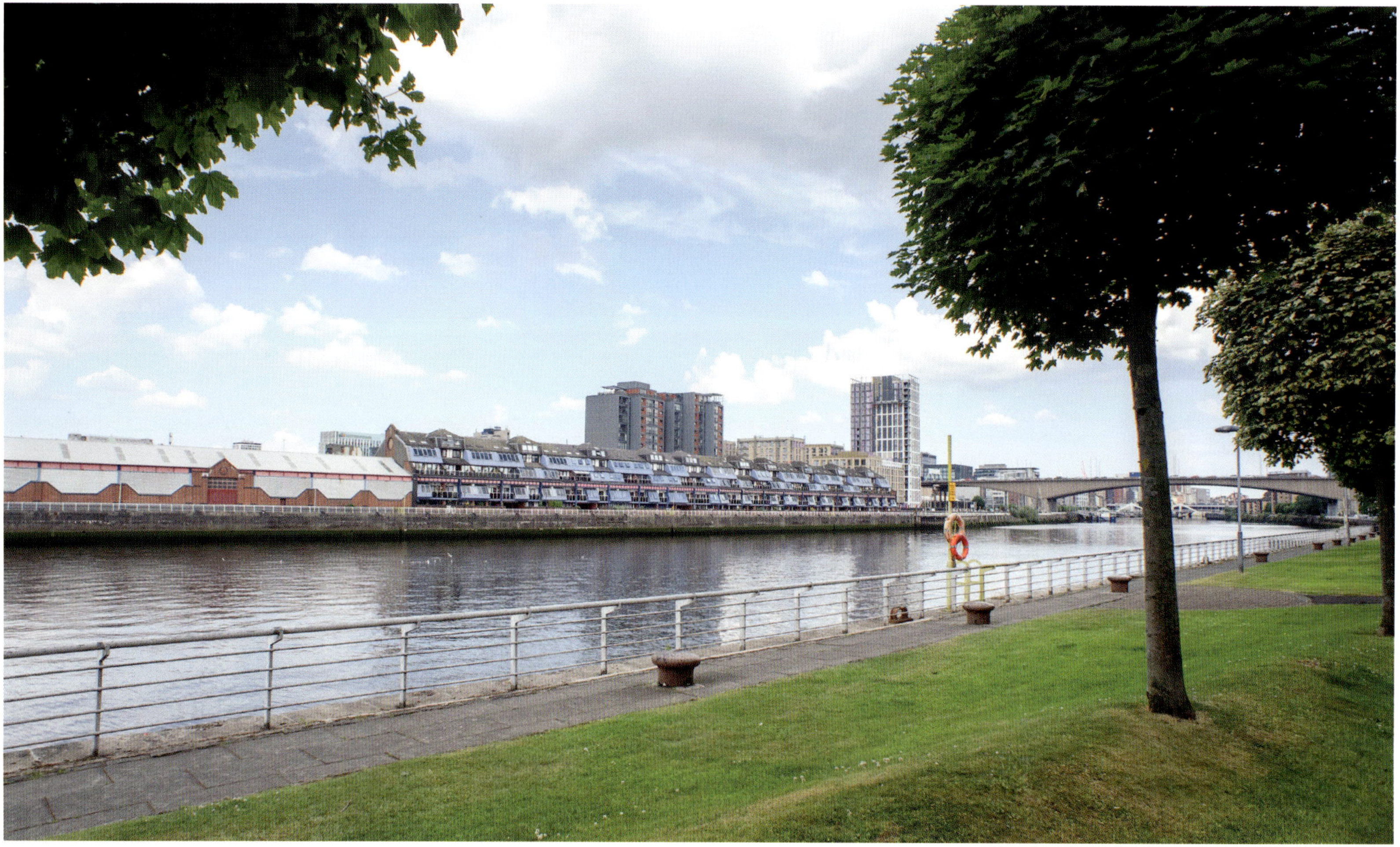

General Terminus Quay today, looking towards Anderston Quay and Kingston Bridge.

NAVIGATING A FUTURE

As ever, opportunities arise with changes in trade. The advent of containerisation and airlines carrying both passengers and substantial freight meant that many cities, including London, Liverpool, Manchester and Glasgow, had docklands that no longer met requirements. The first major shipyard to withdraw from the Glasgow epicentre was Harland & Wolff, its main site becoming new council houses built by Glasgow Corporation on the former slipways, with Queen Elizabeth II opening its riverside walkway in 1977.

In the capital, London Docklands Development Corporation, following the success of new town development corporations from 1947 onwards, started in 1981 with powers to regenerate the docklands area of East London. In the late 1970s the newly formed Scottish Development Agency (SDA) was given broadly similar powers to improve the economy of Scotland, take over and run the Scottish Industrial Estates Corporation, increase land renewal, develop urban renewal of existing cities and towns (until then the New Towns had received most of the attention), provide business advice and stimulate investment.

Emphasis was placed on new research and technologies, service industries and tourism and a need for a slice of the lucrative international conference business. The aim was to create a new shop window for Scotland to tempt the world. SDA bought Queen's Dock, completing its infill and stabilisation. It built the Scottish Exhibition & Conference Centre, opening in 1985 (successor to the Kelvin Hall), and cofunded the multi-storey hotel on the banks of the Clyde, which was fully opened in 1989. Both had space for parking and development of more venues and hotels was anticipated. The Clyde Auditorium (Armadillo) opened in 1997 and the circular Hydro arena in 2013.

Shortly after starting the Queen's Dock work, SDA conceived the possibility of Glasgow hosting a national garden festival with former industrial land being renewed and put to new uses while also marketing the area internationally. This was a new turning point for the city and a prelude to it becoming the European City of Culture in 1990. On the southside of the river the SDA bought Prince's Dock and its quays – a total of 120 acres – recently acquired from Clydeport by housebuilder John Laing. For Laing, the Agency funded offset sites elsewhere in Glasgow, allowing the company to build there instead. SDA relocated remaining businesses, cleared the site of industrial workings, partly filled the dock and totally redesigned the area for the Glasgow Garden Festival, 1988. (Kingston Dock – not part of the site – was filled in before this and houses built.)

Operated by an arm of SDA, the Festival attracted 4 million visitors. Afterwards commercial developments, encouraged by SDA and the city council, gradually emerged, led mainly by housing but firstly a cinema and restaurants at Springfield Quay. The Prince's

Dock area was marketed as 'Pacific Quay' because the Broomielaw was now being marketed as 'Atlantic Quay'. Glasgow Science Centre and visitor centre opened in 2001, followed by STV and BBC Scotland studios, businesses and hotels.

In the mid-1980s SDA initiated the Broomielaw project of urban renewal, buying up vacated properties and old bonded warehouses, assembling land and supporting major new office buildings, hotel development and housing. From the 1990s this became the International Financial Services District, led by the city council and reaching up to Bothwell Street and extending across the river to Tradeston. The area mainly attracted financial-technology firms and banks.

Where the Kelvin joins the Clyde, the city council opened its Riverside Museum visitor centre in 2011, partly in response to the proposal in 1988 for a major Glasgow World Maritime Heritage Centre that aimed to adapt and reuse the immense Yorkhill Quay and buildings. The nearby Queen's Dock hydraulic pumphouse and Italianate tower has become the Clydeside Distillery and visitor centre. In Govan, Fairfield Heritage museum and visitor centre opened in 2013.

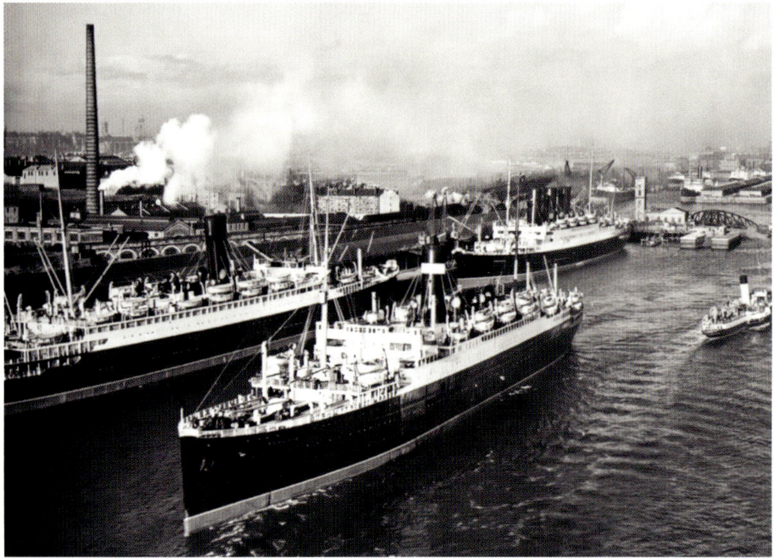

Donaldson Line's *Athenia* en route to Canada, passing Yorkhill Quay.

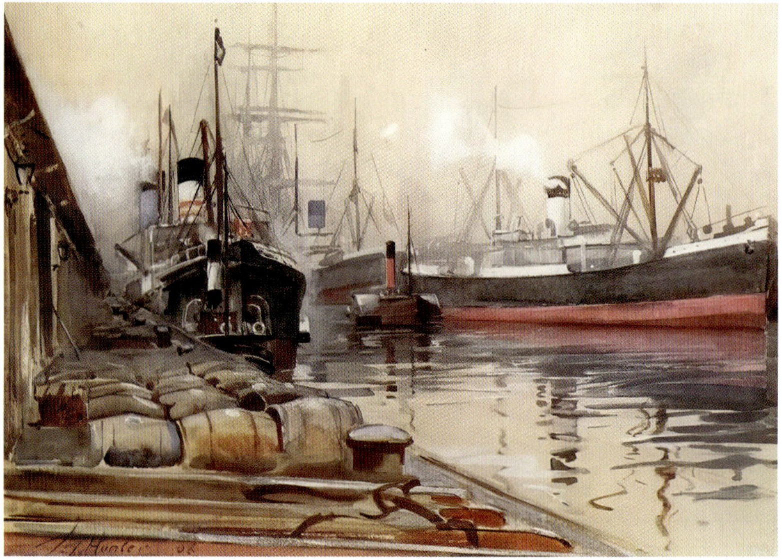

Queen's Dock south basin, painting by Leslie Young Hunter, 1900s.

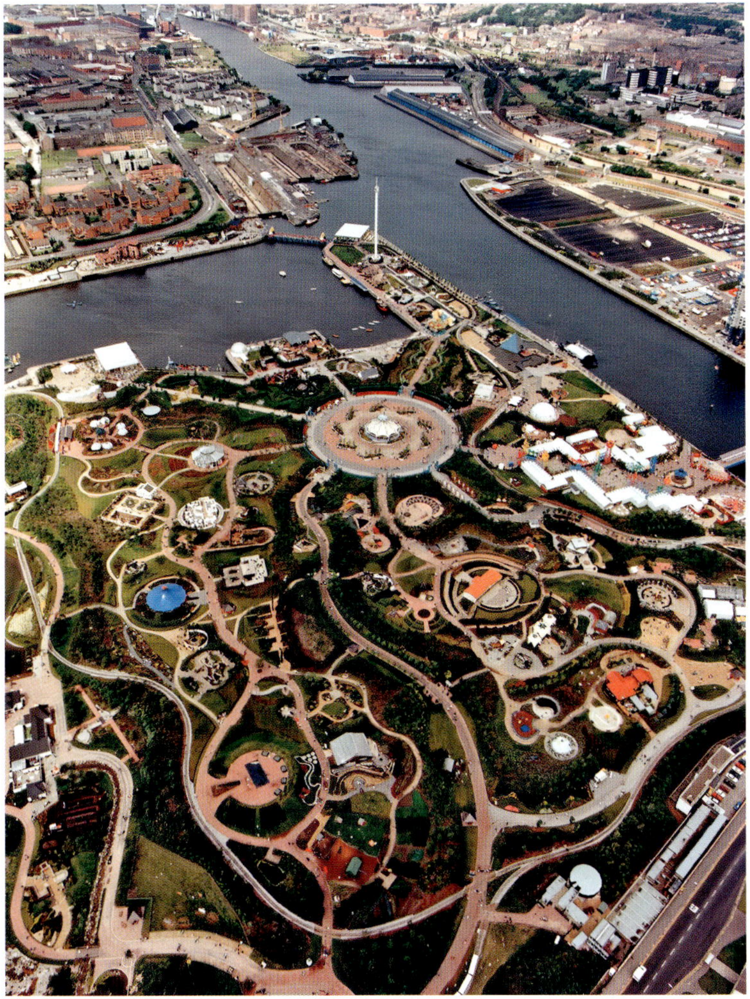

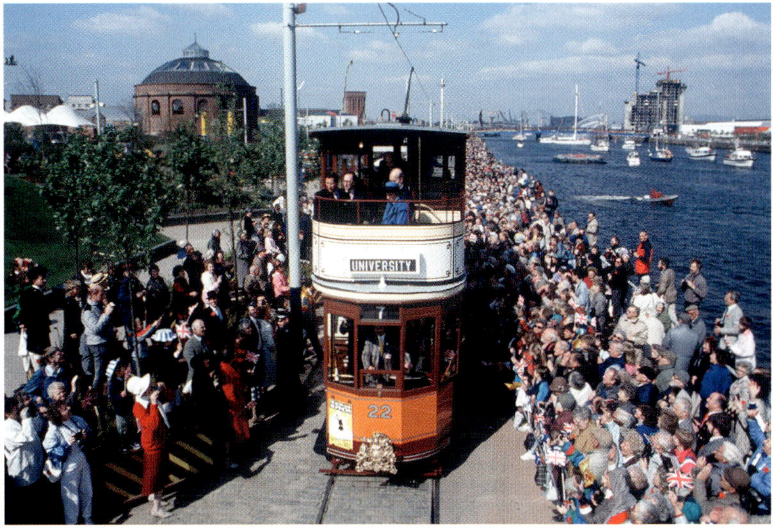

Above: The opening day of the Glasgow Garden Festival, May 1988. The Prince and Princess of Wales are in the leading tramcar.

Left: Prince's Dock and quays developed as the Glasgow Garden Festival, 1988. Yorkhill Quay and Basin can be seen in the distance.

Glasgow Garden Festival, 1988

Occupying Prince's Dock and quays, the new undulating landscaped setting showcased the city and region with themed gardens, pavilions, bandstands, performance areas, amusements and the festival village. The Garden Festival was officially opened in May by the Prince and Princess of Wales. On the other side of the river is the new Scottish Exhibition & Conference Centre, and beyond that Yorkhill Quay.

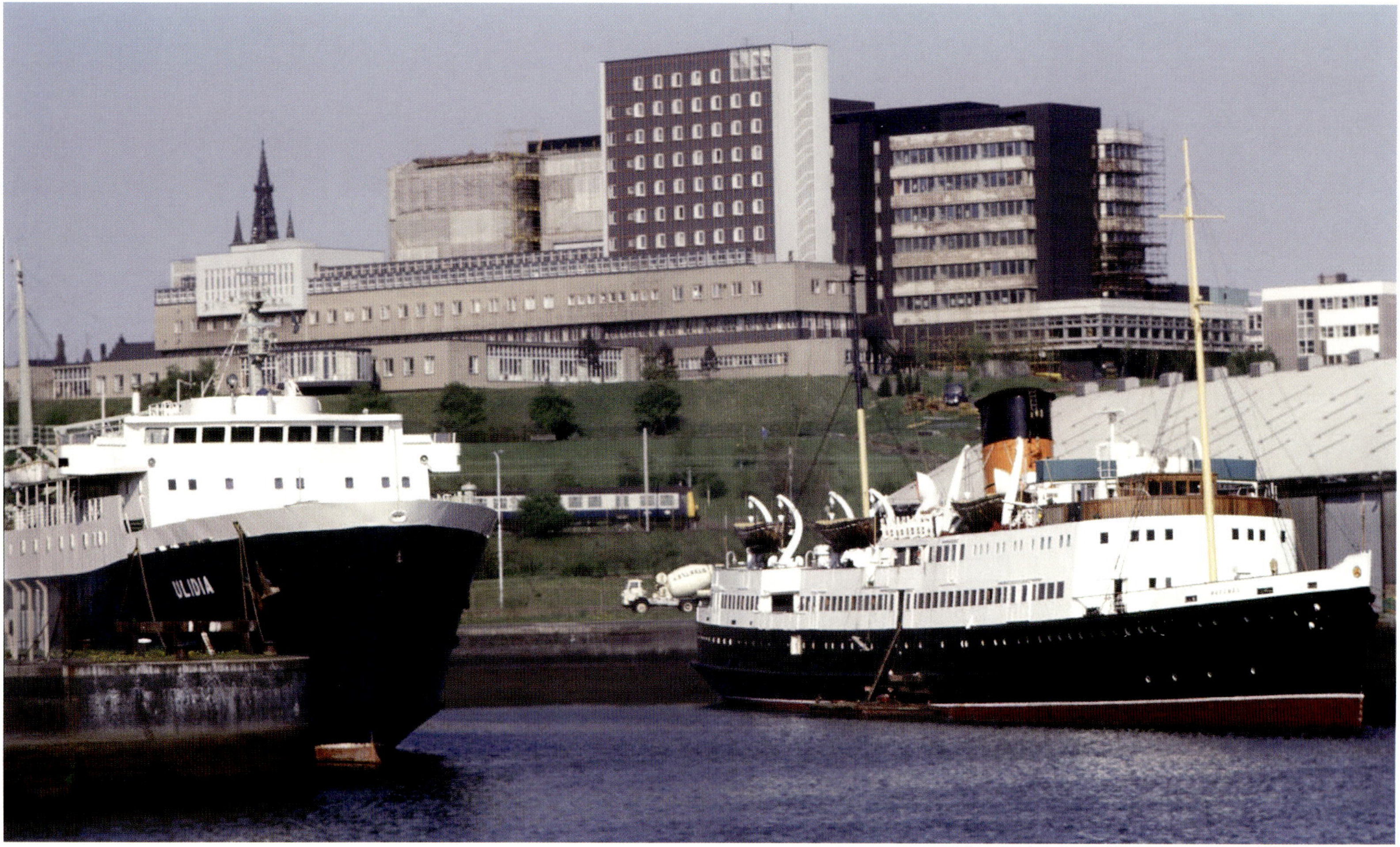

Yorkhill Basin; beyond is Yorkhill Children's Hospital and the Queen Mother's Maternity Hospital.

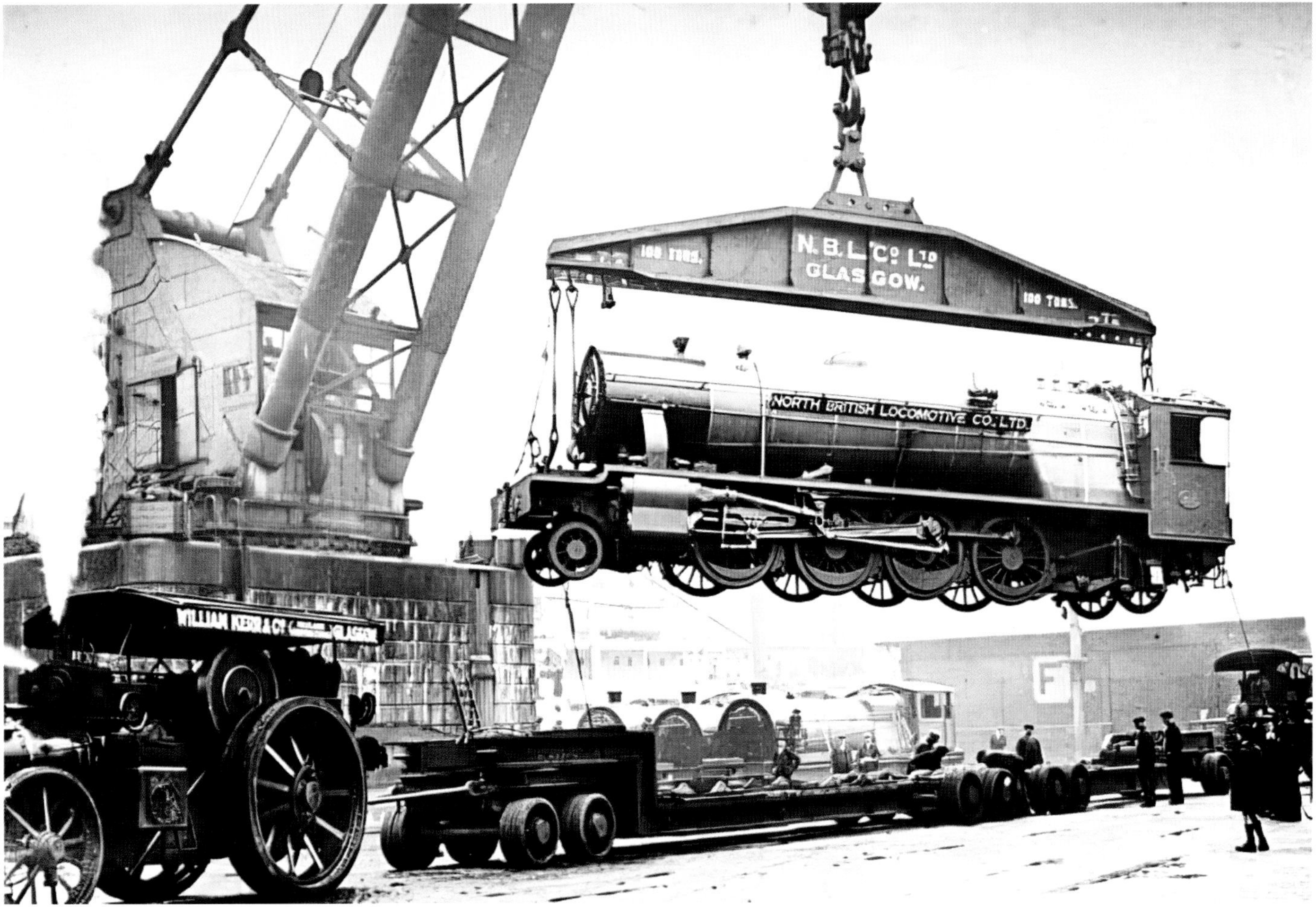

Loading locomotives at Prince's Dock.

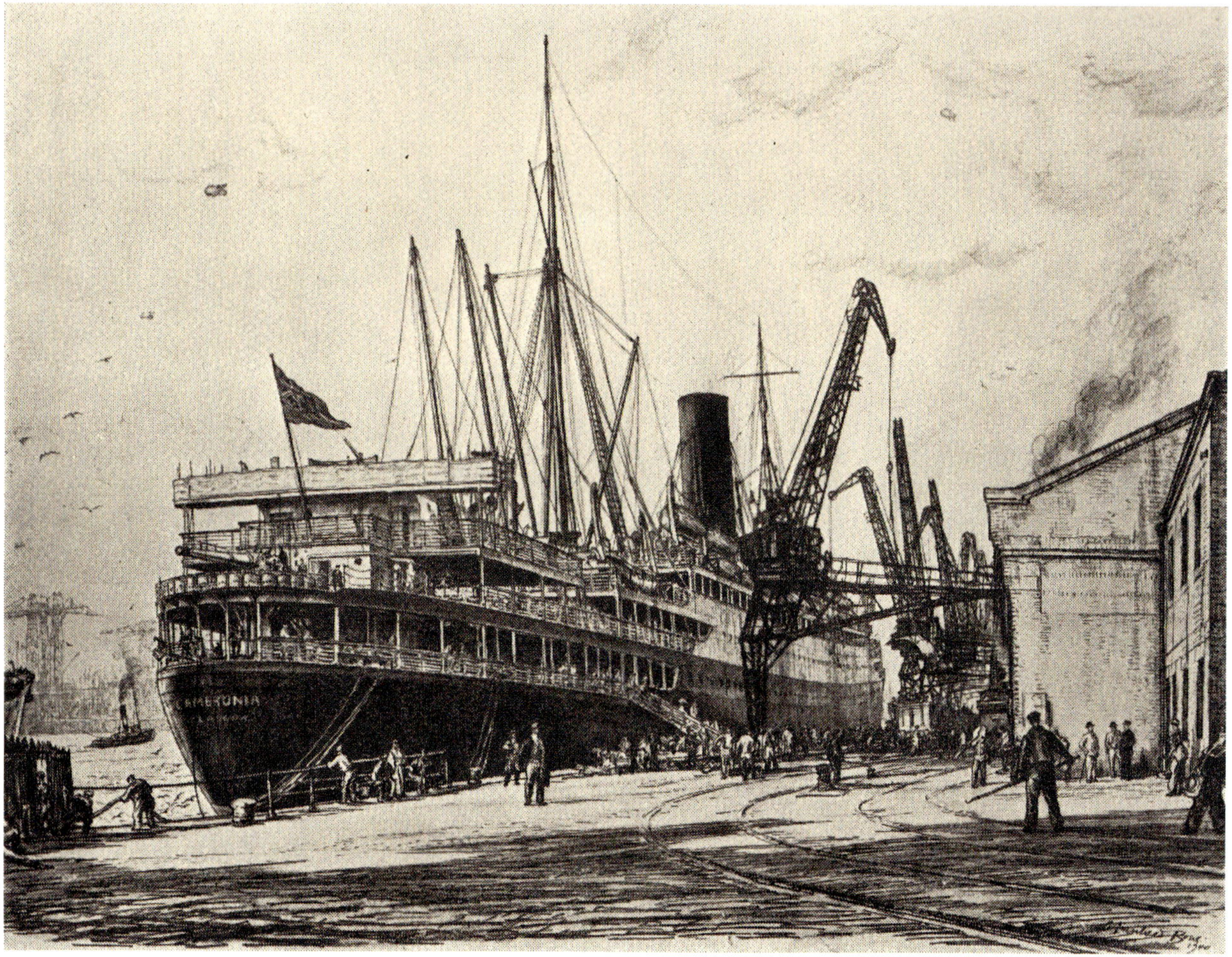

Unloading an ocean liner at Yorkhill Quay, drawing by Sir Muirhead Bone, 1940.

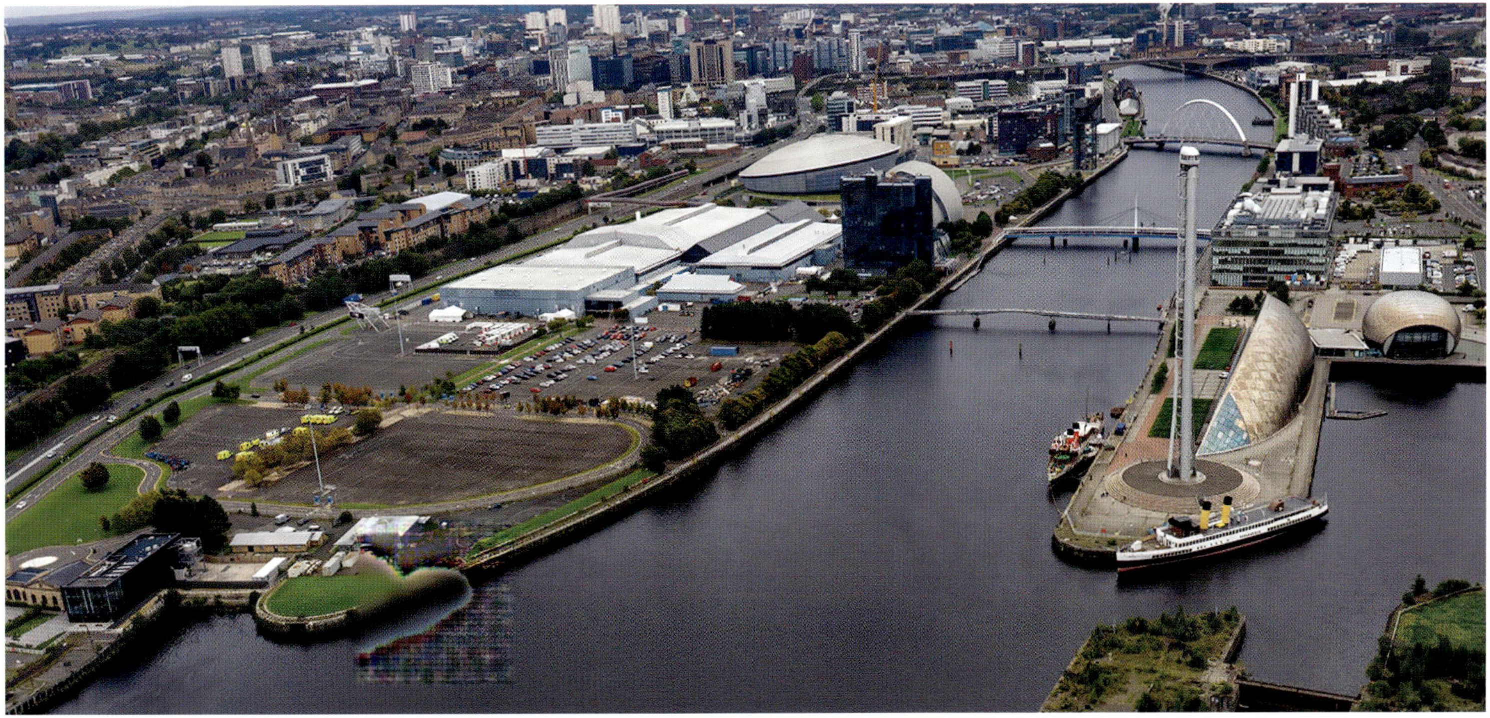

Panoramic view of Queen's Dock and Prince's Dock today.

Bird's-Eye View

The vast Queen's Dock contains the now-named Scottish Event Campus (SEC) with the Scottish Exhibition Centre in the middle and, beyond, the first hotel. The SEC Armadillo, designed as a series of interlocking ships hulls, is an auditorium seating 3,000 people. The Hydro arena can accommodate 14,000 people. There are more hotels beyond these complexes. Next to Yorkhill Quay, lower left, the Queen's Dock hydraulic power station houses the Clydeside Distillery.

To the right, Prince's Dock houses the Pacific Quay area, firstly the Glasgow Science Centre buildings, followed by BBC Scotland and STV studios, businesses and more hotels.

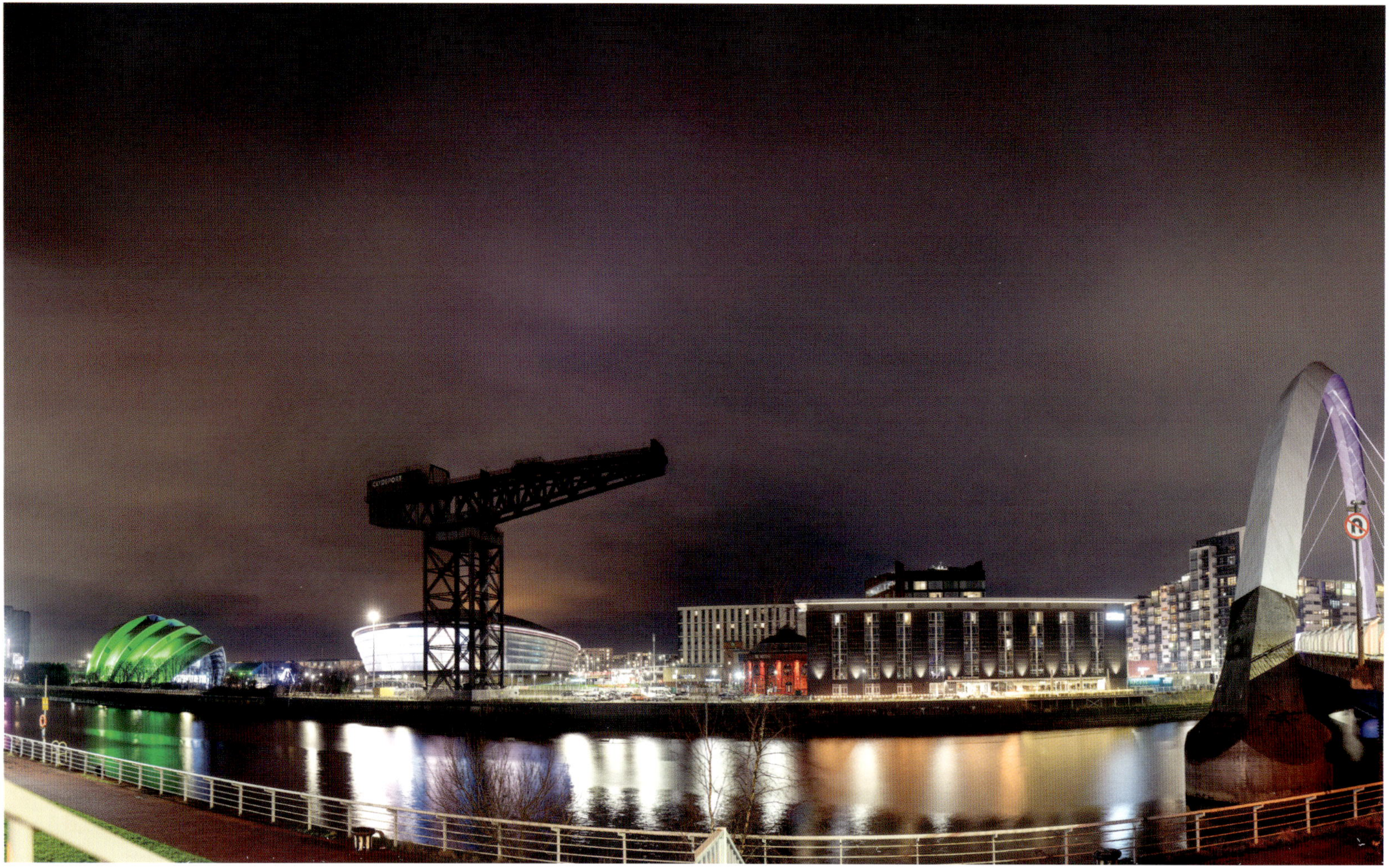

Looking north west towards Queen's Dock.

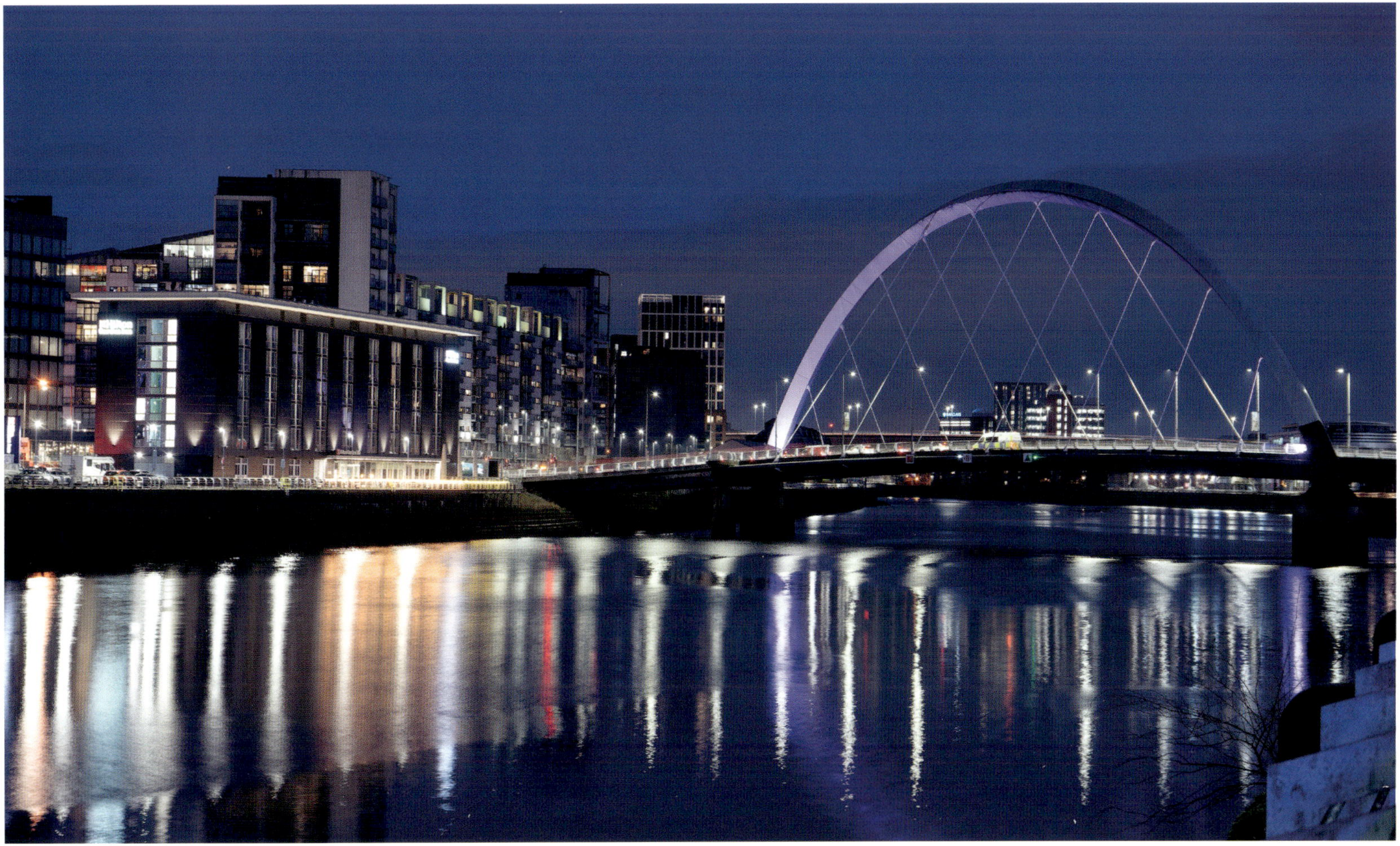

The view east through the Arc Bridge (Squinty Bridge) towards the city centre.

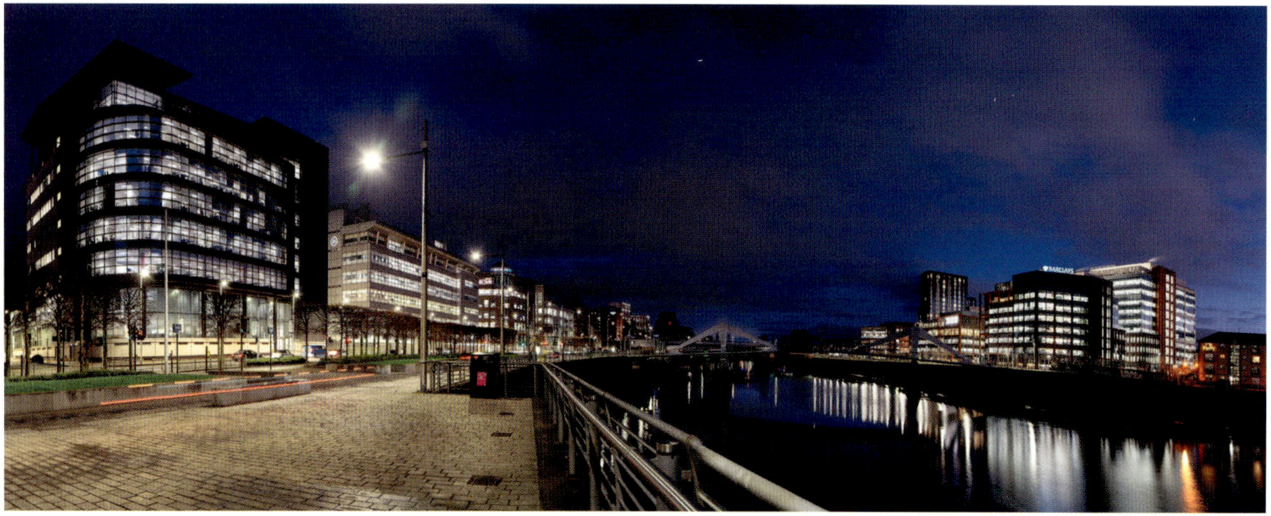

On the left are office buildings at Broomielaw. To the right is Tradeston.

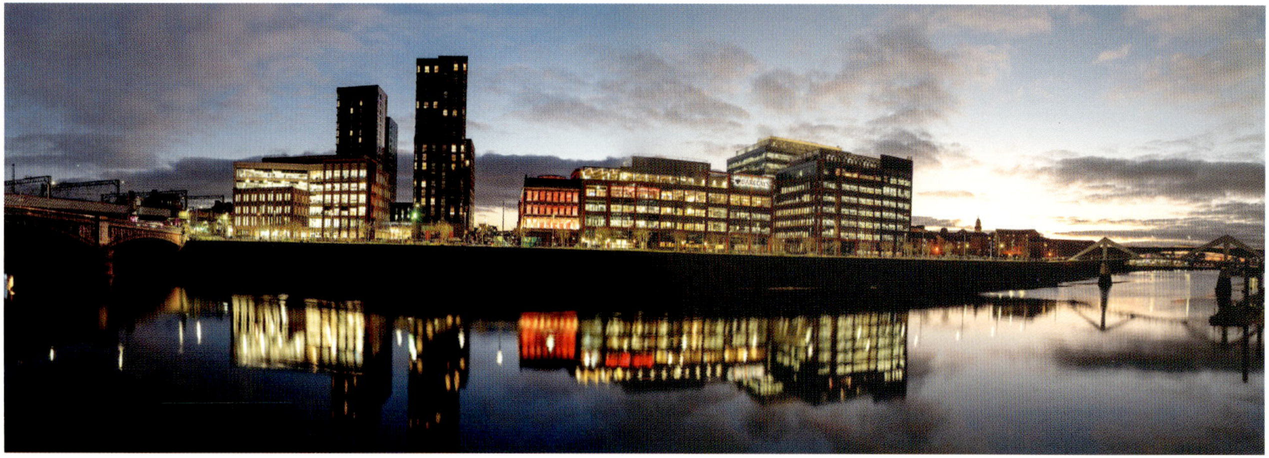

Bridge Wharf/Tradeston today, an extension of the financial district in the city centre.

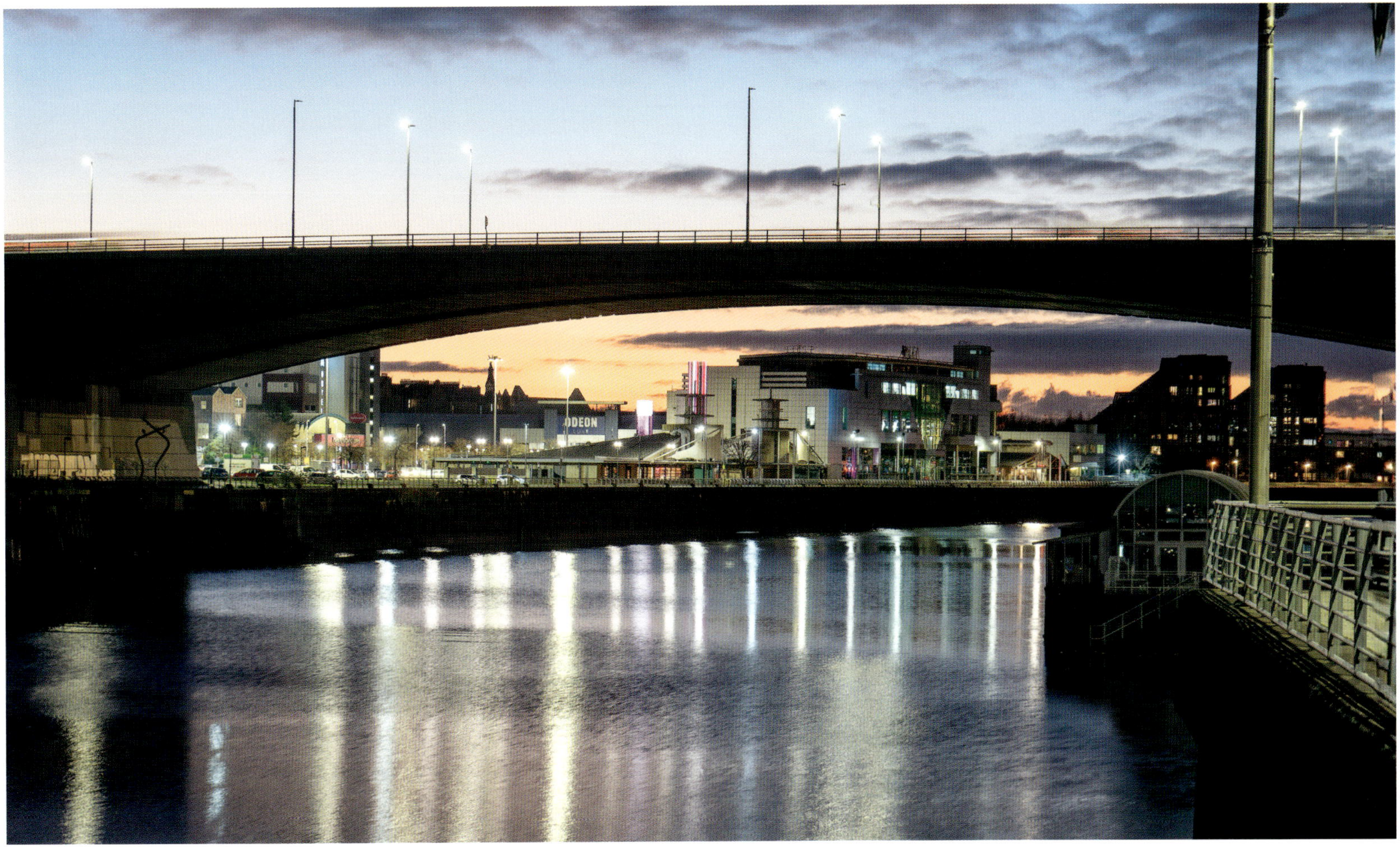

Kingston Bridge and beyond Springfield Quay and General Terminus Quay today.

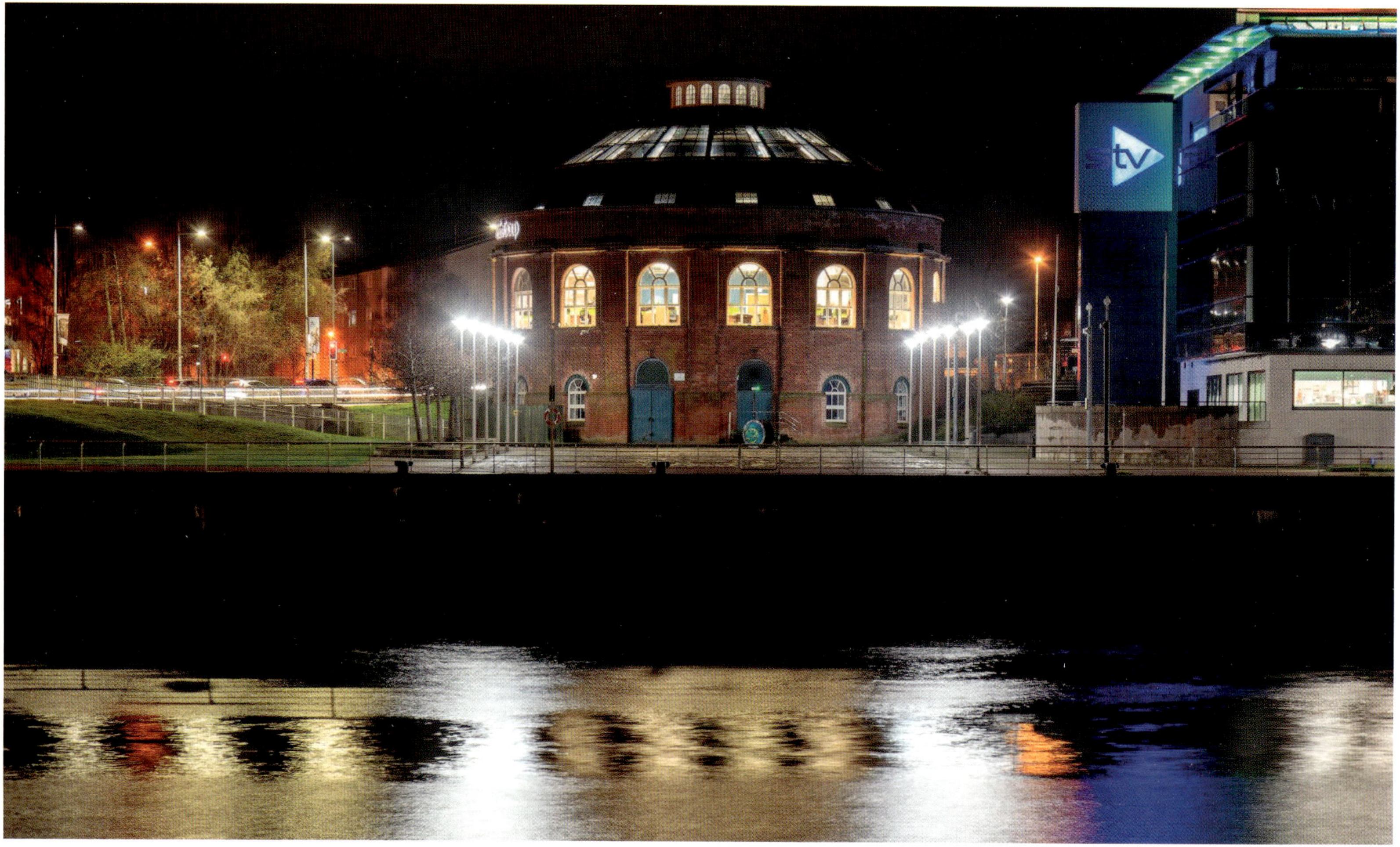

The harbour tunnel's South Rotunda today, home to offices. The North Rotunda houses restaurants.

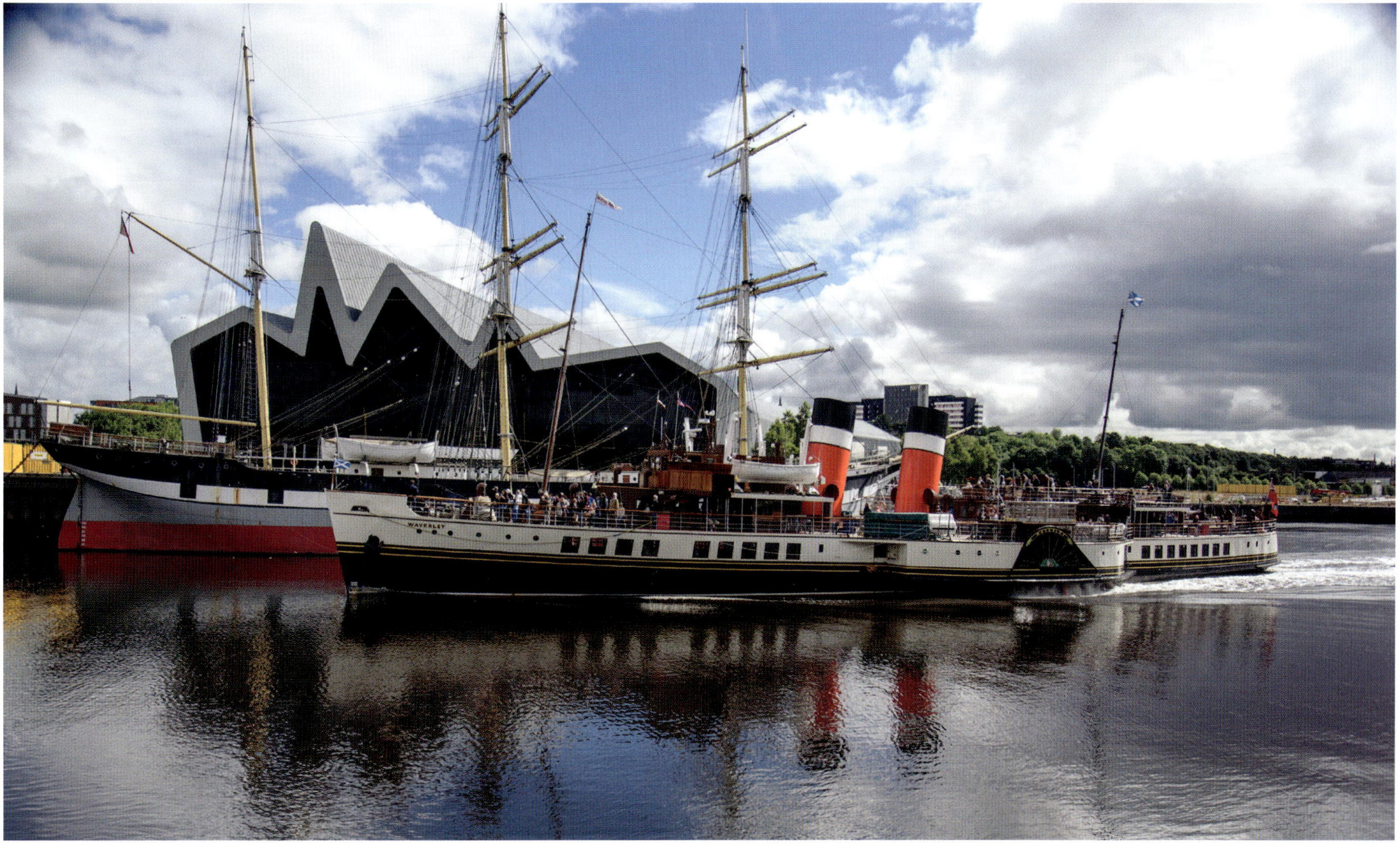

PS *Waverley* coming downstream, past Riverside Museum and sailing ship *Glenlee*. Yorkhill Quay is on the right.

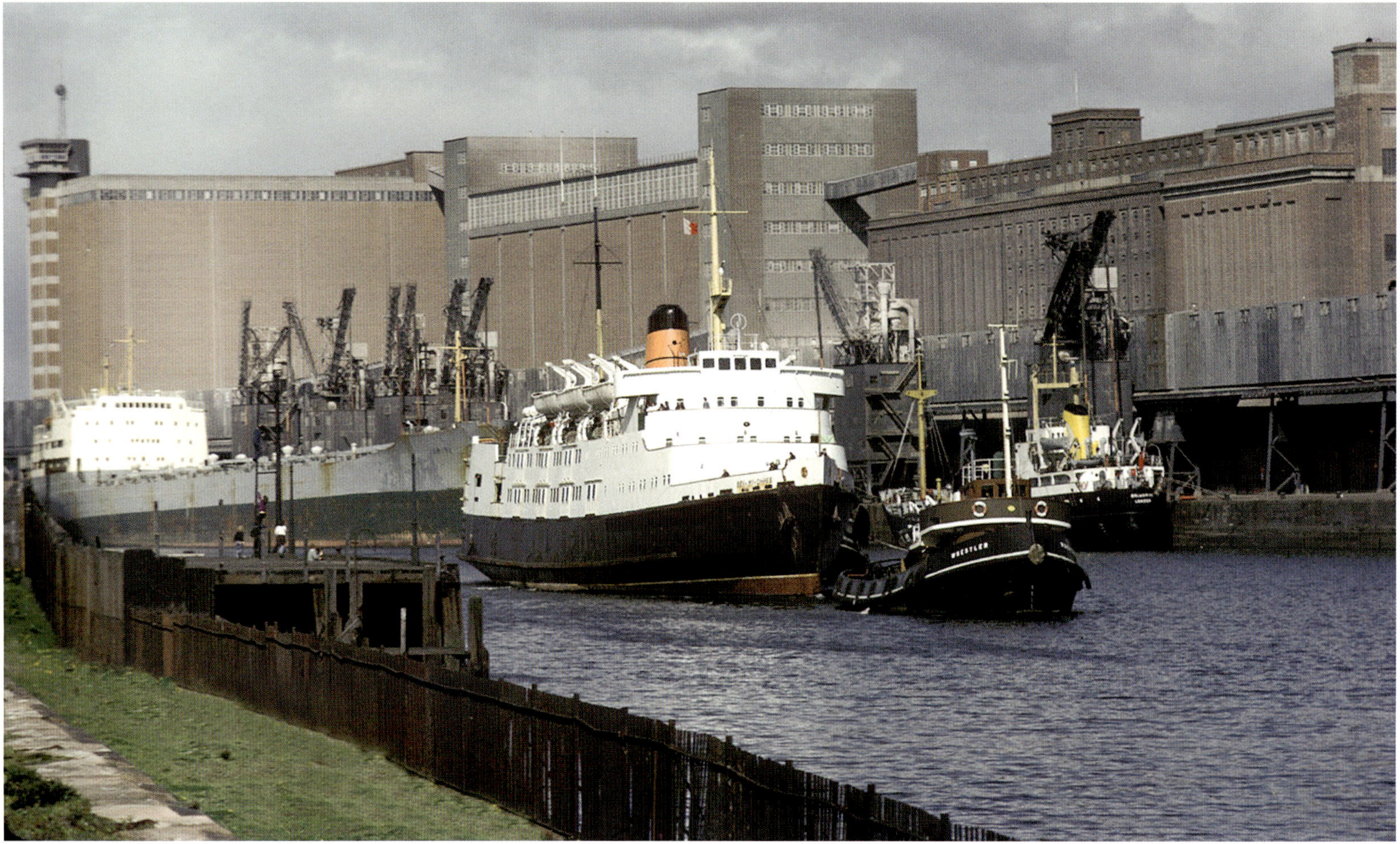

Meadowside Granaries with its 1967 addition on the left. Atop is Clydeport Operations Room, controlling river movements (now located at Greenock).

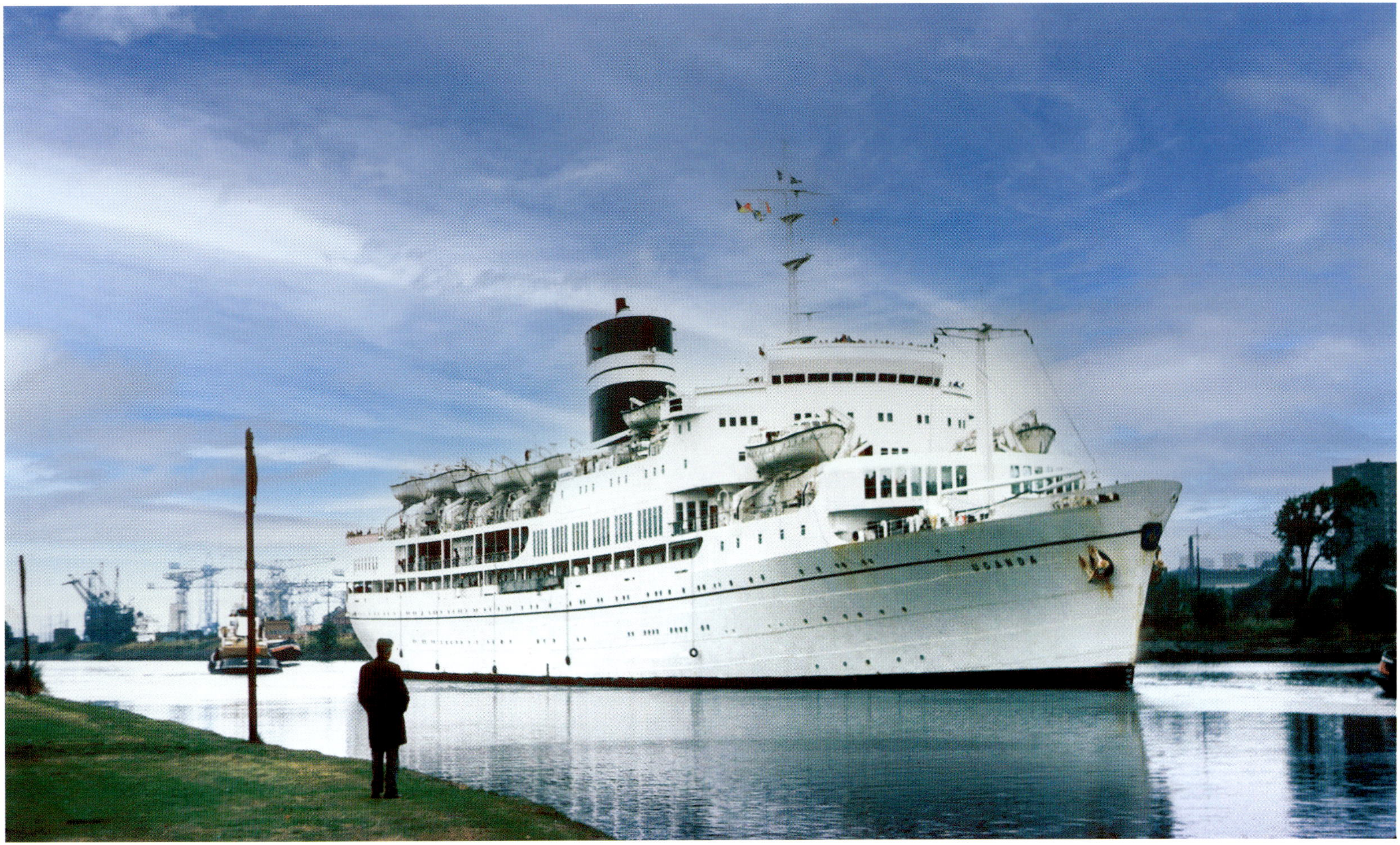

Union-Castle liner *Uganda* moving upriver at Renfrew, with John Brown's yard at Clydebank in the distance.

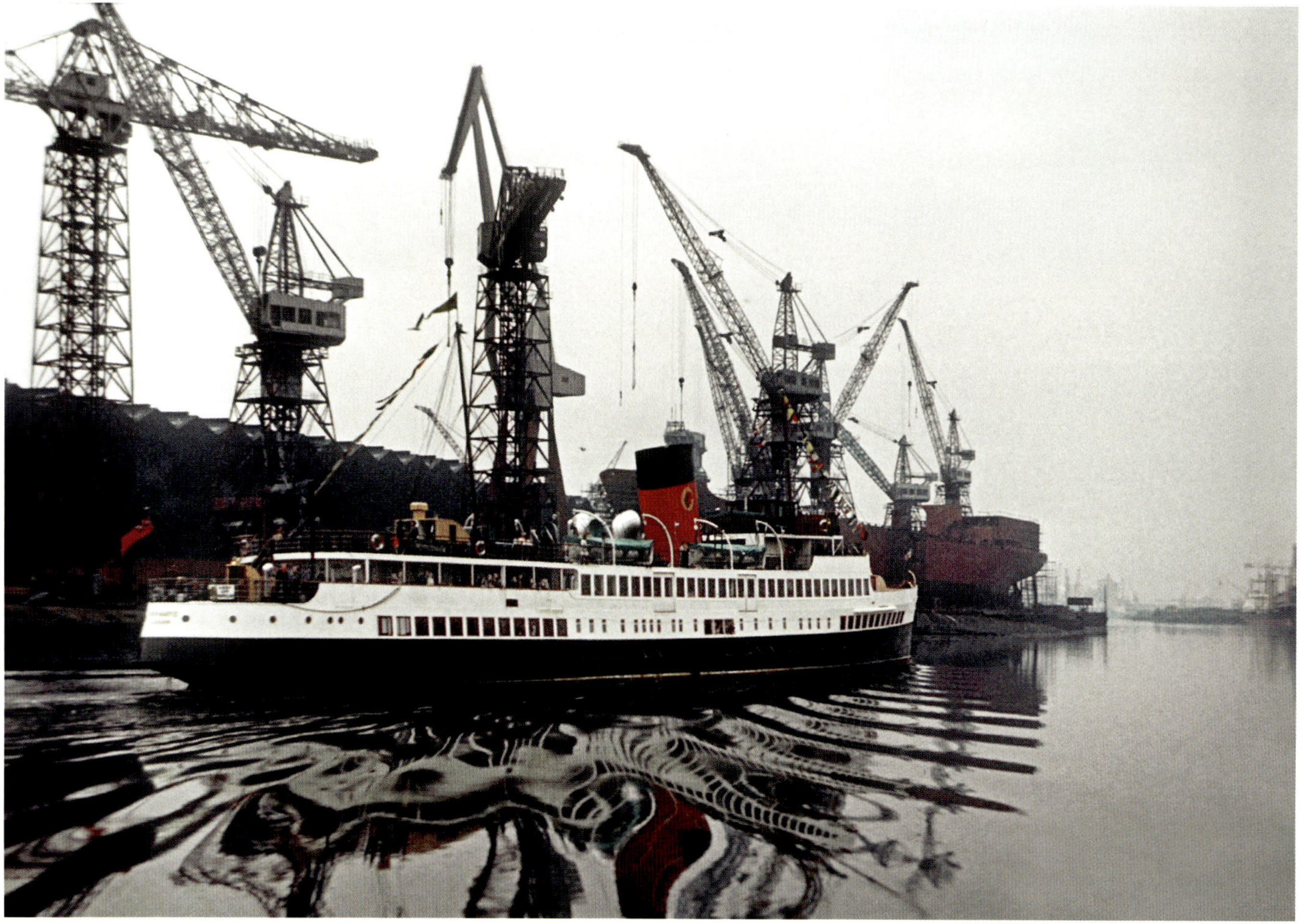

Pleasure steamer *Queen Mary* approaching Fairfield's, Govan.

SHIPBUILDING COMPANIES

Ten major shipyards are described in the following pages. Large shipbuilders had their own engine and boiler works for their shipping clients and for industrial clients and power stations. Yards also contracted engines, boilers and systems from other major firms, notably David Rowan, British Polar Engines, John G. Kincaid, Babcock & Wilcox, G. & J. Weir, James Howden and Rolls-Royce.

Quality steels, timber and deckings took their shape. Floor covering and furniture-making involved the yards' own craftspeople and leading firms such as James Templeton, Wylie & Lochhead, Archibald Stewart, Rowan & Boden, Waring & Gillow, and Morris & Co. In voyaging, refrigeration mattered, as did air-conditioning for people and freight – an invention created by the Stewart family of Thermotank Ltd, headquartered in Glasgow, benefitting merchant fleets, navies, railways, planes, offices and hotels internationally. Each yard's marine superintendent took ships out on trials to satisfy their clients.

By the late 1950s containerisation and aviation brought ship construction to a new low in many countries. Some Continental governments gave yards hidden subsidies to win contracts. With lower costs and larger yards, the Far East concentrated on ultra-large container ships and tankers. Shipping companies in the UK were offered government loans to order new ships, but with no restriction as to the country of building.

On the Clyde, Denny of Dumbarton retired from business in 1963. Fairfield's shocked the industry in 1965 by declaring it had run out of money despite its order book and modern equipment. Geographical group mergers of yards would become government policy. On the Clyde this would be Upper Clyde Shipbuilders (UCS) for the upper reaches, and for the lower reaches Scott-Lithgow, being Scotts of Greenock and Lithgows of Port Glasgow.

Before that, industrialist Sir Ian Stewart of Thermotank Ltd had the vision for Fairfield to bring unions, workers, management, investors and government together with new practices and shared approaches to building. Shipping firms placed orders and the Fairfield Experiment began in 1966. Two years later it was bounced into the ill-fated UCS grouping and reform stagnated. On the north side of the river, Yarrow's with its naval orders resisted re-grouping but they too were bounced into UCS for a time. Barclay Curle had already decided their contracts would switch to their parent company, Swan Hunter, based in the North East of England. All government-inspired groupings across the UK failed. Shipyards – those remaining – were then nationalised and then de-nationalised.

On the Clyde two would emerge out of this: Fairfield's under various names, in particular Kvaerner, the Norwegian company focusing on the vision and methods of the Fairfield Experiment, reaping rich reward for all; and Yarrow's, who insisted they could keep their head just above the water (financially). Today, both yards are BAE Systems.

Harland & Wolff

Harland & Wolff, based in Belfast from 1861, grew to become the largest shipbuilders in the world and part of the largest shipping group in the world. They also owned the Colvilles group of steel-making companies, headquartered in Glasgow. Concerned about possible civil war in Ireland following publication of the Irish Home Rule Bill, they bought three historic yards at Govan in 1912.

The combined complex was totally rebuilt with enlarged building berths, vast new platers and steel working shops, and re-equipping the recently opened fitting-out basin. A new iron foundry – Clyde Foundry, also known as the Glass House – was built in Helen Street, the largest glass-clad building in the world. On the north side of the river, they developed engine works in Finnieston and Scotstoun. They also bought and ran more yards, including Caird in Greenock and, directly across from Govan, D. & W. Henderson at Meadowside and A. & J. Inglis at Pointhouse.

The company had seven building berths at Govan for ships up to 750 feet long. Each of the slipways had mini dockgates allowing building to continue at all heights of the tide. By 1962 some 325 ships had been built, including passenger liners but principally cargo ships and tankers. Business reverted to Belfast after 1962. The group was profitable, but soon required government support.

Henderson's, with five berths up to 600 feet long, built some 470 ships from 1873 to 1936 after which it was used for repair work, Inglis, with five berths up to 425 feet long, built around 500 ships from 1862 to 1962. For some years after 1962 Alexander Stephen & Sons of Linthouse used the large basin for fitting out and for ship repairs, also leasing and using the adjacent Govan Dry Docks.

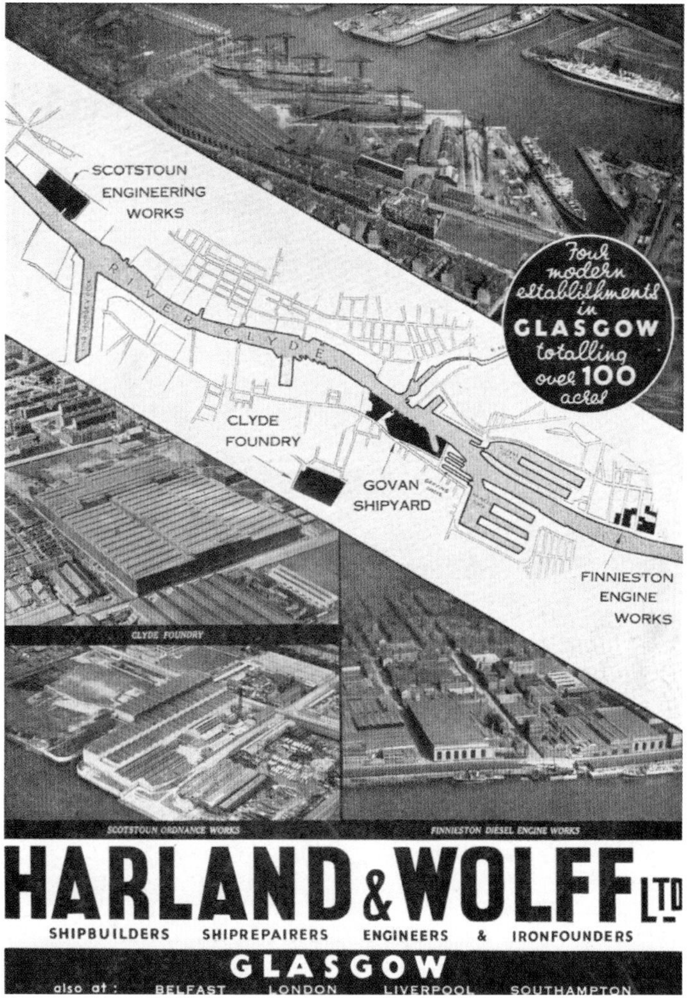

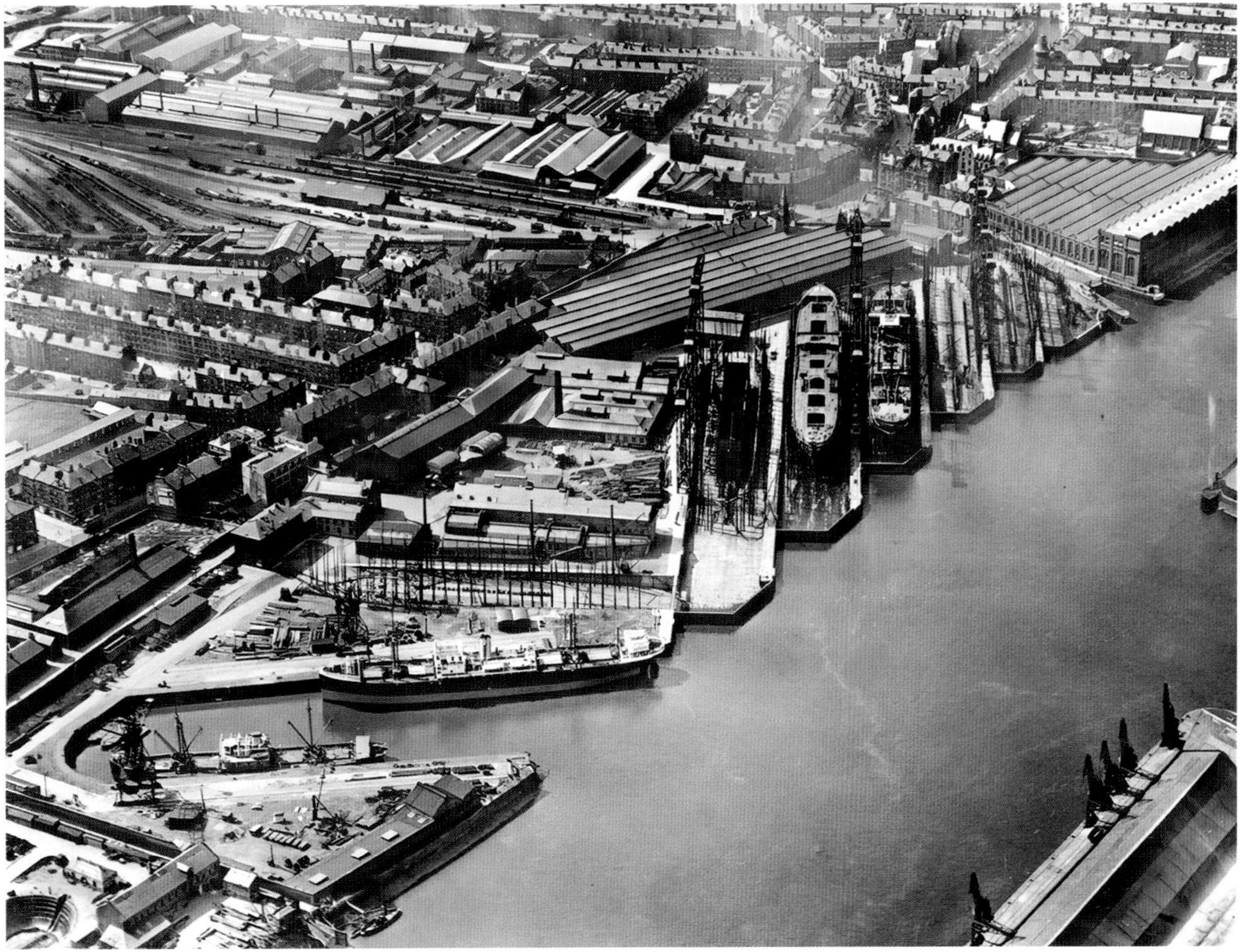

Harland & Wolff shipyard and basin, looking towards Govan Cross.

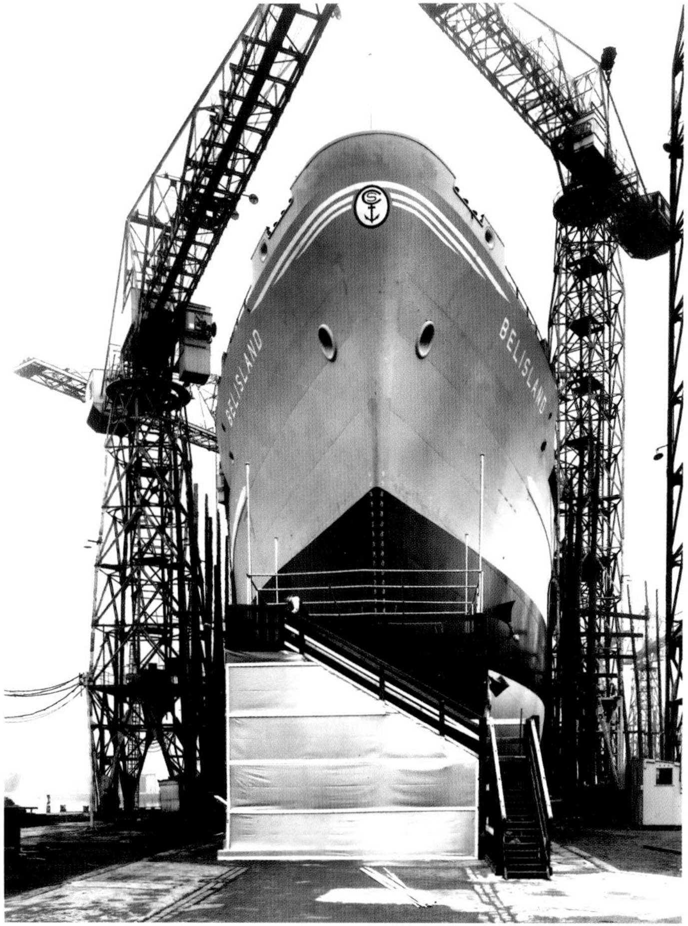

Awaiting her launch, MV *Belisland*, built for Bellships Co.

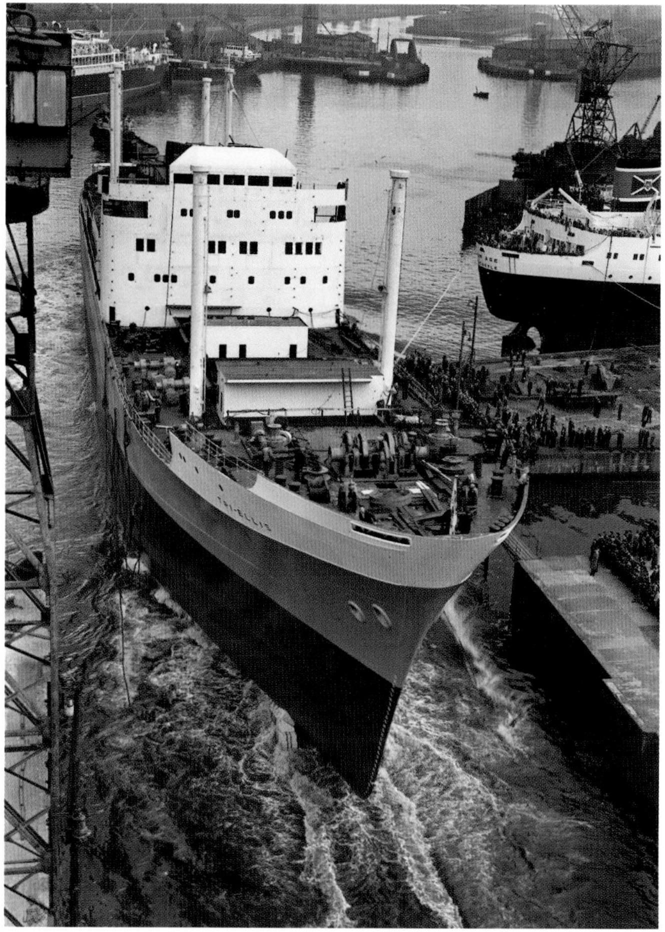

MV *Tri-Ellis* launched for the British Phosphates Commissioners. Yorkhill Quay and Queen's Dock are behind.

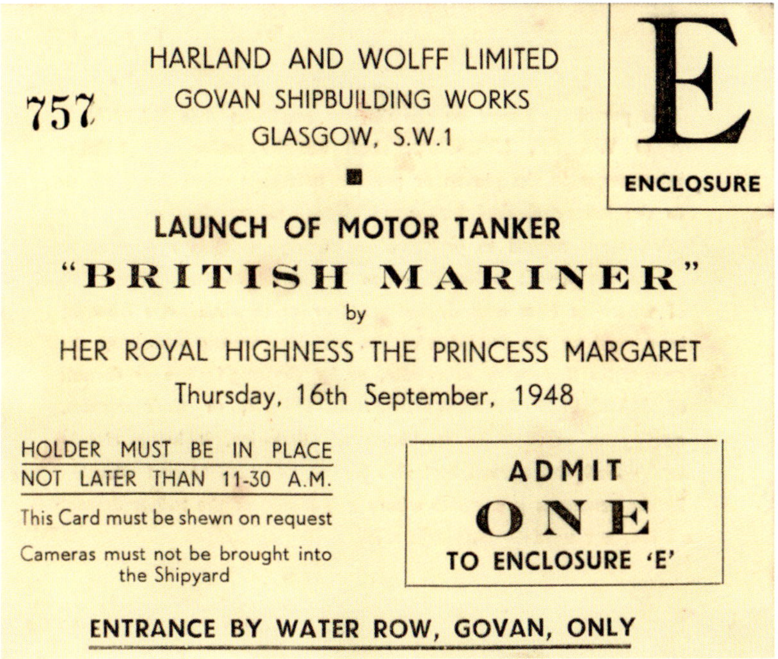

757

HARLAND AND WOLFF LIMITED
GOVAN SHIPBUILDING WORKS
GLASGOW, S.W.1

E
ENCLOSURE

LAUNCH OF MOTOR TANKER
"BRITISH MARINER"
by
HER ROYAL HIGHNESS THE PRINCESS MARGARET
Thursday, 16th September, 1948

HOLDER MUST BE IN PLACE
NOT LATER THAN 11-30 A.M.

This Card must be shewn on request

Cameras must not be brought into the Shipyard

ADMIT
ONE
TO ENCLOSURE 'E'

ENTRANCE BY WATER ROW, GOVAN, ONLY

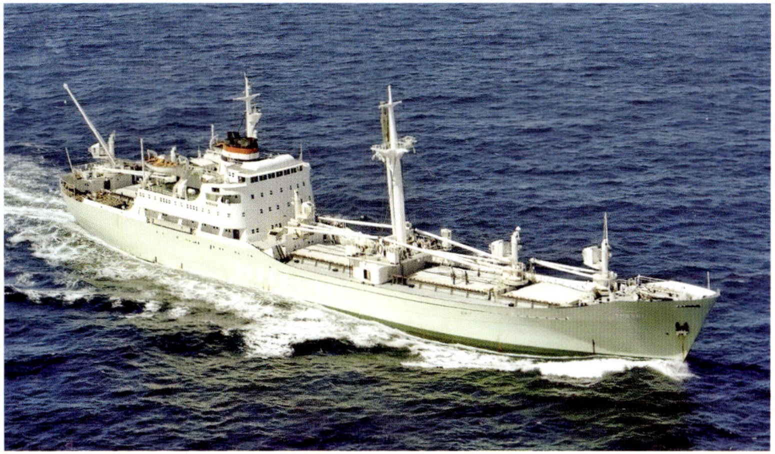

Built for British India Steam Navigation, MV *Bombala*, later named MV *Shendi*.

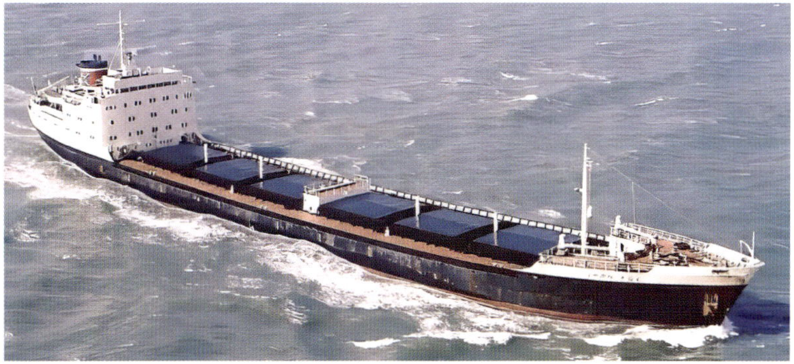

MV *Iron Age* for Vallum Shipping.

BAE Systems

Warship building in Glasgow is designed and constructed by BAE Systems at its shipyard, which combined two sites, Govan from 1999 (formerly Fairfield's) and Scotstoun from 1985 as GEC-Marconi (formerly Yarrow's). Ship halls replace slipways. The earlier Fairfield's hall enabled frigates to be built in two sections before being welded together outside. The very new ship hall building on the former West Basin at Govan allows two frigates, each around 8,000 tons, to be built entirely side by side, before roll out. Assembly cranes and gantries are internal, and out of public view. Steelwork transformation at Govan involves a new panel line with more capacity, greater speed, automation and robotic equipment.

Conventional ship launches are replaced by new ships being rolled on to semi-submersible barges. Each is towed to Loch Long, where, at Glen Mallan, the barge removes and the new ship is towed upstream to Scotstoun for final fitting out and weaponry, using the dry docks as required. Design and manufacturing are sited at Scotstoun.

The new Applied Skills Academy is for naval business and employee training and is also available to other companies. Digital-based shipbuilding ensures all employees have information instantly on demand at their place of work, with live data at all times.

BAE is one of the largest defence manufacturers in the world, formed from a merger of Marconi, General Electric and British Aerospace. BAE Systems also constructs submarines at its vast complex in Barrow-in-Furness, and operates equally modern digital shipyards in Canada and Australia.

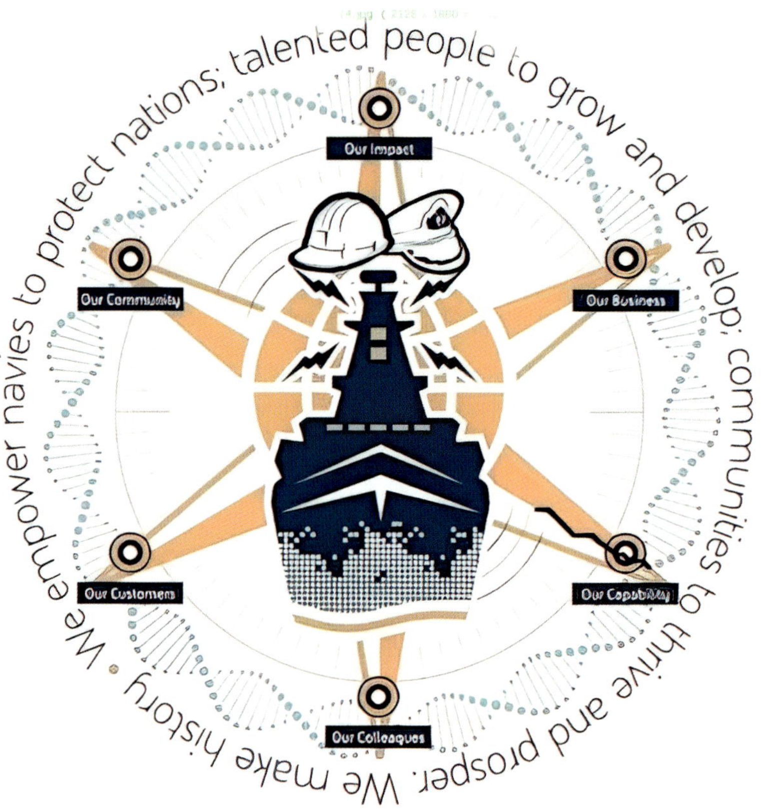

BAE SYSTEMS

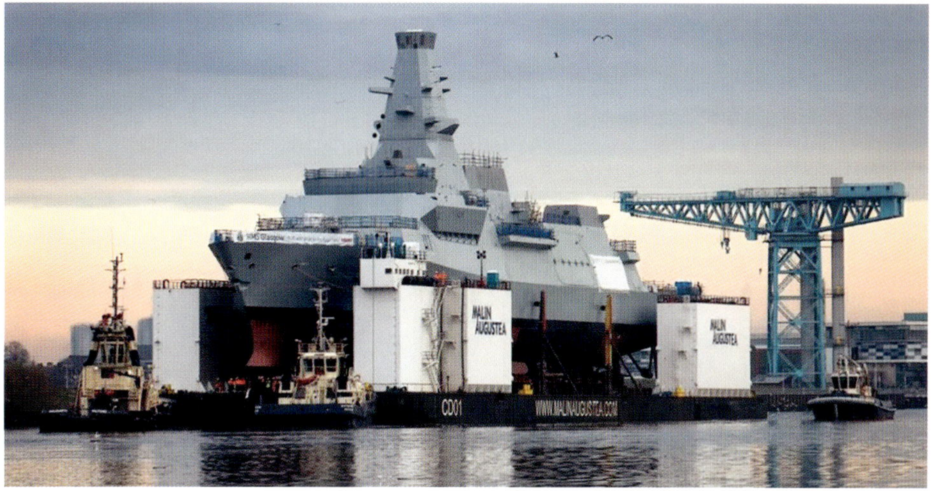

Right: HMS *Glasgow* on a specialist barge on the journey to fitting out at Scotstoun.

Below: The new Shipbuilding Hall at the western end of the Govan yard.

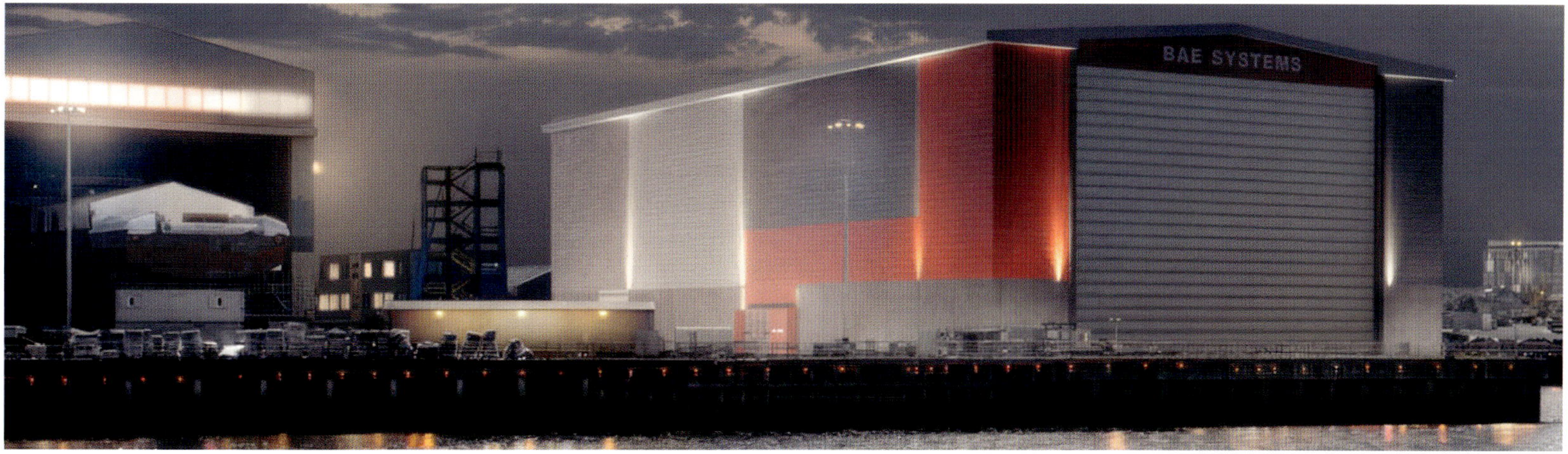

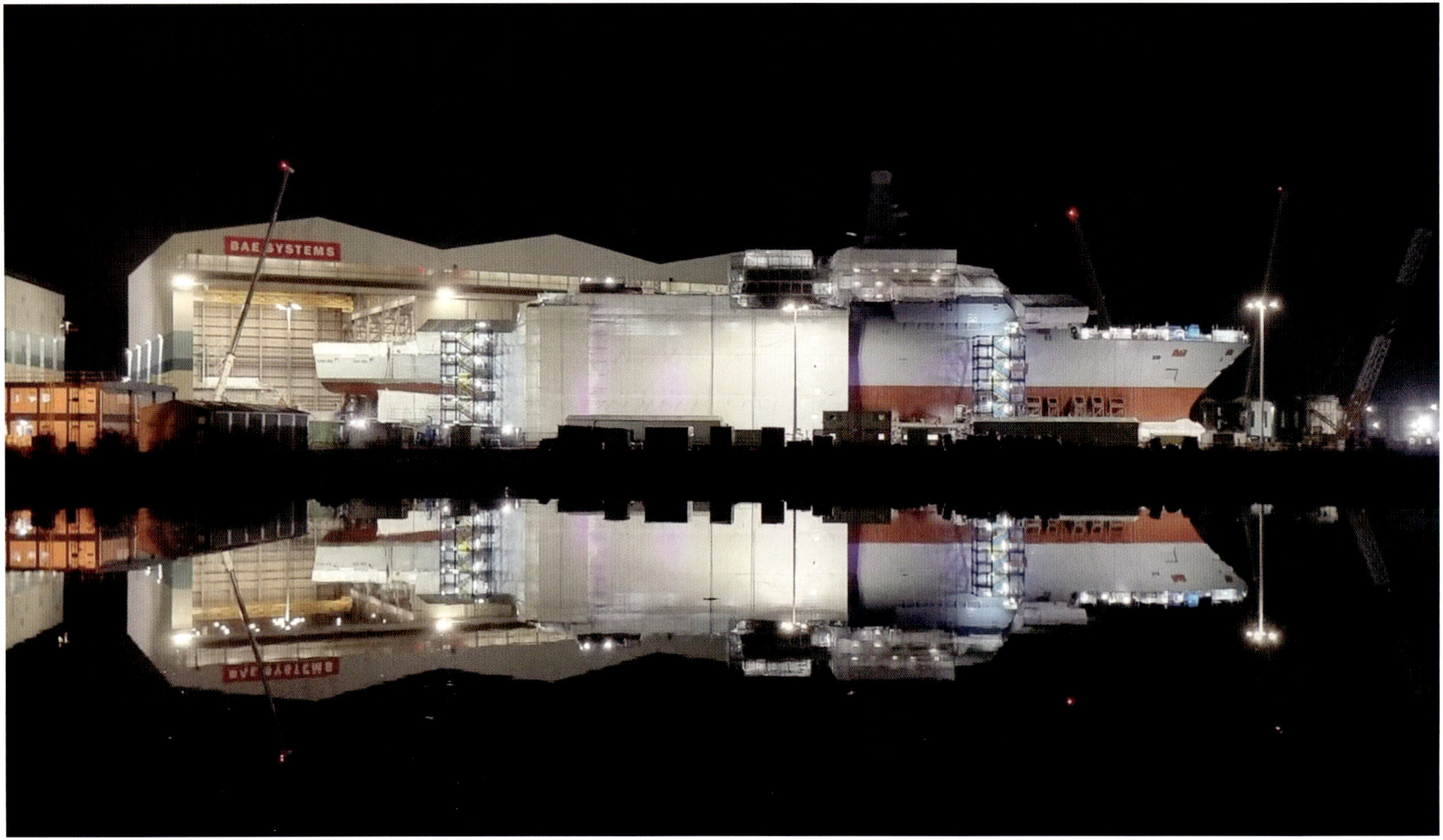

HMS *Cardiff* completing its build at Govan.

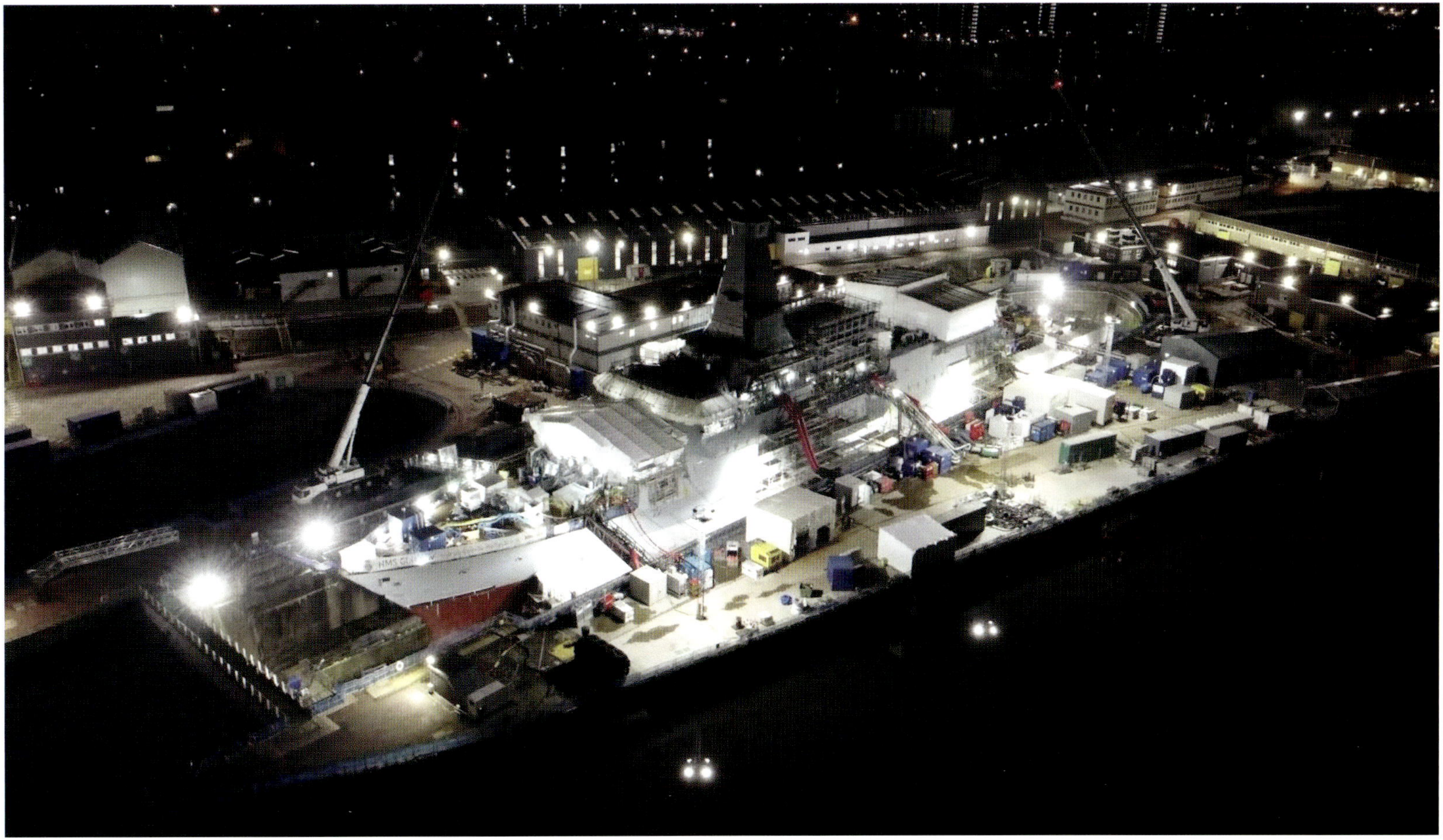

HMS *Glasgow* fitting out at Scotstoun.

Fairfield

John Elder and Charles Randoph founded the Fairfield Shipbuilding & Engineering company in Govan in 1860, expanding to its present site in 1864. From 1852 they had been in partnership as engineers, but not yet shipbuilding. The new business soon became the largest and most productive yard in the world. Like other yards on the Clyde, many of its clients were international.

On John Elder's early death, his widow, philanthropist Isabella Elder, continued the business, and was to be joined by William Pearce, who equally committed to the firm's growth and the welfare of its workers and their families.

In 1935 majority control of the company was bought by industrialist and Port Glasgow shipbuilder Sir James Lithgow and his brother, Henry. This helped the business to recover from the financial difficulties experienced by one of its largest clients, the Anchor Line. The yard thrived. The new chairman, Sir James, also conceived the idea of holding the Empire Exhibition 1938, attracting 13 million visitors to its art deco site in Bellahouston Park. The complex had six building berths – later changed to five – accommodating vessels up to 1,000 feet long, principally warships, passenger liners, cargo ships, tankers and carriers as well as large yachts. Its large pioneering indoor fabrication unit opened in the late 1950s, christened then as the 'Shipbuilding Hall'.

From 1966 onwards the business has been called Fairfield (Glasgow), Govan Shipbuilders and Kvaerner; it is now part of BAE Systems with indoor ship construction halls replacing all slipways. Having built well over 800 ships at Govan from 1860, it continues in business today. The distinguished red sandstone head office, built in 1891, now houses Govan Workspace businesses and Fairfield Heritage visitor centre, celebrating shipbuilding past, present and future.

The
FAIRFIELD
Shipbuilding & Engineering Co. Ltd
GOVAN, GLASGOW
Telegrams—"Fairfield Glasgow"

Designers and Builders of all classes of
WARSHIPS, MAIL AND PASSENGER VESSELS, CARGO BOATS, OIL TANKERS, CROSS CHANNEL STEAMERS, TRAIN FERRIES, CABLE SHIPS, YACHTS, Etc.

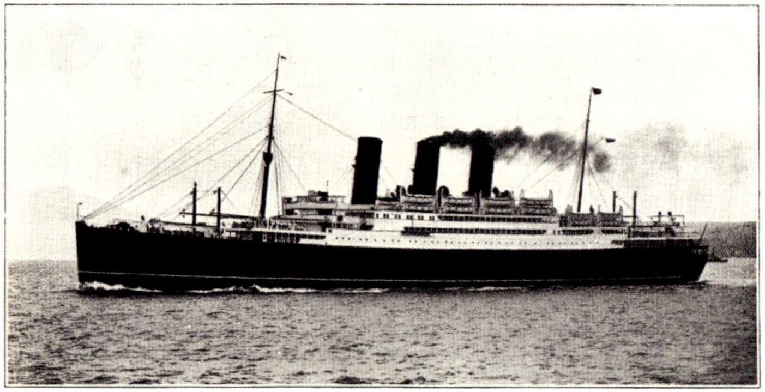

T.S. "Transylvania," built for The Anchor Line (Henderson Bros.) Ltd.

MAKERS OF DIESEL MACHINERY
OF FAIRFIELD-SULZER AND FAIRFIELD-DOXFORD TYPES
ALSO
STEAM RECIPROCATING ENGINES AND TURBINES
Ship and Machinery Repairers

CONSTRUCTIONAL STEELWORK DEPARTMENT
Chepstow Works, Chepstow, Mon.
Constructors of all Classes of Steelwork for Bridges, Wagons, Oil Storage Tanks, Buildings, etc.

LONDON OFFICE - - 9 VICTORIA STREET, WESTMINSTER, S.W.1

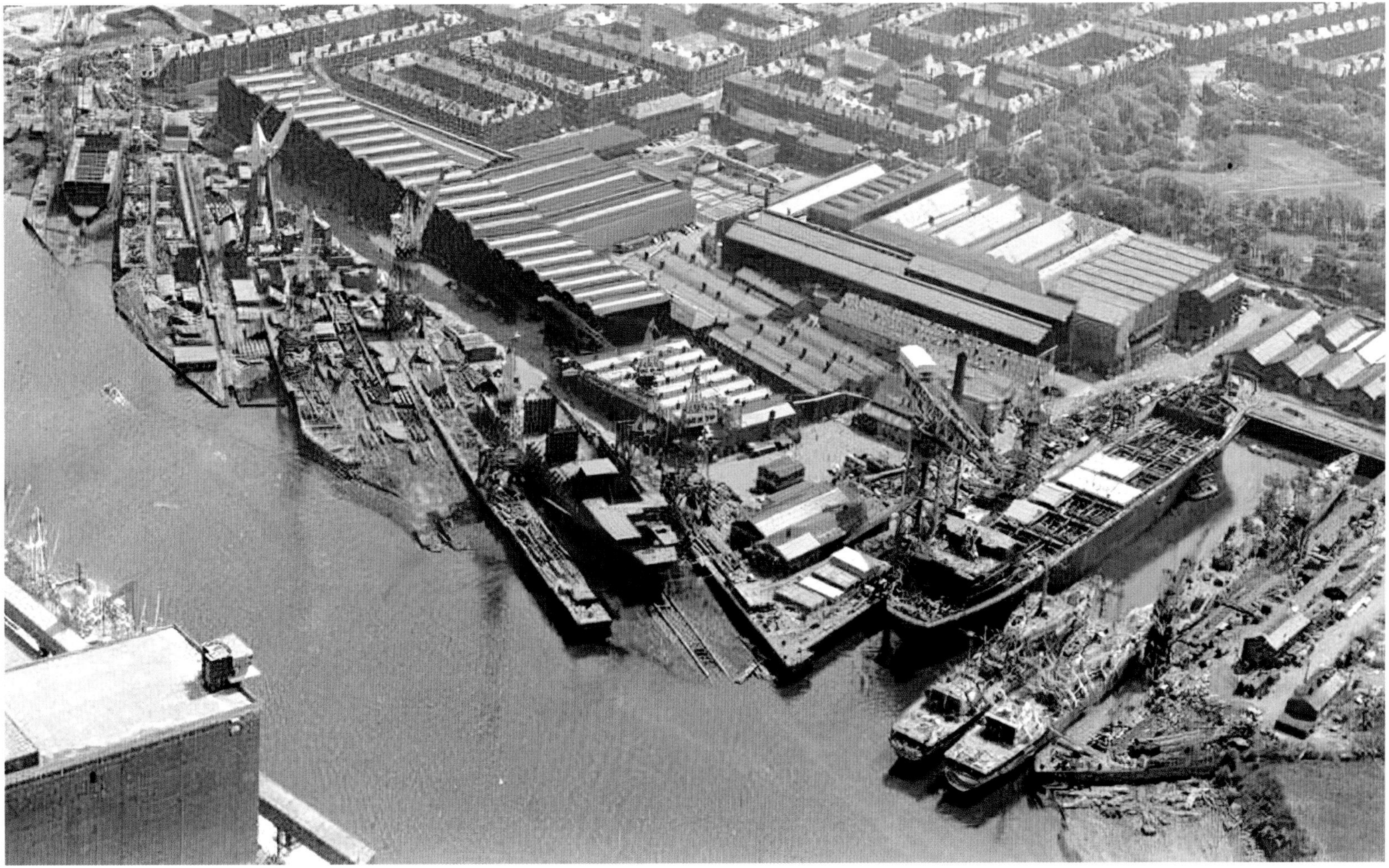

Fairfield's shipyard and basin operating when part of Upper Clyde Shipbuilders Ltd.

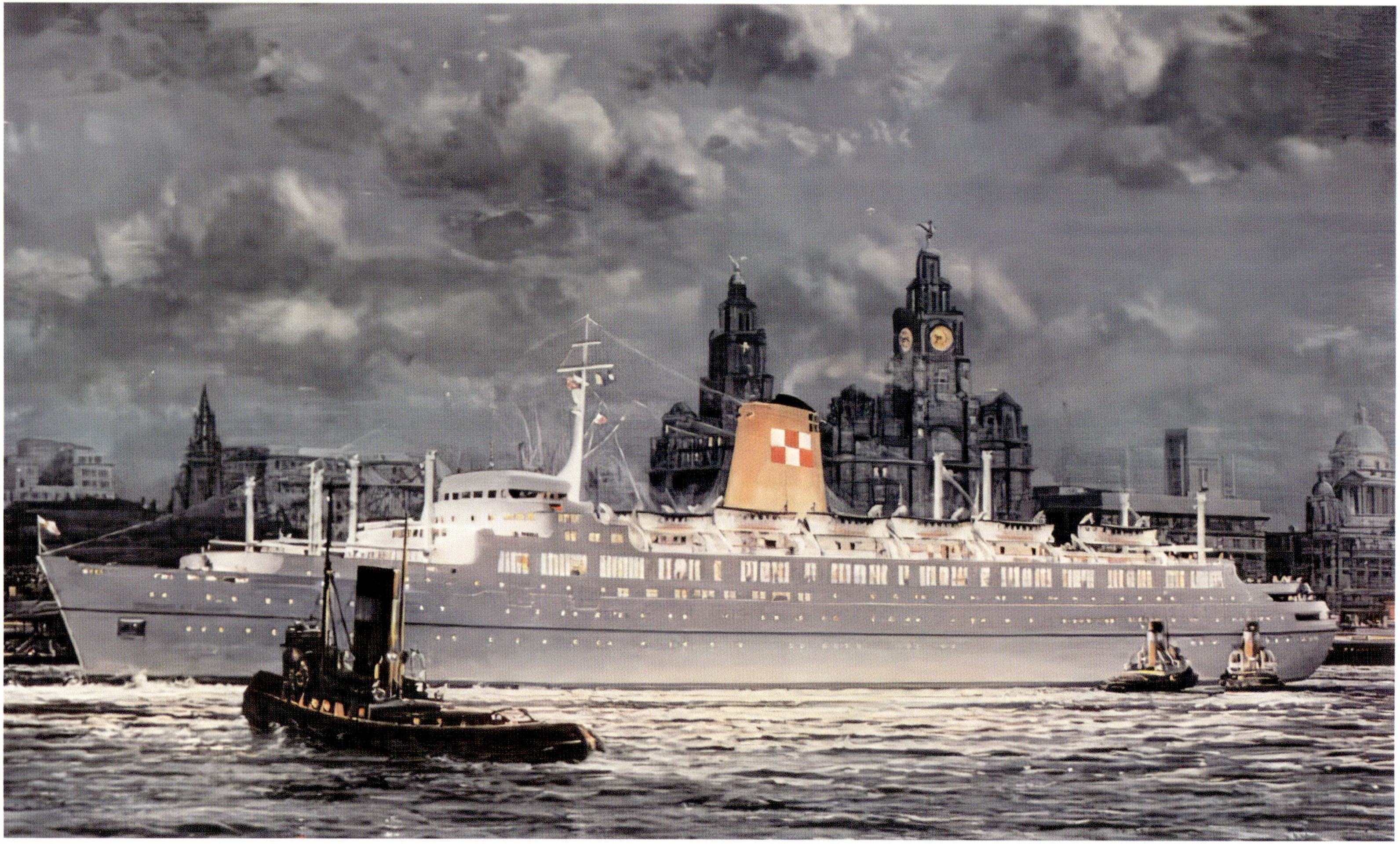

Canadian Pacific Line's TSS *Empress of Britain*.

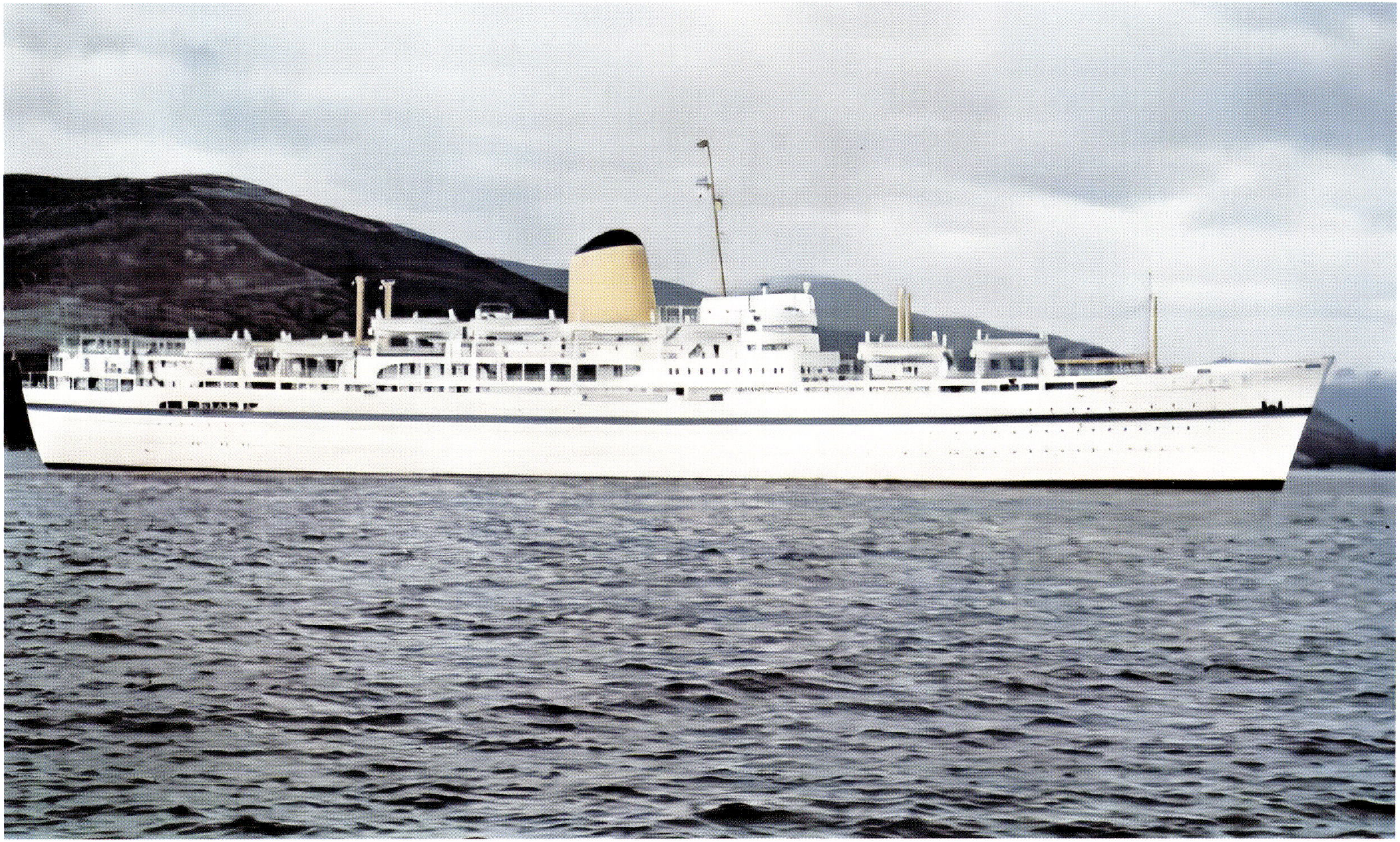

TSS *Oxfordshire*, built for the Bibby Line.

Alexander Stephen & Sons

Of long heritage and with an active shipyard in Dundee, Alexander Stephen & Sons became shipbuilders on the Clyde, this being the premier shipbuilding river. Firstly based at Kelvinhaugh in 1851, they made way for the construction of Queen's Dock and moved across to the southside at spacious Linthouse in 1871, beside Whiteinch Wharf, west of Fairfield's hive of activity. They had started on the north-east coast, boat building in Burghhead from 1750 and then moved down to Aberdeen, then to Arbroath and to Dundee from 1843, building ninety-seven ships there up to 1893.

As Glasgow Harbour kept expanding ever west, Stephen's soon had regular use of the extended Shieldhall Wharf for fitting out. They became co-owners of the Steel Company of Scotland. Having six berths at Linthouse for ships up to 700 feet long, they built some 550 ships between 1871 and 1968 (and before that, 147 ships at Kelvinhaugh). These ships were principally warships, passenger liners, cargo ships, tankers and carriers but also included some large yachts.

When the company and yard became part of UCS, but with no new ships there, Stephen's independently continued engineering and ship-repairing using the Harland & Wolff basin in Govan, and leasing and using the adjacent dry docks until 1977. The company retired from all business in 1982. A major occupant of Linthouse today is Thales UK, aerospace, defence and security developers and manufacturers and successor to Barr & Stroud Ltd.

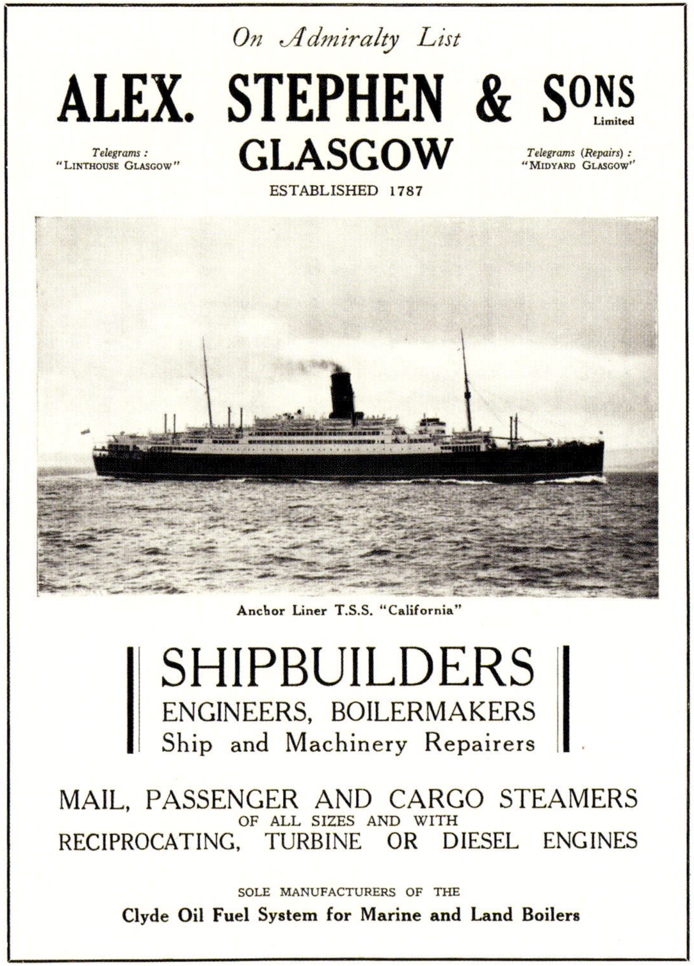

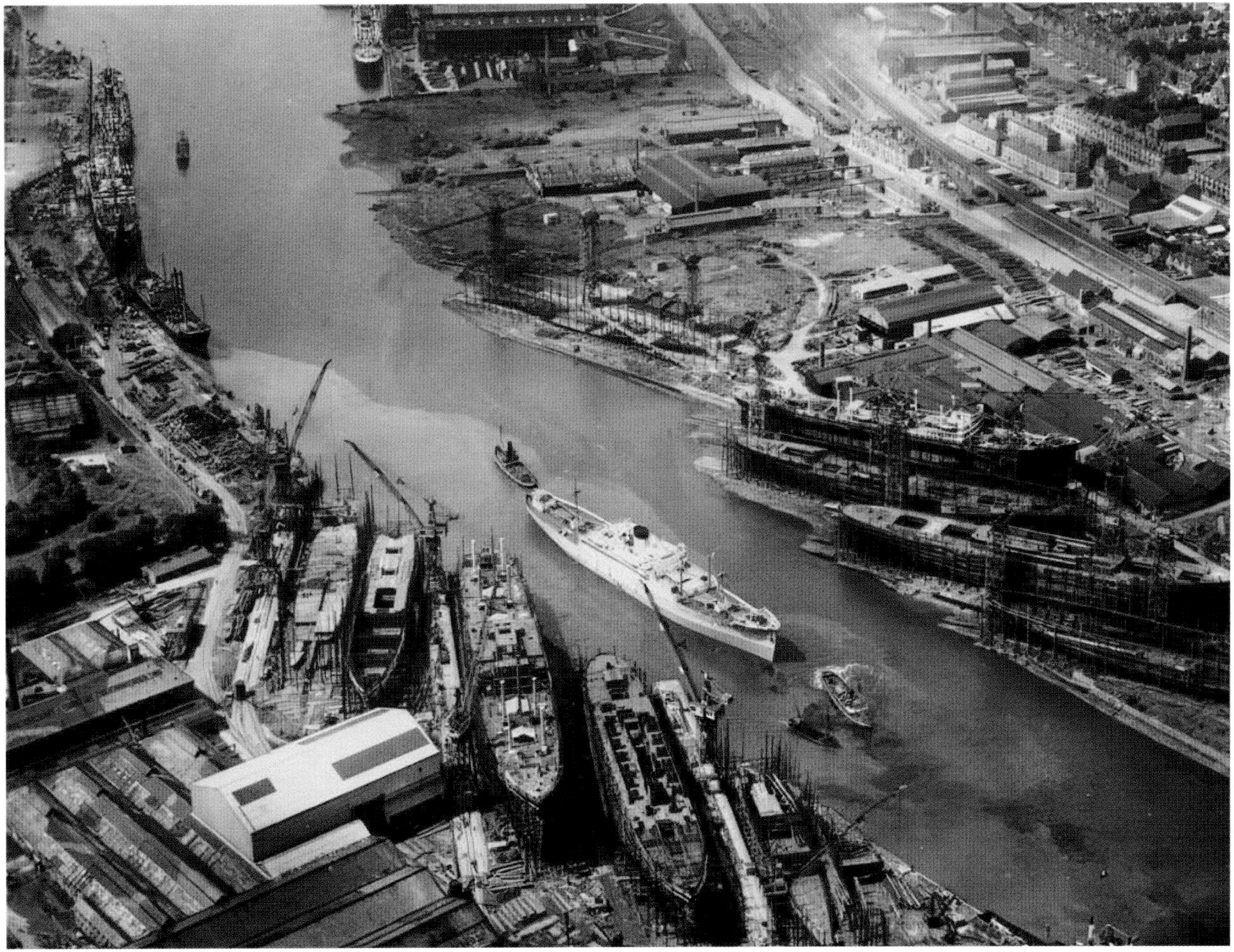

View over Stephen's shipyard and Shieldhall Wharf on left. Across the river is Barclay Curle's Clydeholm yard.

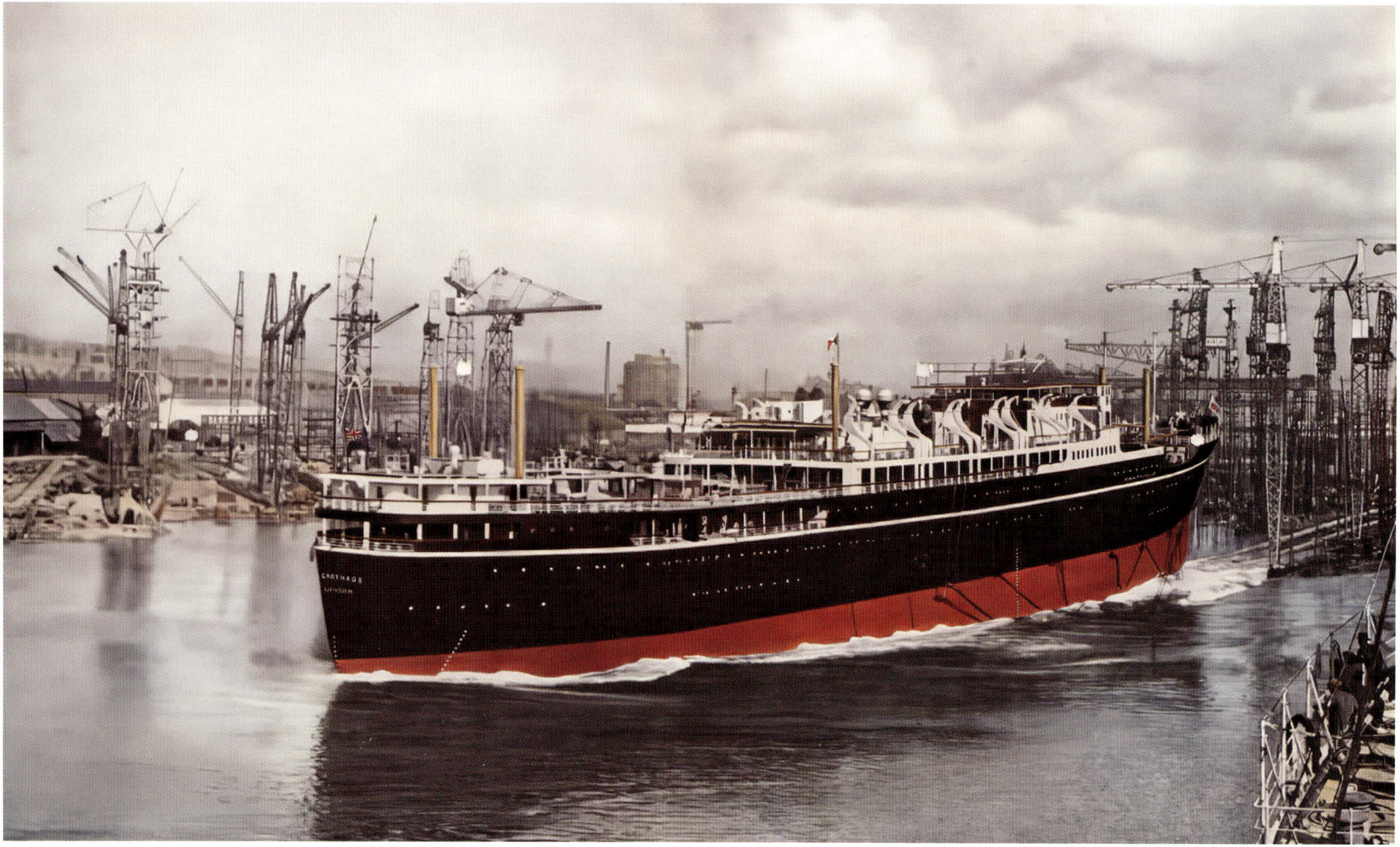

Launch of TSS *Carthage* for Peninsular & Oriental Steam Navigation Company.

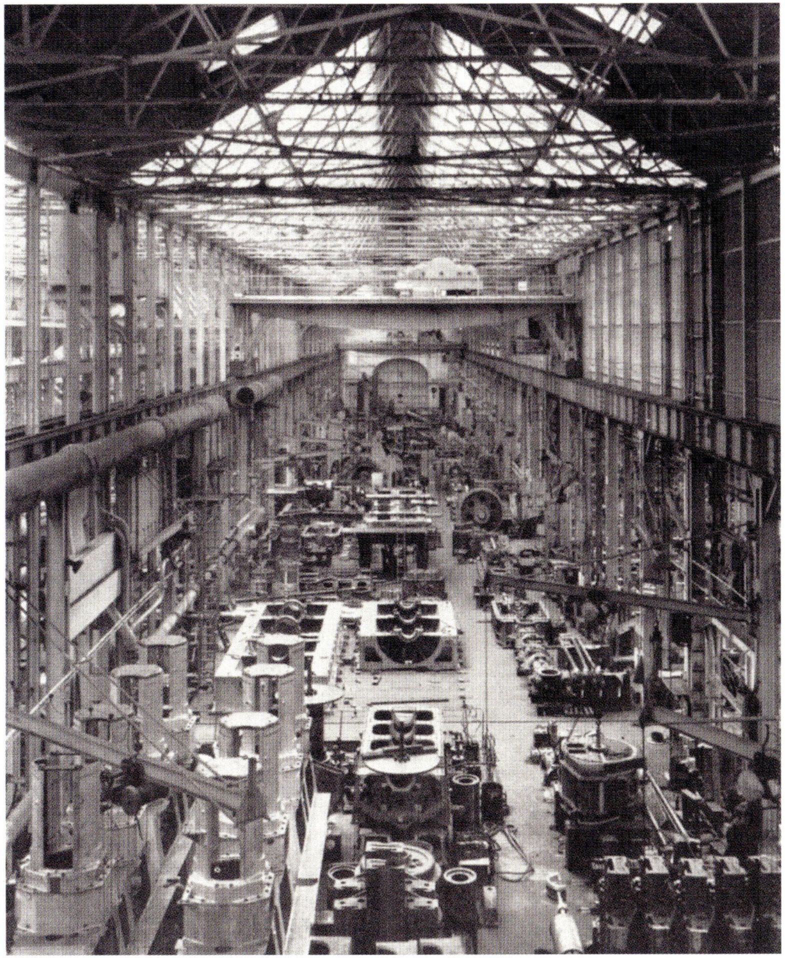

One of the bays of Stephen's Engine Works.

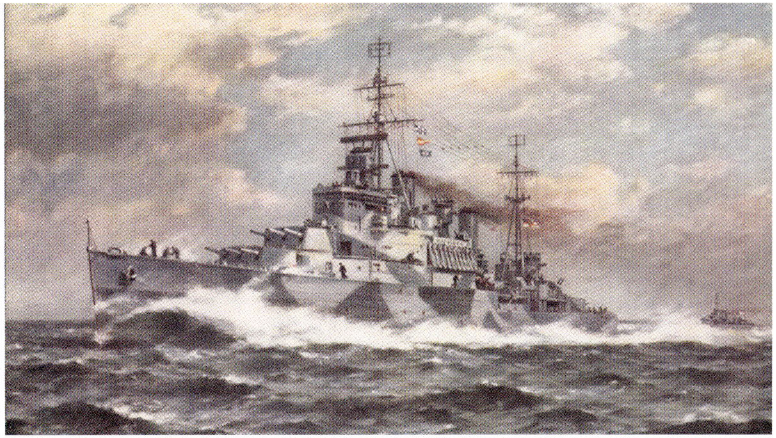

HMS *Ceylon*.

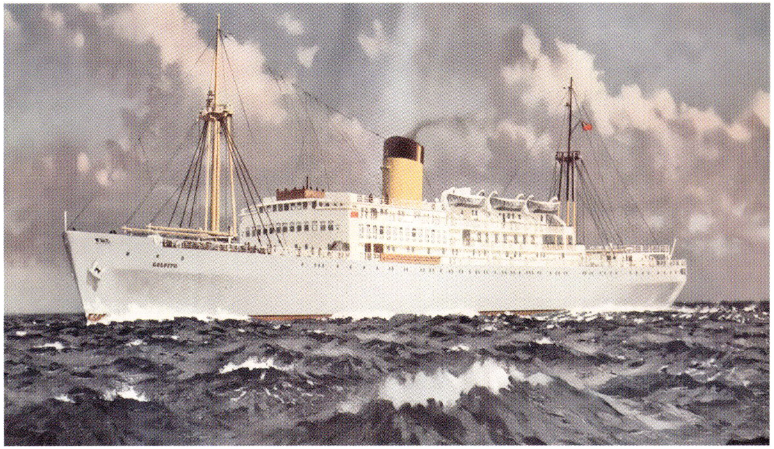

TSS *Golfito*, built for Elders & Fyffes Ltd.

Barclay Curle

On the north side of the river one of the first modern ship carpenters, John Barclay, started his family business of shipbuilding in 1818. Glasgow's first new shipyard, at the Stobcross pool – known as The Hole – was deep enough to allow ships of up to 200 tons to be launched. In the 1840s his son, Robert Barclay, invited Robert Curle and others to join the firm, becoming known internationally as Barclay, Curle & Co. Two graving slip docks were built to enhance their repair business, otherwise shipowners had to go to Greenock.

In 1855 the firm's shipyard moved west to Clydeholm at Whiteinch to compete for ever-larger ships, while developing major engine works back in the Finnieston area.

In 1912 the company merged forces – but not names – and shared directors with Swan Hunter of the North East of England. Chaired by a fellow Scot, this was to become one of the largest group of shipbuilders in Britain. Barclay Curle bought the nearby Elderslie shipyard and dry dock at Scotstoun and would add two more dry docks there (all still used today) and a fitting-out wharf of 2,000 feet. In 1913 they took over the North British Diesel Engine works adjacent to Clydeholm, adding a hammerhead crane at the quayside for transferring engines.

Barclay Curle were principally builders of passenger and cargo liners, cargo ships, tankers and bulk carriers. Having five berths up to 700 feet long, the firm built over 750 ships between 1818 and 1967. The company's ship-repairing and conversion business was one of the largest in Britain, continuing into the 1970s. In 1974 the dry docks were bought by Yarrow's.

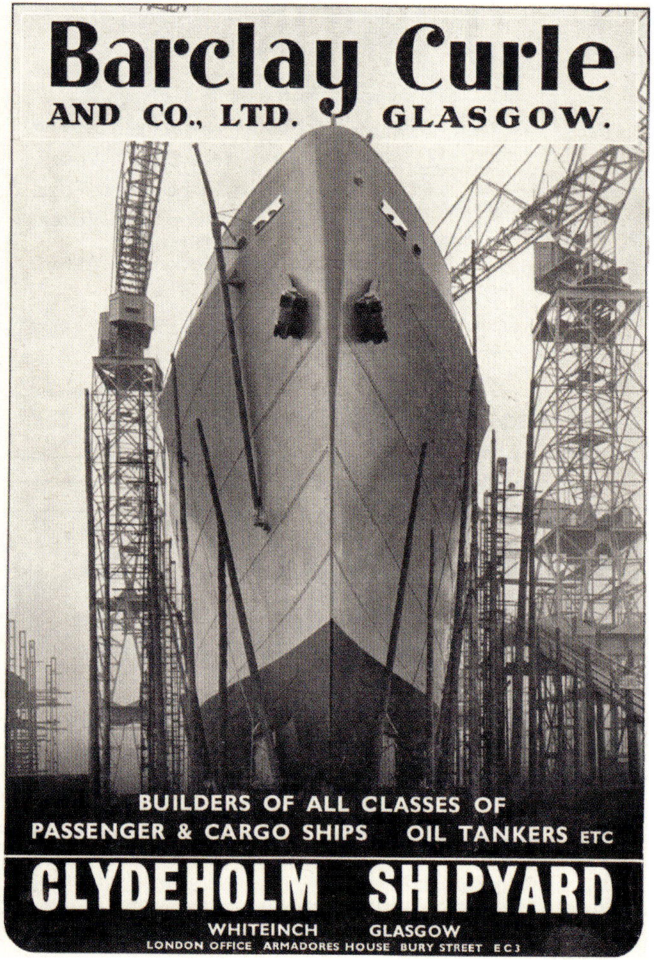

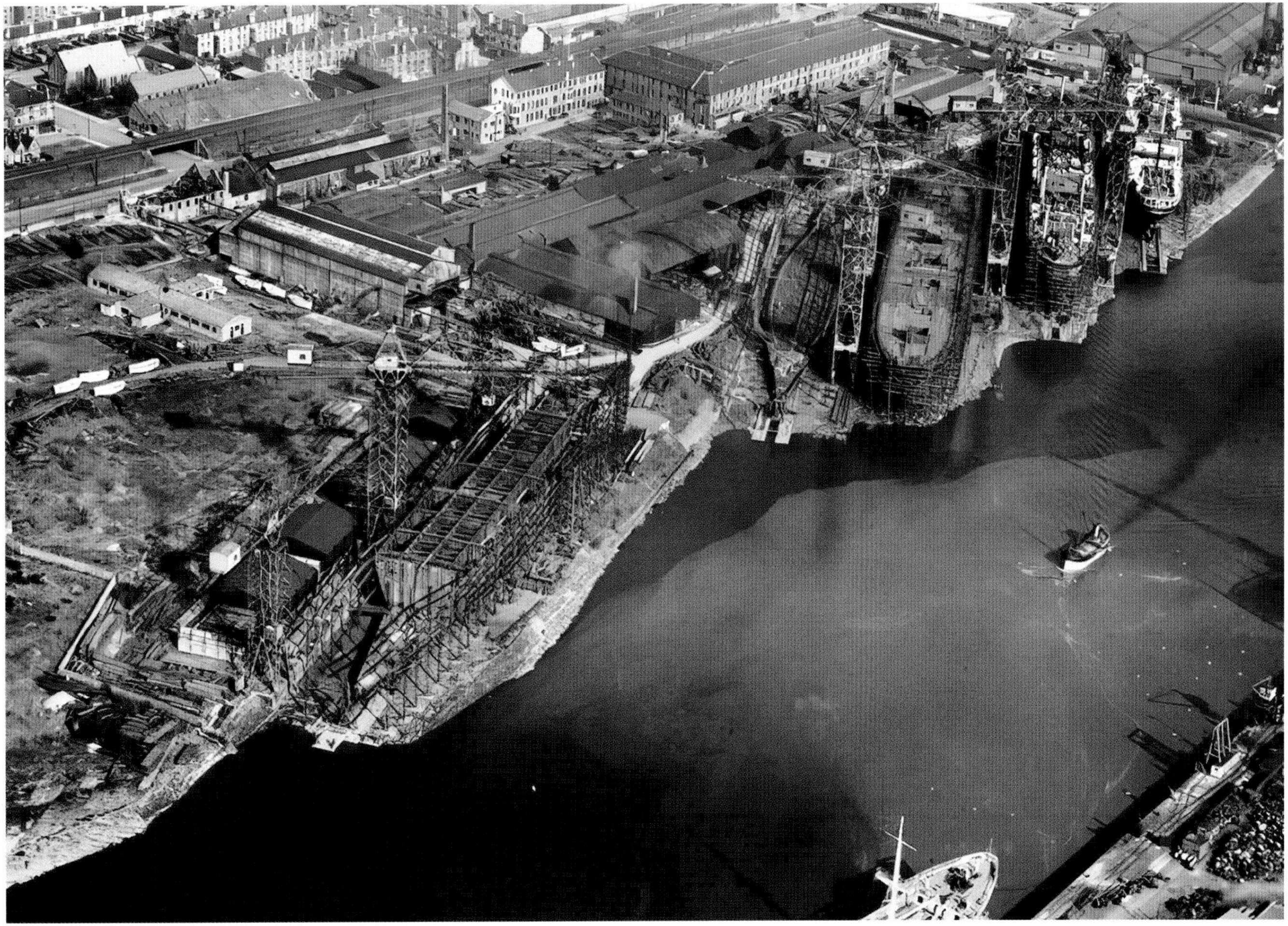

Barclay Curle's Clydeholm shipyard.

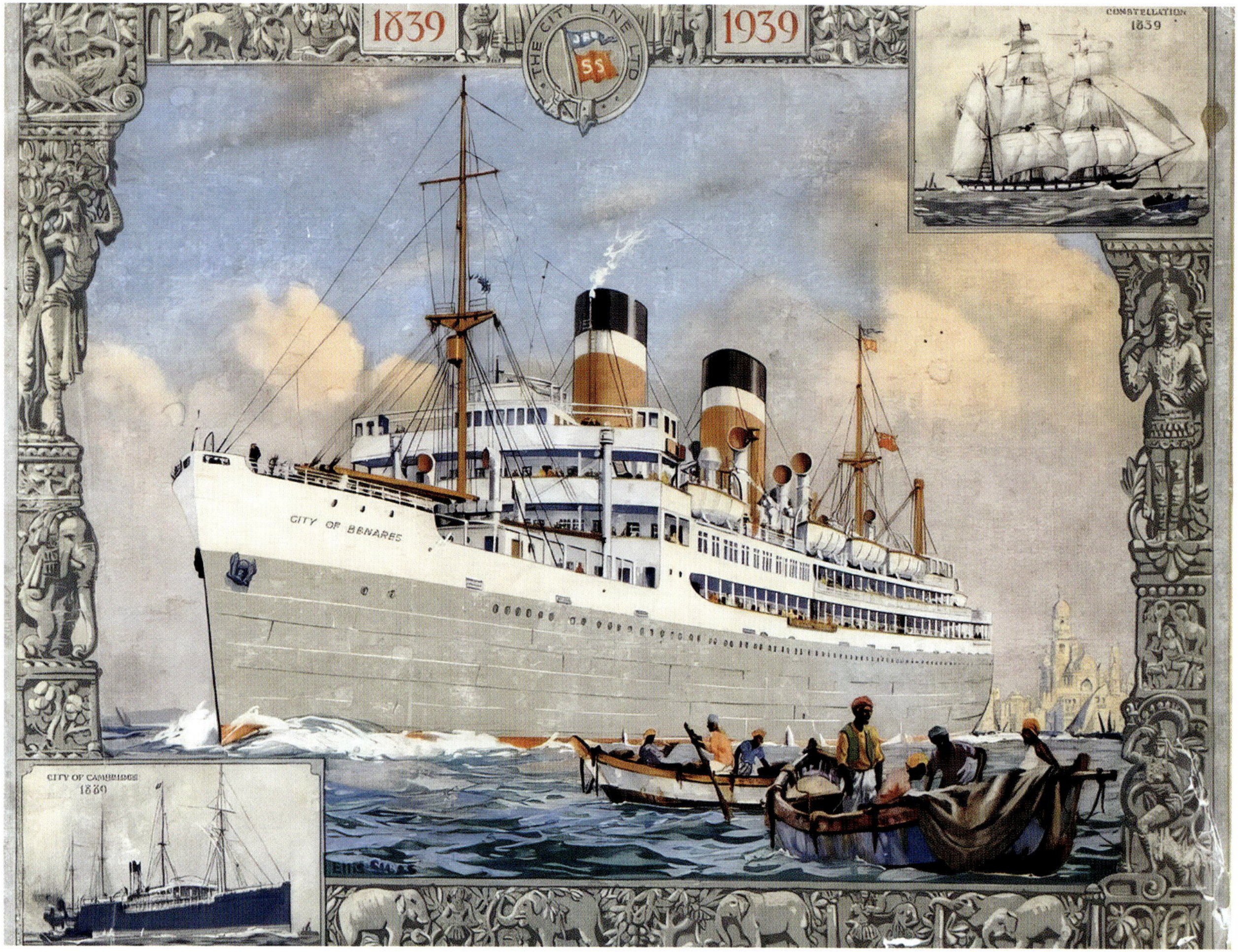

SS *City of Benares*, built for the City Line and depicted in a City Line centenary print.

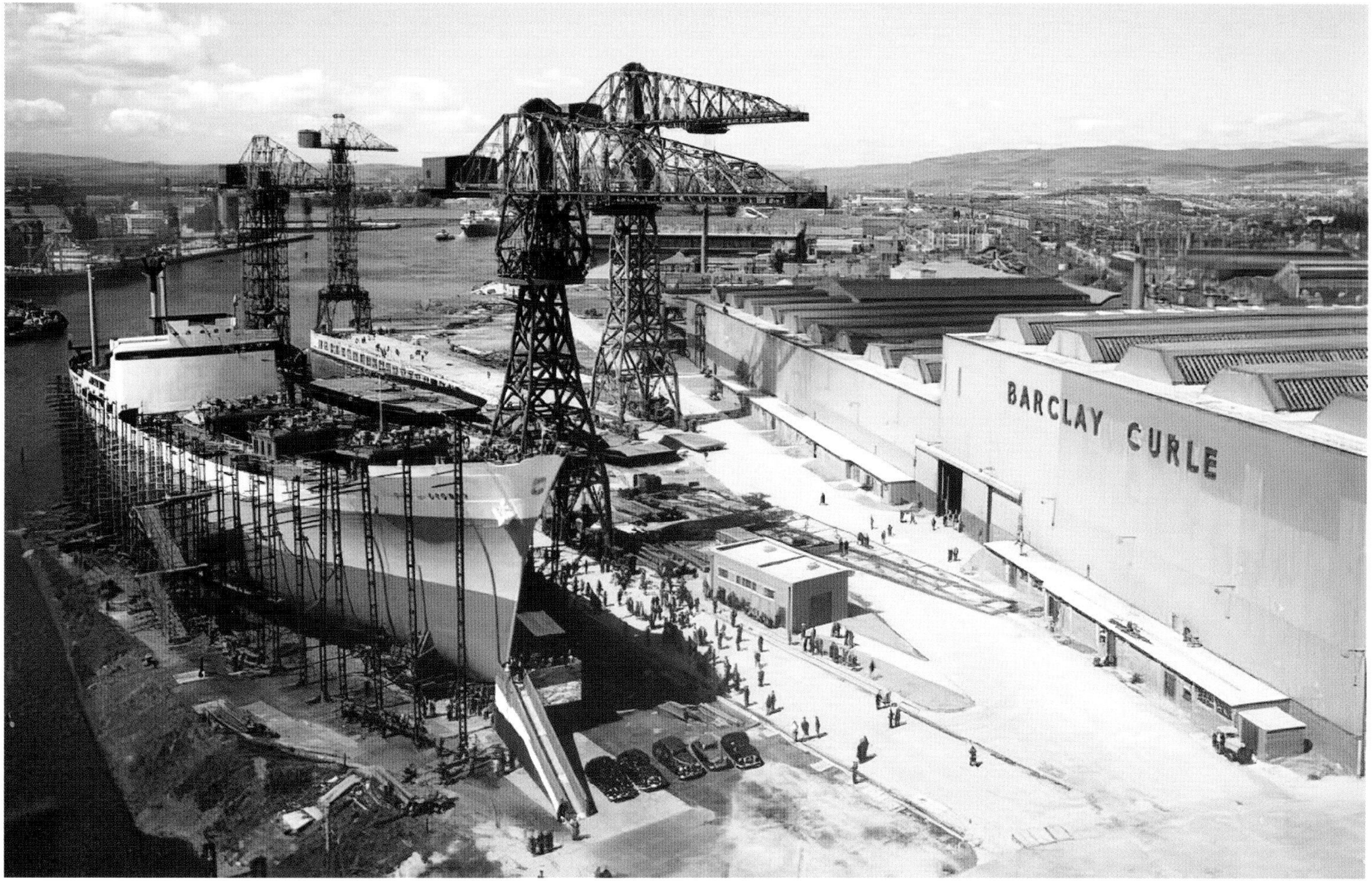

MV *City of Sydney*, ready for launching for Ellerman Lines.

Charles Connell

In 1861 Charles Connell started his own business building ships at Kelvinhaugh, next to Alexander Stephen & Co., where he had become manager. A few years later the new business moved to Scotstoun facing over to lands that much later would become home to new docks, notably King George V Dock.

Tea clippers and passenger ships gave way to a concentration on passenger-cargo ships, transport ferries and later tankers and bulk carriers. Charles Connell did not make ships' engines and instead used engines built by others. For a time, Connell's supplied machinery to the shipbuilding industry. Having six berths up to 700 feet long, the firm built 510 ships up to 1968.

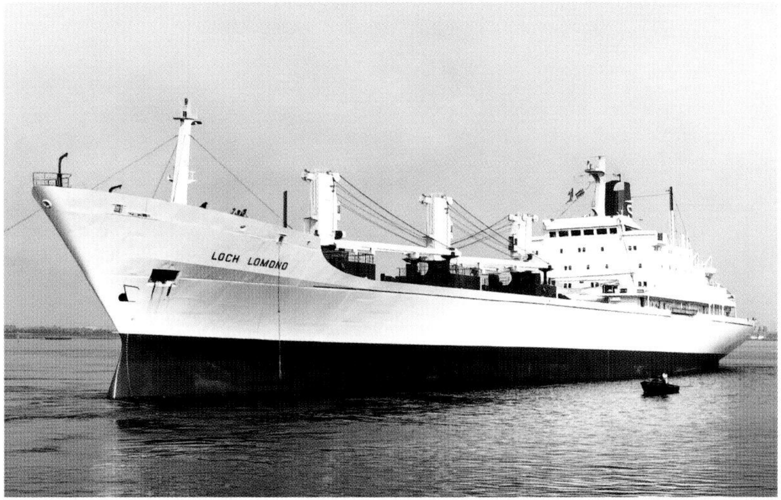

MV *Loch Lomond*, built for Glenfarg Shipping Co. by Scotstoun Marine.

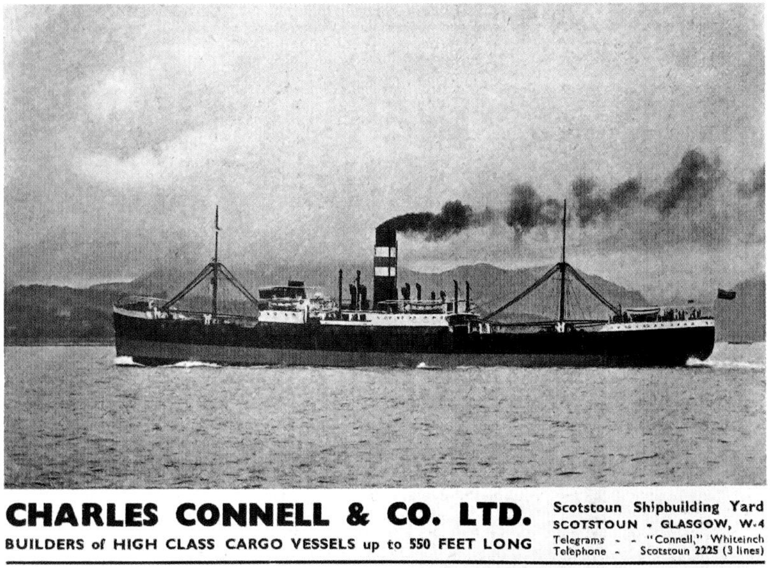

The yard became the Scotstoun Division of UCS and quickly became Scotstoun Marine Ltd, part of Govan Shipbuilders Ltd across the river (at Fairfield's) before UK shipyards were nationalised in 1977. Scotstoun built eighteen ships.

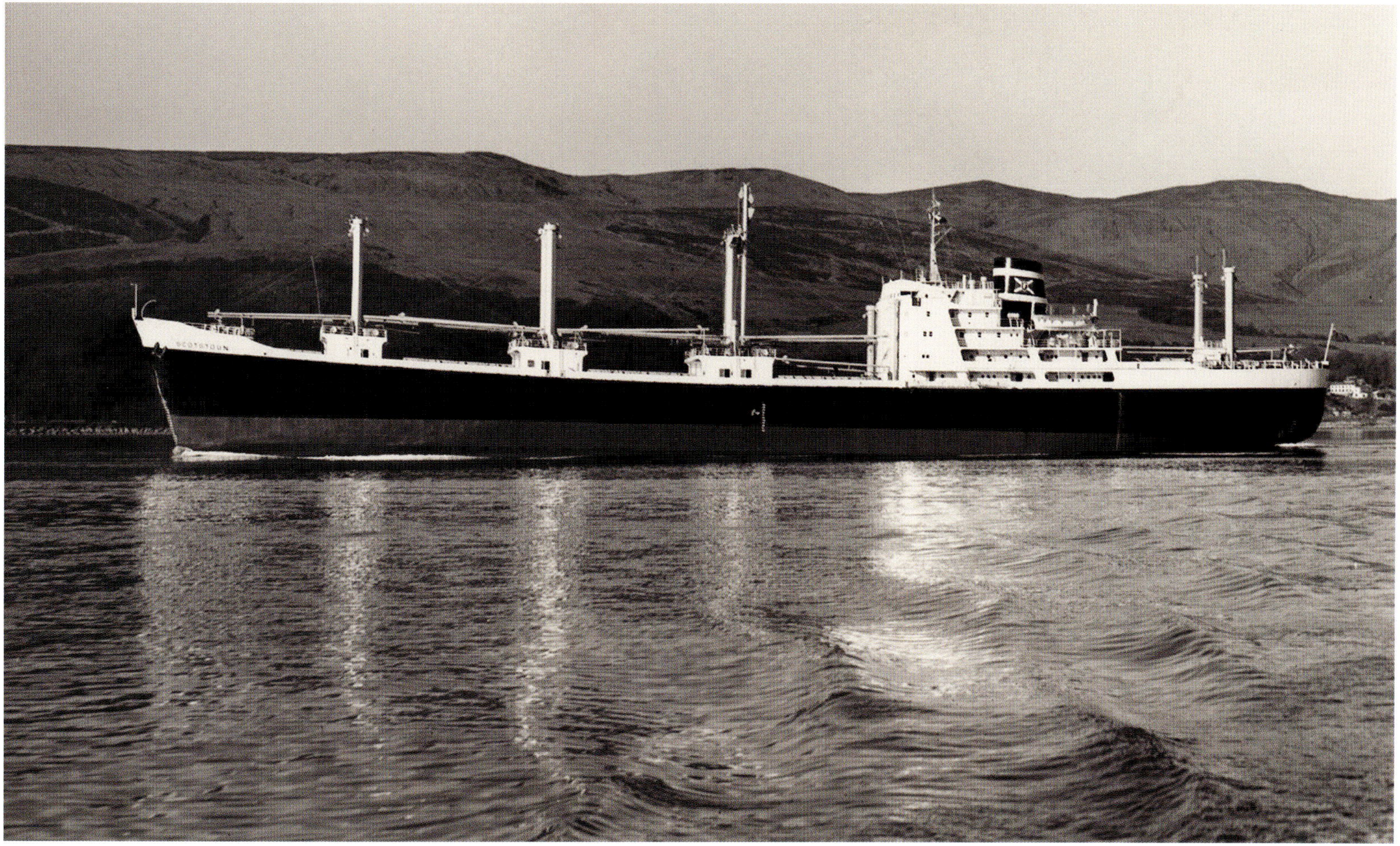

MV *Scotstoun*, built for Falkland Shipowners.

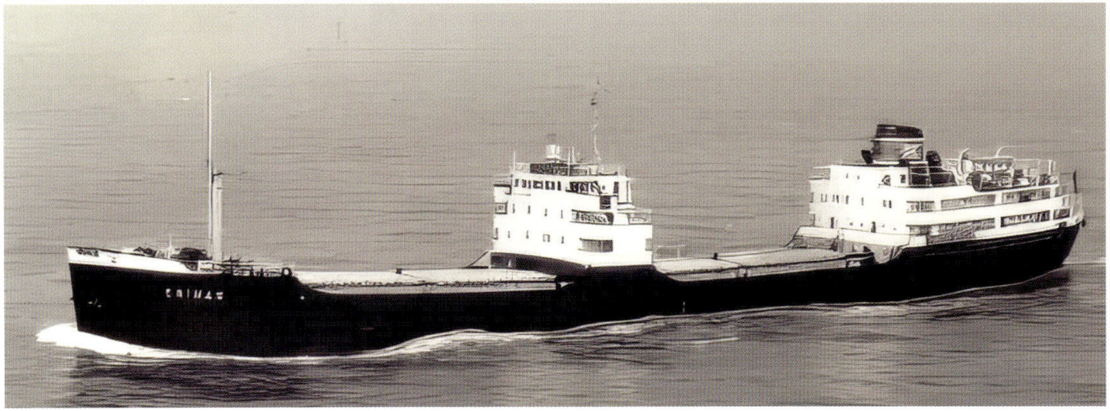

MV *Crinan*, built for Scottish Ore Carriers.

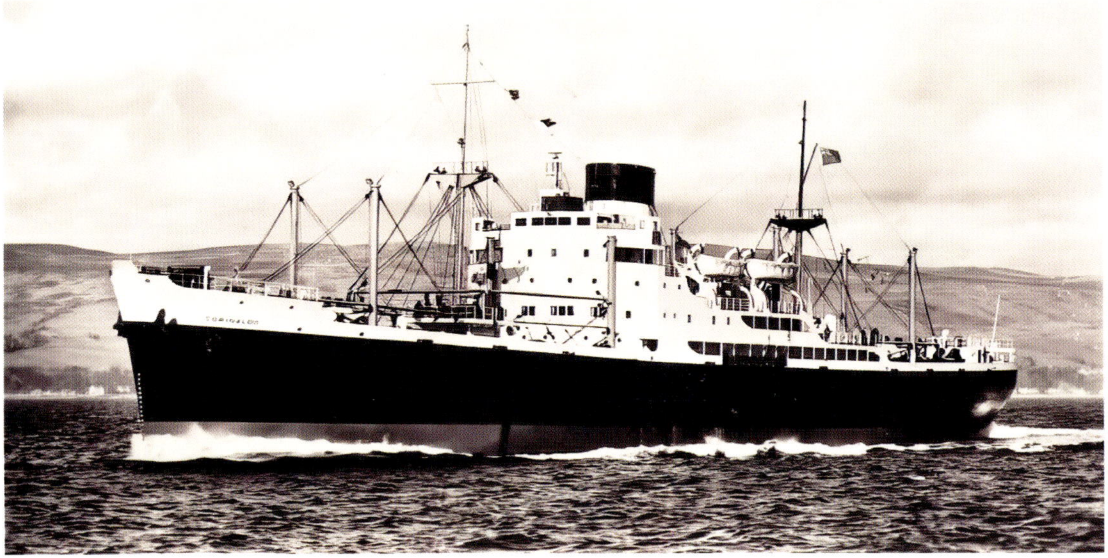

MS *Corinaldo*, built for Donaldson Line.

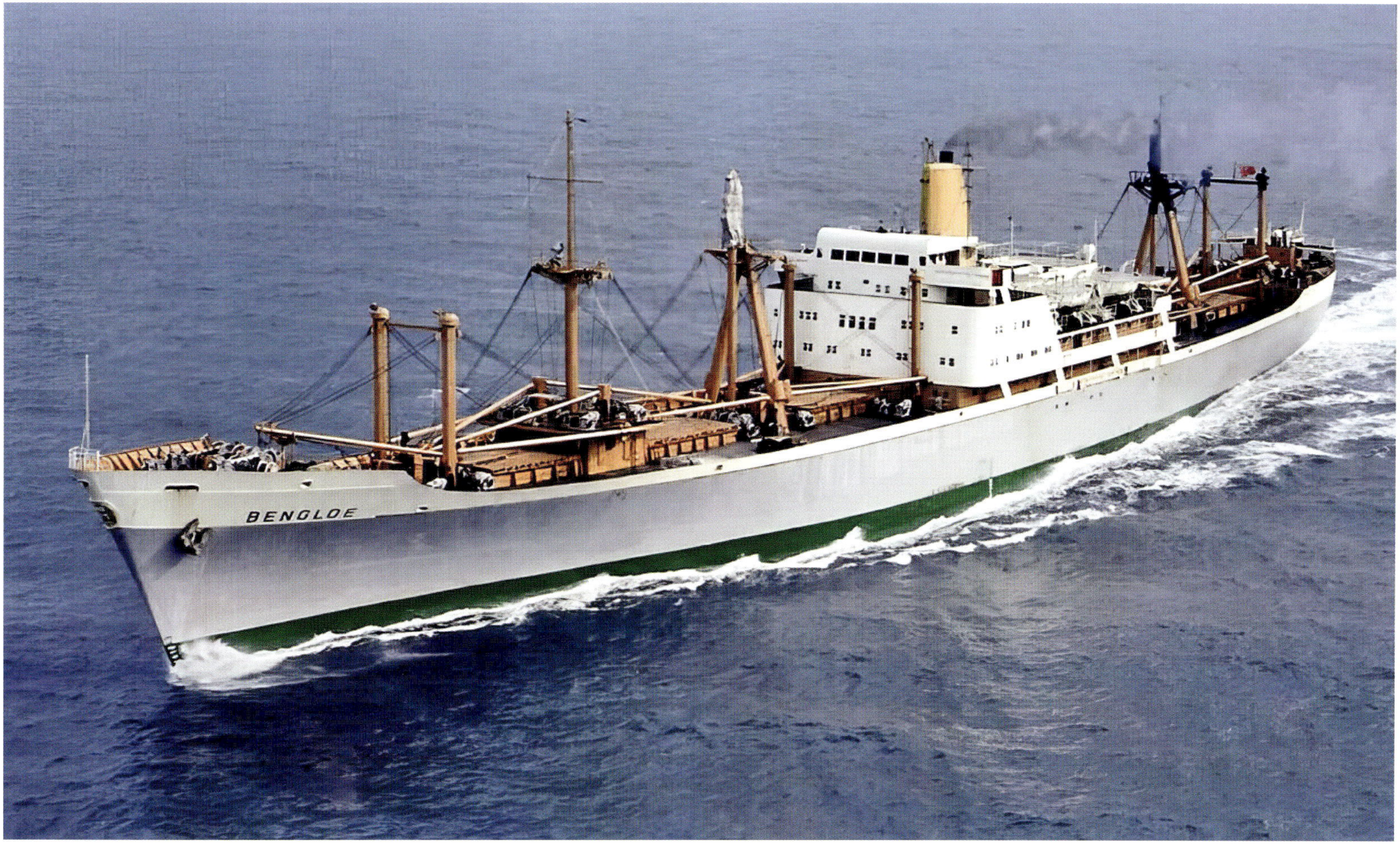

ST *Bengloe*, built for Ben Line.

Blythswood

Keen on developing further the building of oil-carrying vessels, in 1919 Hugh MacMillan, from Fairfield's, and Donald Bremner, from Dunlop, Bremner in Port Glasgow, founded the Blythswood Shipbuilding Company at Scotstoun. Oil was increasingly replacing coal as the fuel for ships and the same was true for many industries. In addition to tankers, they also built passenger cargo ships and bulk carriers.

Blythswood did not build ships' engines, instead commissioning them from other makers. The firm had five berths up to 600 feet long, facing over to Braehead, Renfrew, where the firm had its ship repairs and finishing department. They built 140 ships between 1919 and 1964, when the firm withdrew from shipbuilding. The following year the company sold its yard to its westerly neighbour, Yarrow's, who extended across the site, constructing covered shipbuilding halls and new buildings for their land boiler division.

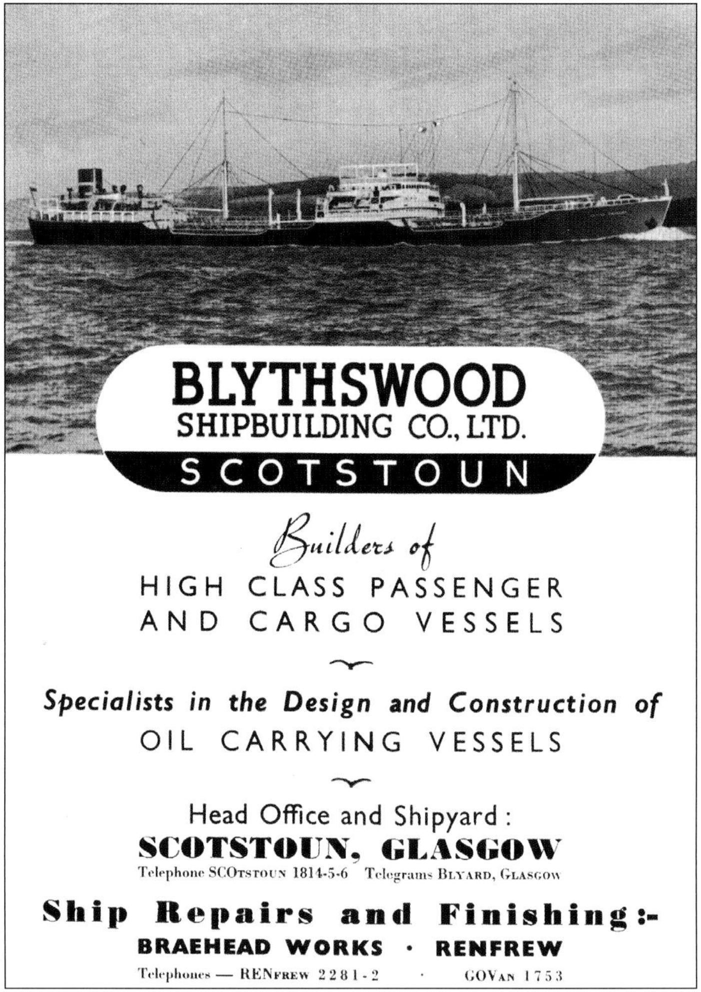

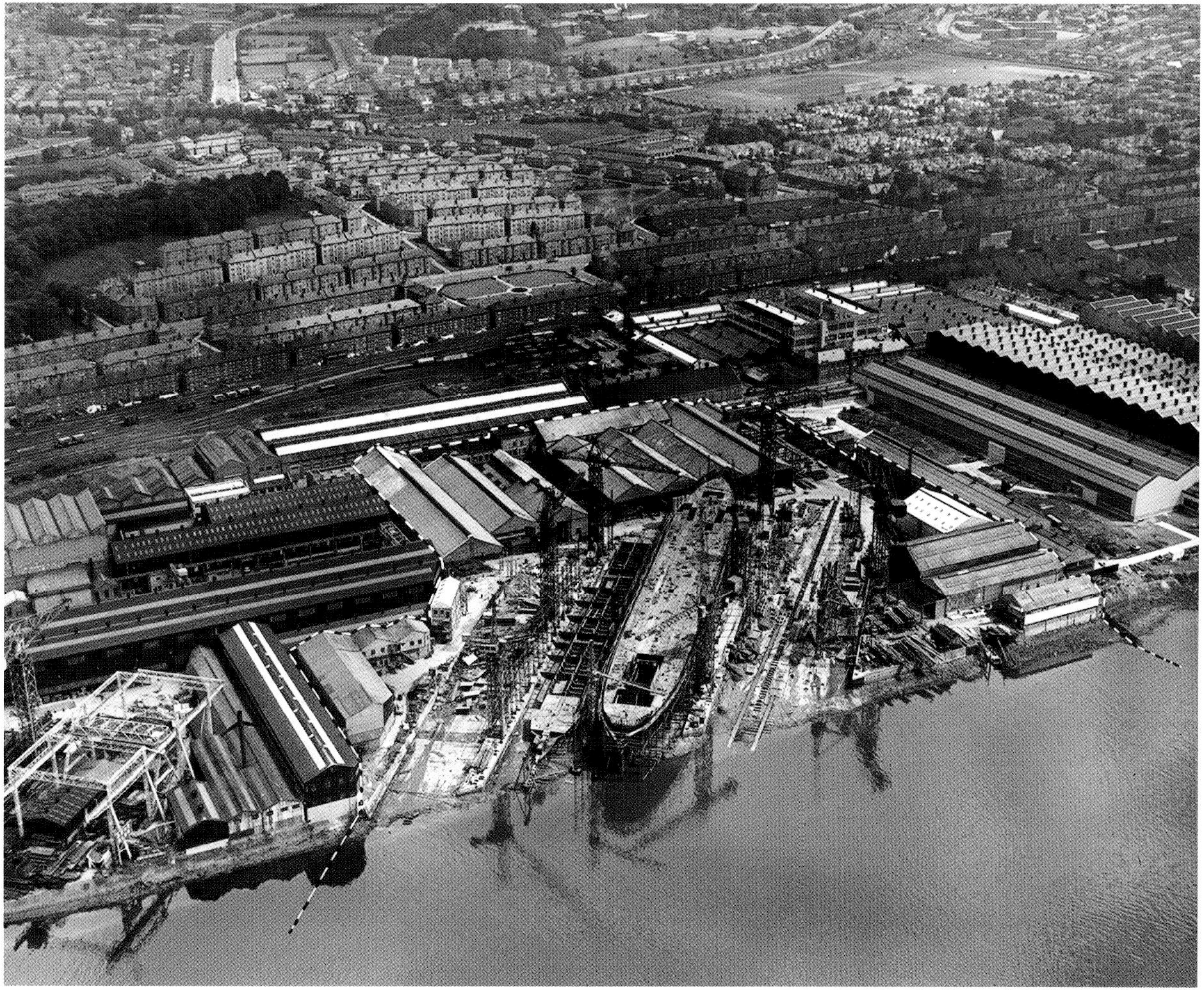

Blythswood shipyard looking north, next to Yarrow's on left.

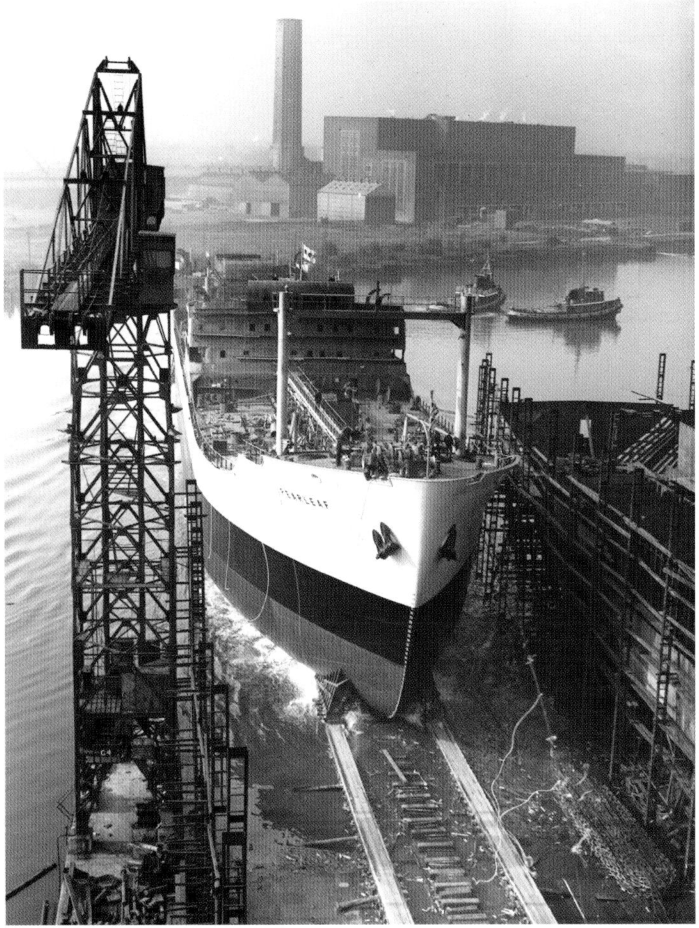

MV *Pearleaf* enters the water for John I. Jacobs & Partners. On the other side is Braehead Power Station.

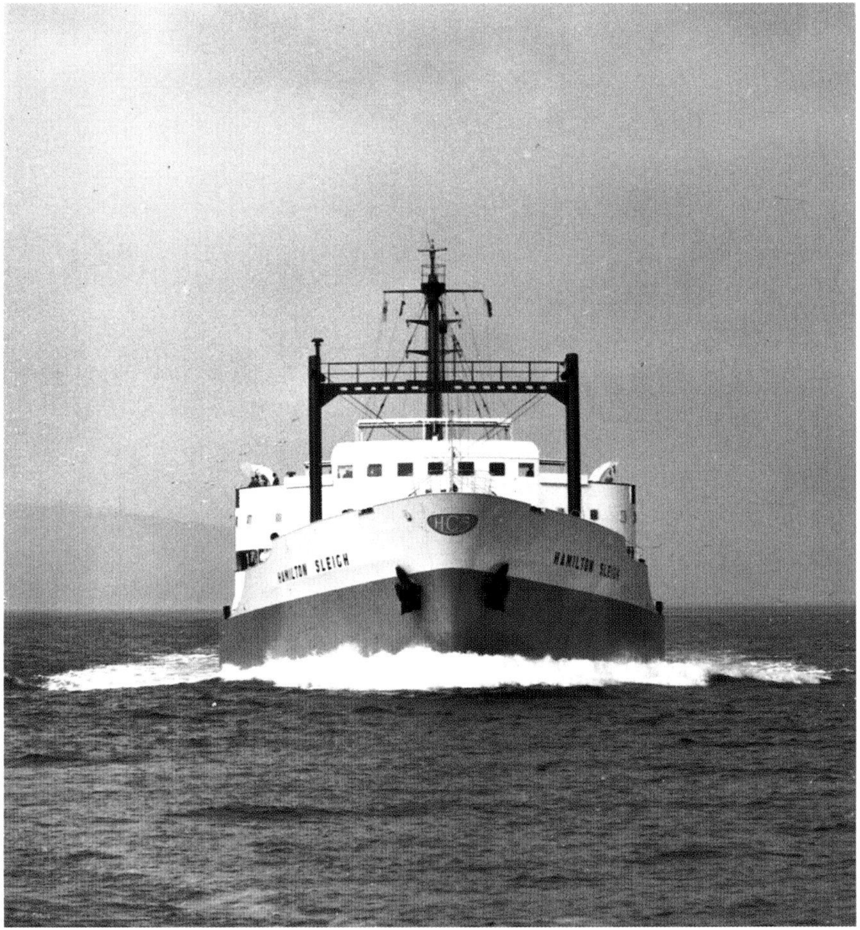

ST *Hamilton Sleigh* on trials for Dominion Navigation Co.

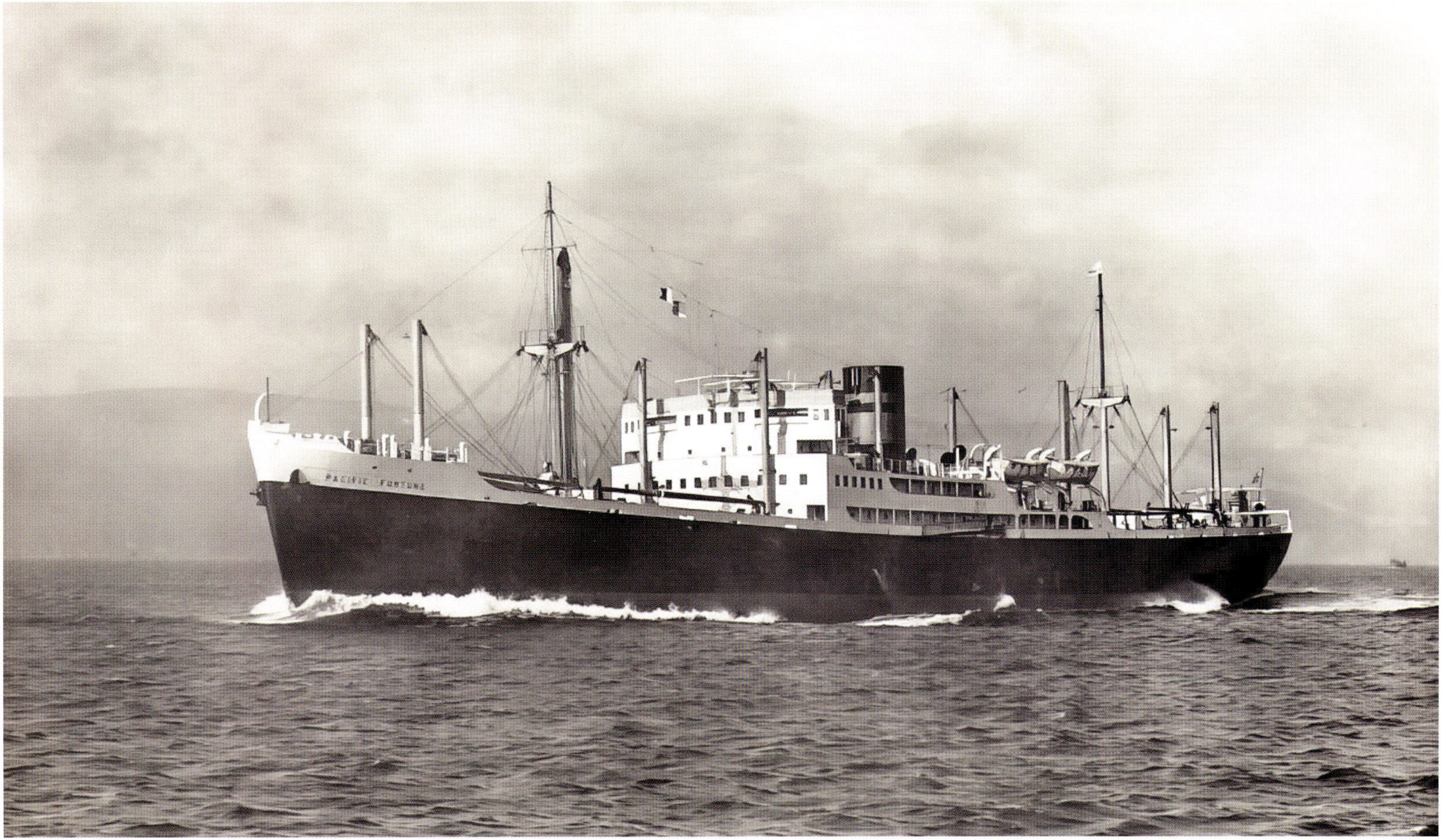

SS *Pacific Fortune*, built for Furness Withy.

Yarrow's

A son of Scotland, inventor and future benefactor, Alfred Yarrow started in 1865 on the River Thames, East London, building steam launches for rivers and lakes, followed by fast torpedo boats and then torpedo boat destroyers for the Royal Navy. The firm also devised high-pressure Yarrow boilers for marine and land uses.

To be at the centre of shipbuilding, and have a larger pool of employees, Yarrow & Company moved to Glasgow in 1906, creating its yard on the open fields of Scotstoun. The firm became a major builder of destroyers and frigates for many navies and some merchant ships, especially for inland waters worldwide.

From the end of the Second World War onwards, the new Yarrow-Admiralty Research Department (Y-ARD) at Scotstoun, and then Charing Cross, ensured the firm's dominance in the supply of fast medium-sized naval ships.

The yard was extended easterly in 1965 after the purchase of the neighbouring yard belonging to the Blythswood Shipbuilding Company. Here covered shipbuilding halls and new buildings for its land boiler division were constructed. In 1974 the firm bought the three dry docks and wharf westward from Barclay Curle.

With six building berths for vessels up to 6,000 tons and more, over 400 ships have been built by the firm in Glasgow to date. Continuing today as BAE Systems, the firm carries out research and design with final fitting out and weaponry in conjunction with the Govan production yard upstream, formerly Fairfield's.

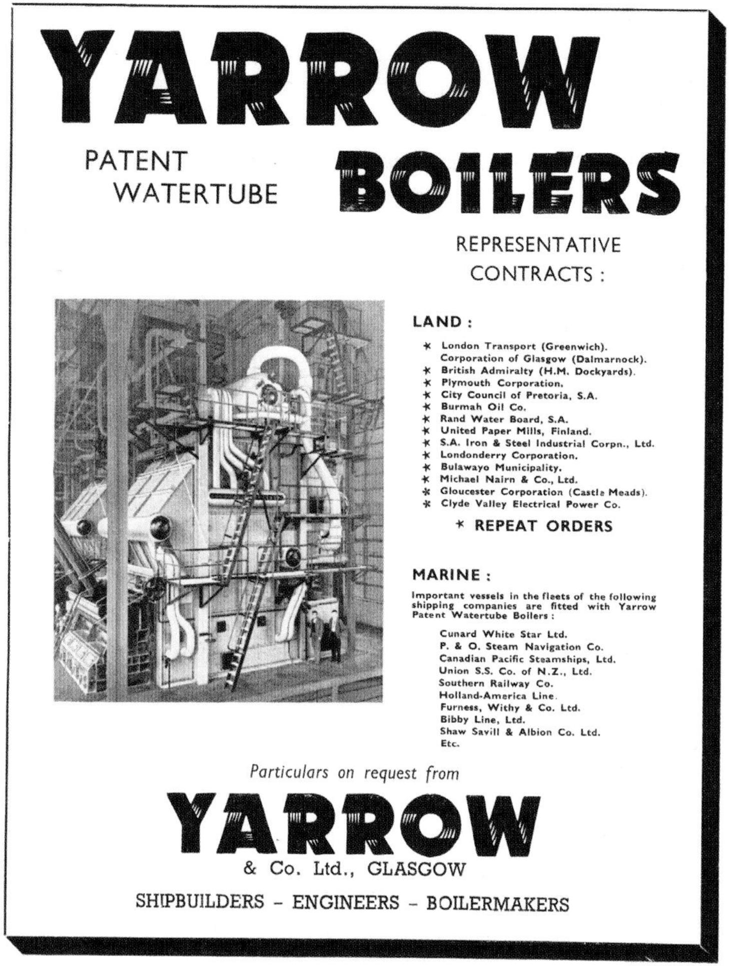

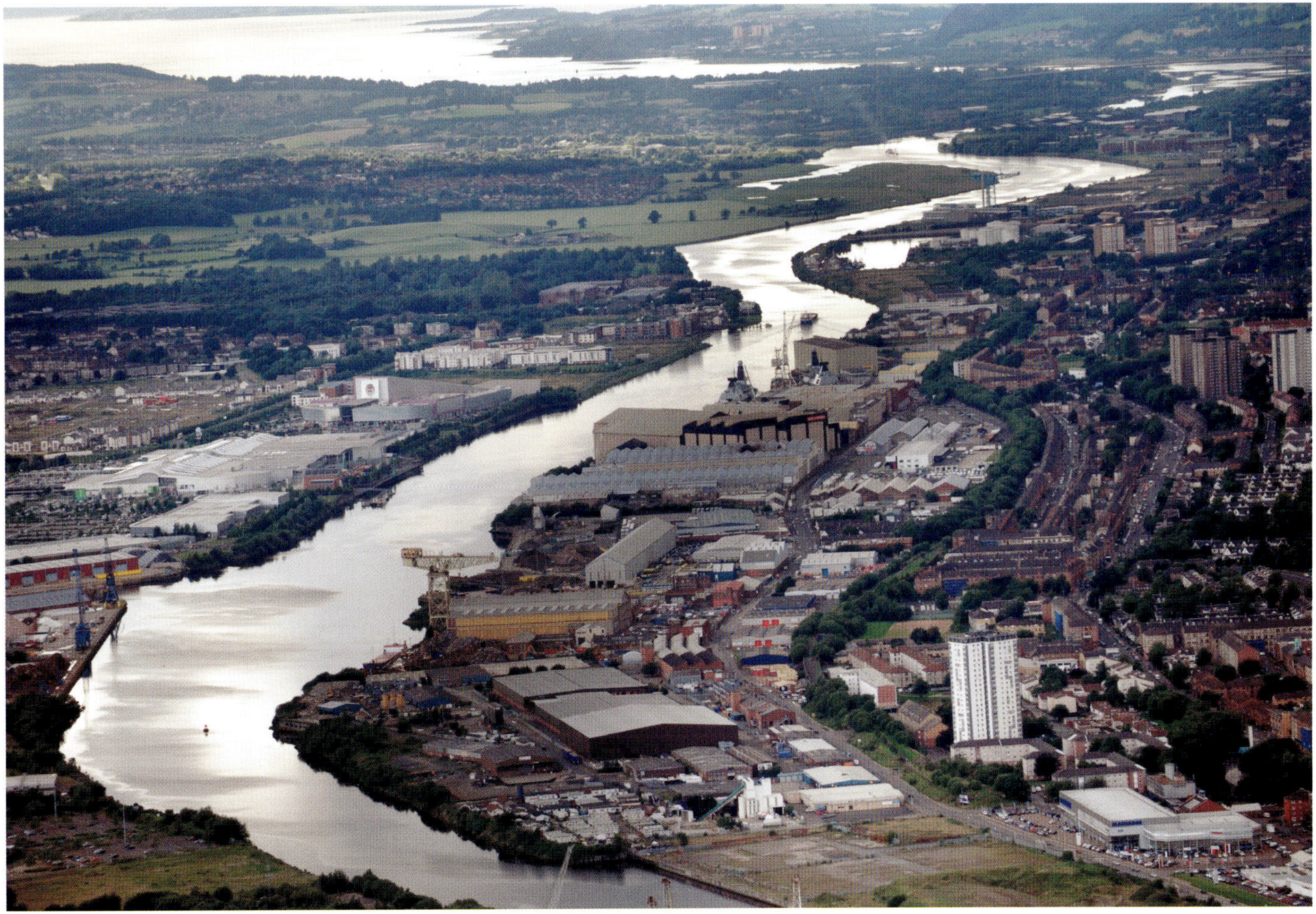

Yarrow's shipbuilding halls and dry docks at Scotstoun are in the centre of this image with Braehead opposite. Beyond is Rothesay Dock and Clydebank.

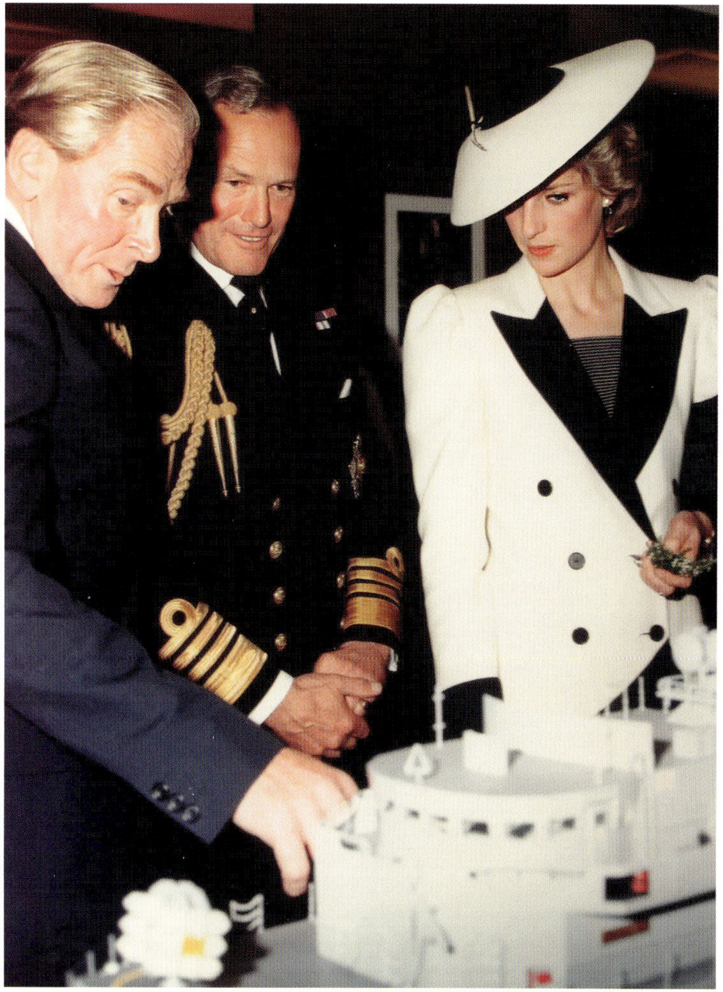

HRH Princess Diana at Yarrow's for the launch of HMS *Cornwall*.

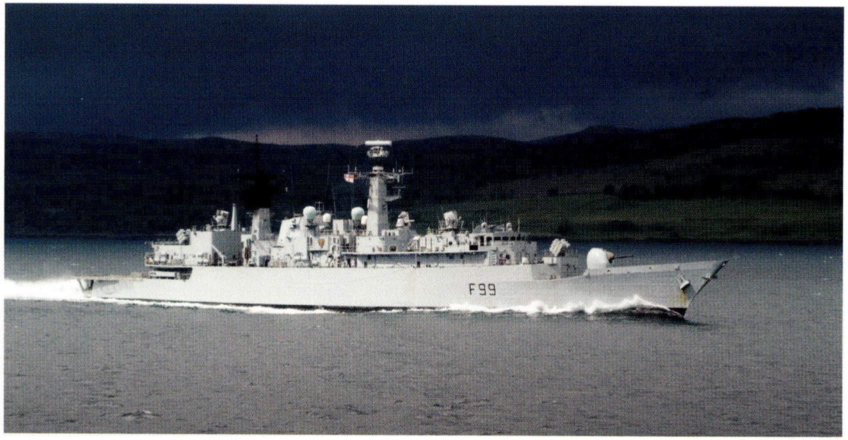

HMS *Cornwall* on trials.

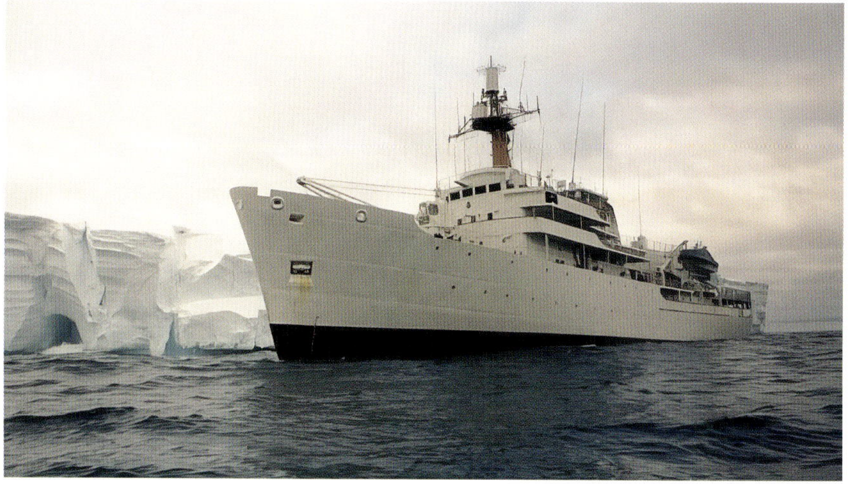

Hydrographic survey ship SAS *Protea* in Antarctica.

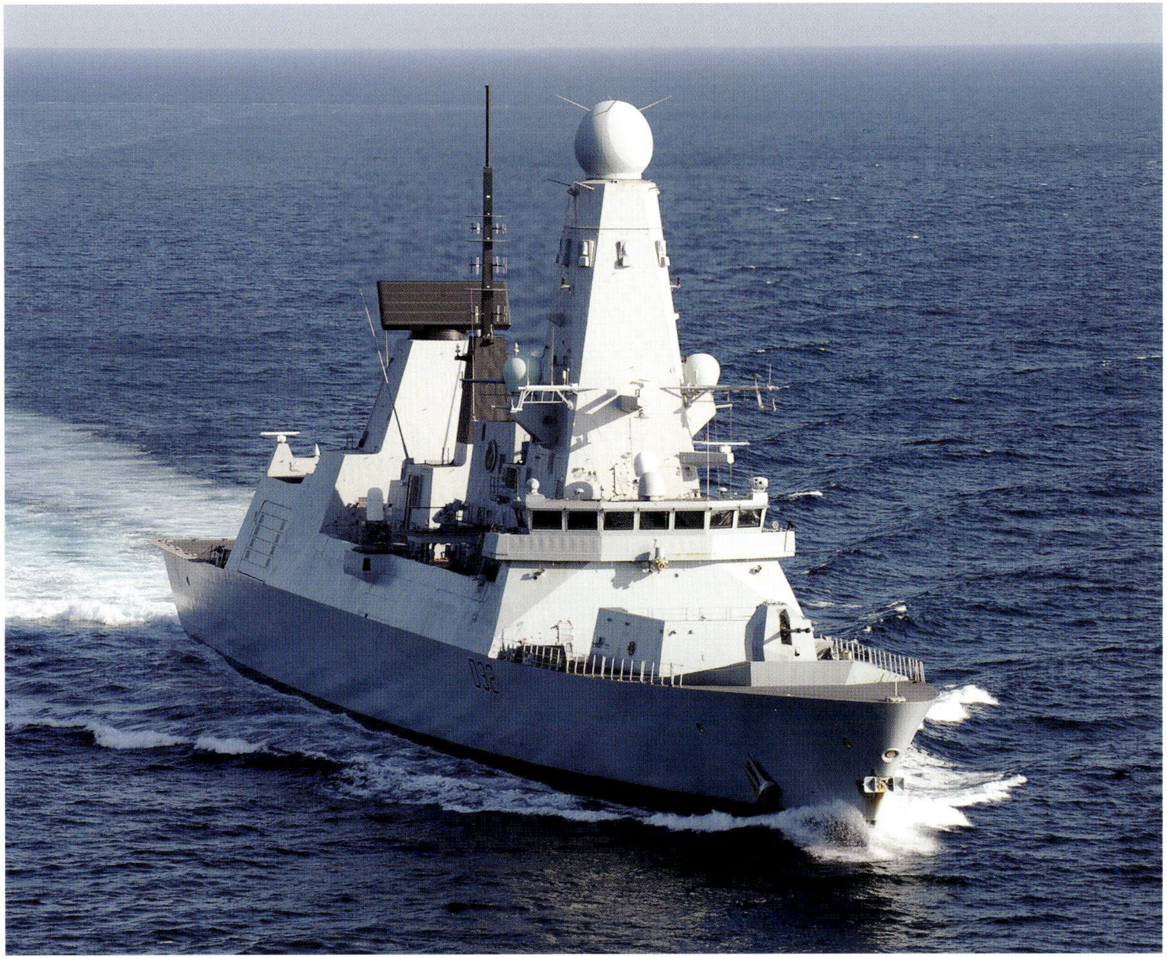

HMS *Daring*.

John Brown

The brothers James and George Thomson started marine engineering at Clyde Bank foundry in Finnieston in 1847 and shipbuilding in Govan in 1851. (A third brother became the first superintendent engineer of the Cunard Line.) The new town of Clydebank was only established in 1871 when the firm of J. & G. Thomson moved their shipbuilding downstream from their Clyde Bank yard at Mavisbank, Govan, to new open land opposite the River Cart. Large, modern engine works opened in 1884, making larger ships and larger launches possible.

The size and international renown of the yard attracted steelmaker and supplier of armour plating John Brown & Co. of Sheffield to purchase it in 1899 and expand it further. The largest ships in the world would be built by the firm.

The company mainly produced warships, passenger liners, cargo ships, tankers and bulk carriers as well as steam yachts. The company also developed and made gas turbines for marine use. It had eight building berths of up to 1,000 feet long. The fitting-out basin sat between the East Yard and the West Yard. The company produced some 750 ships between 1847 and 1971. Oil rig work commenced in the 1960s.

With turmoil in the industry in the 1960s, and losses multiplying at Clydebank, the company became part of the short-lived UCS group in 1968. However, John Brown Engineering in association with the General Electric Company produced gas turbines for land and marine uses from 1967 onwards, and latterly Kvaerner Energy until 1998.

From 1972 other parts of the yard focused on oil rig construction under Marathon of the USA and followed by UiE of France until 2000. The whole yard was cleared in 2001, leaving a hammerhead crane at the river's edge.

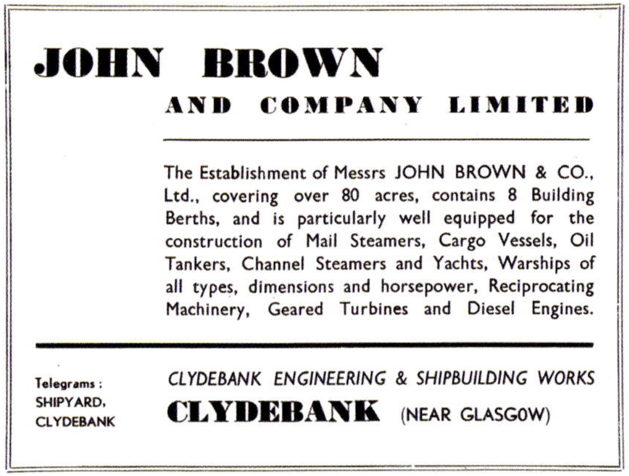

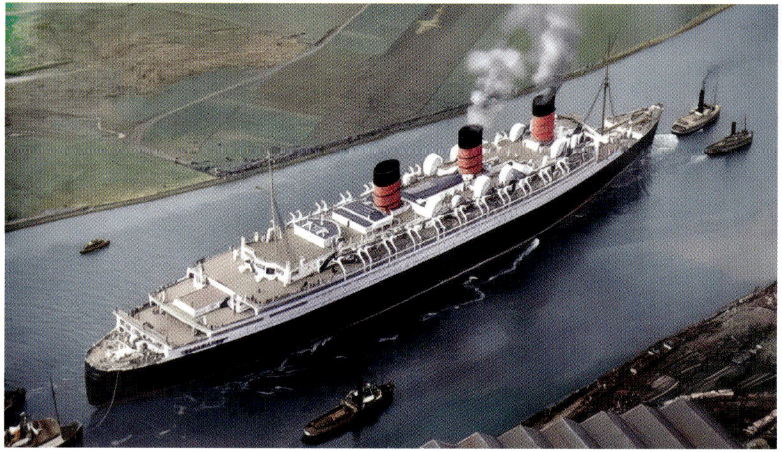

RMS *Queen Mary*, built for Cunard-White Star, sets sail from Clydebank.

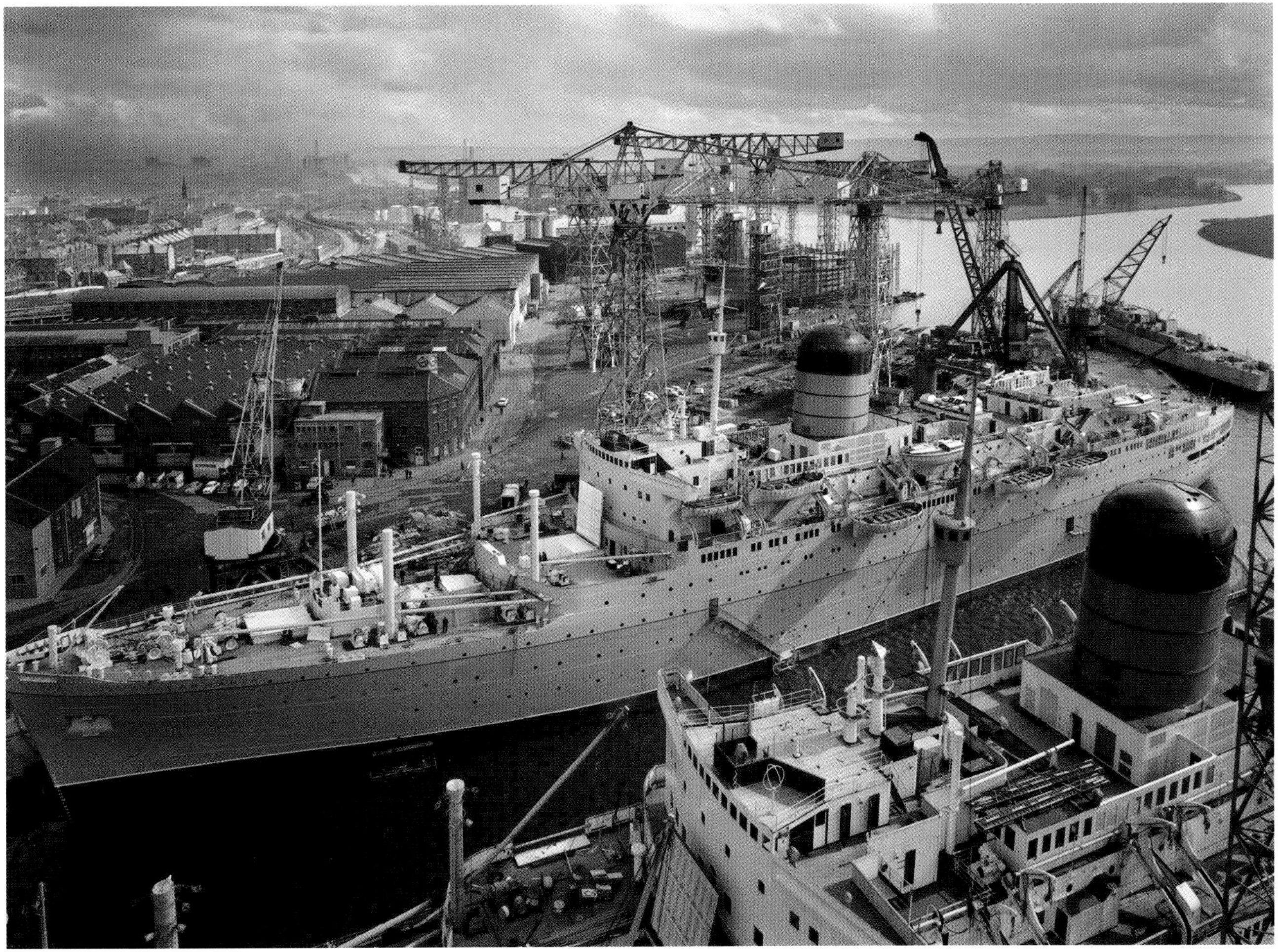

John Brown's shipyard with Cunarders in for a refit, RMS *Carmania* (launched as *Saxonia*) and RMS *Franconia* (launched as *Ivernia*).

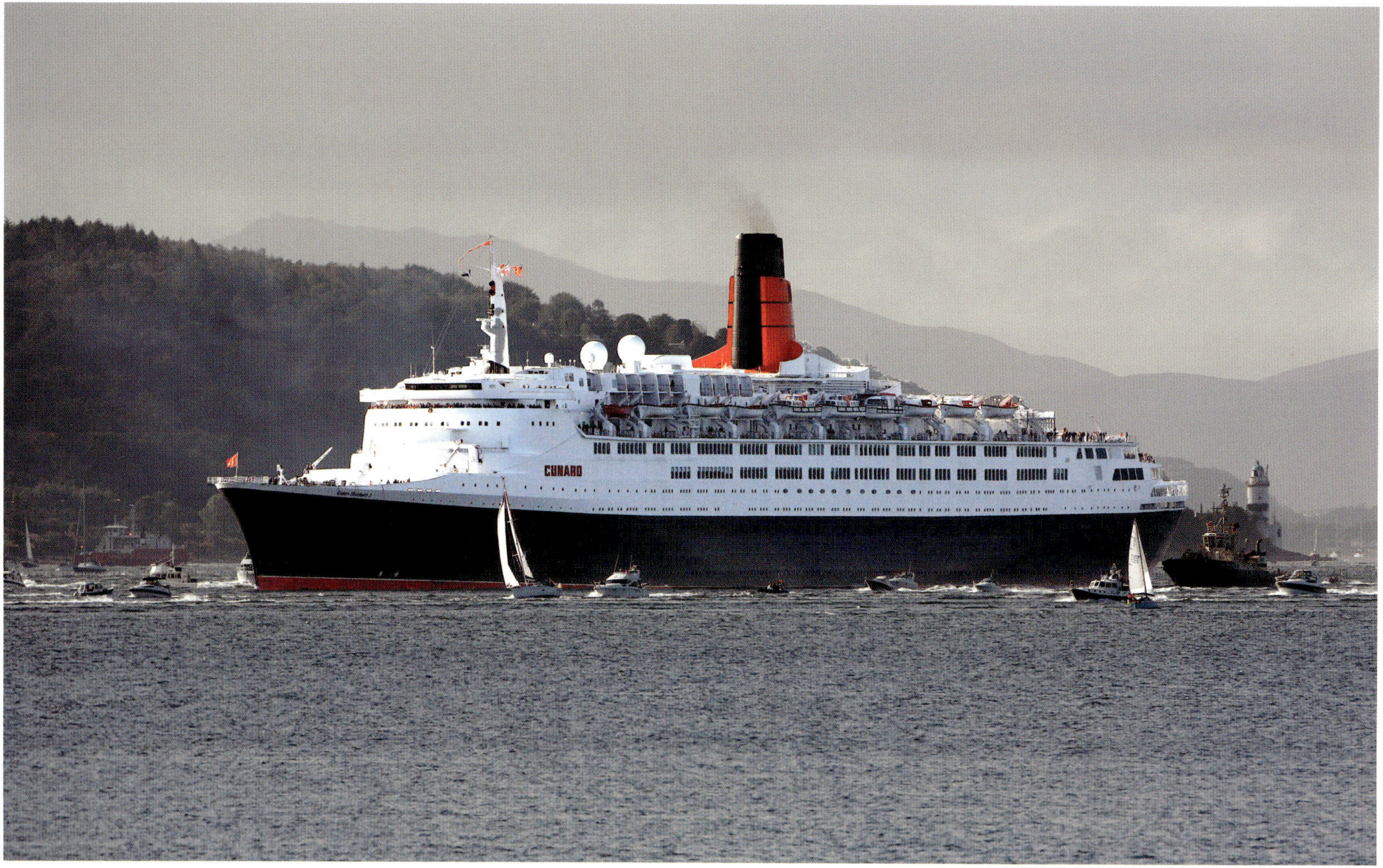

RMS *Queen Elizabeth 2* (QE2), built for Cunard, passing Cloch Lighthouse.

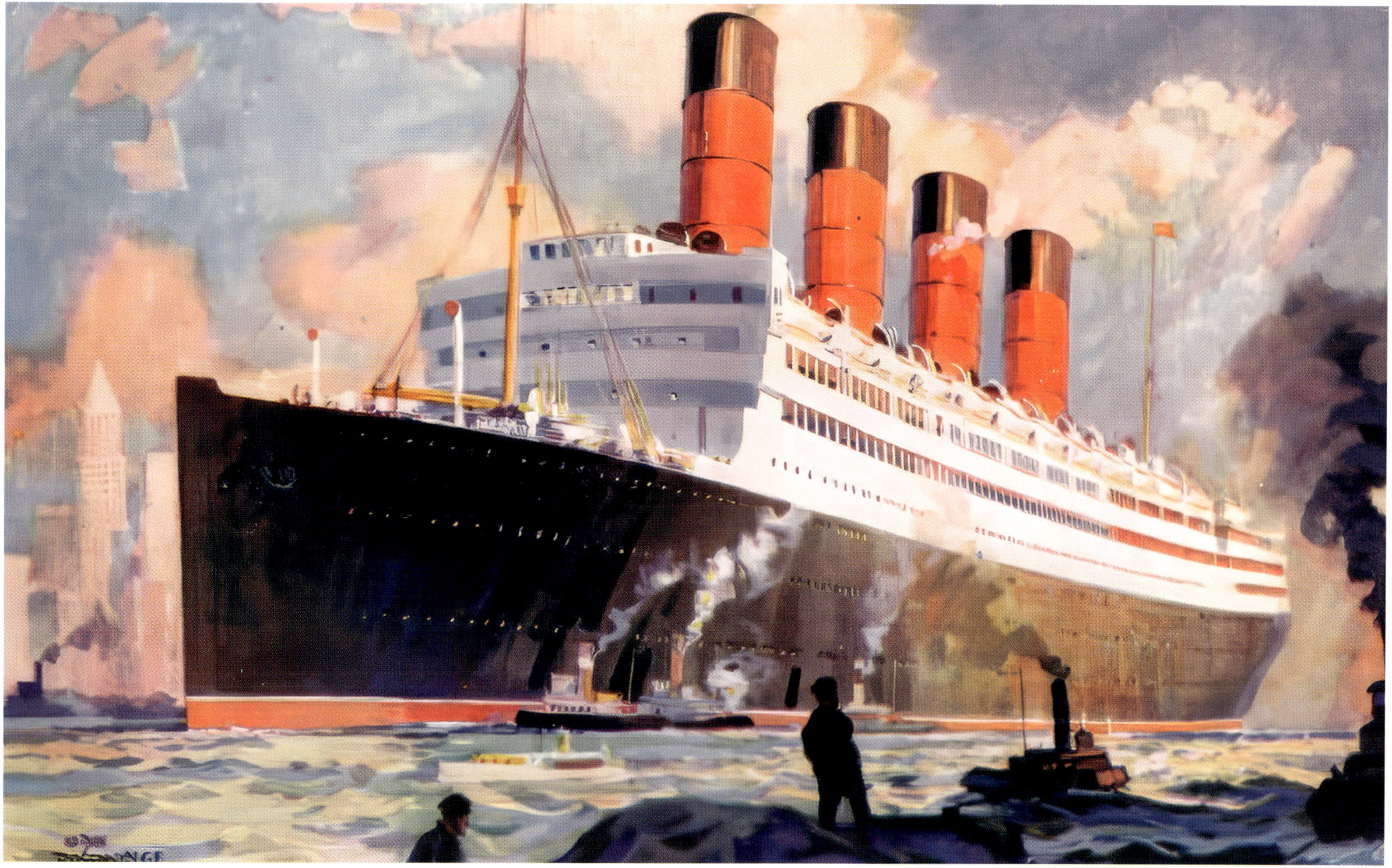

‘The Ship Beautiful’ – RMS *Aquitania*, built for Cunard, painting by Odin Rosenvinge.

Beardmore

(Sir) William Beardmore, dubbed the 'Field Marshal of Industry', already supplied shipbuilders and engineering businesses throughout Britain from his immense Parkhead Forge in Glasgow, which would continue until 1983. He bought Robert Napier & Sons' shipyard in Govan in 1901. He instantly planned to build his own Naval Construction Works downstream at Dalmuir, past Clydebank, with the first naval ship launching in 1906. The extensive yard set new standards in layout and production, completed with a West Yard, fitting-out basin and East Yard.

Beardmore companies formed one of the largest industrial groups in Britain, manufacturing steel, castings, armour plate, armaments, ships, locomotives, airships, aeroplanes, motor cars, taxis, motorcycles and more (even GPO red telephone boxes). At Dalmuir warships, submarines, passenger liners and cargo ships were constructed. There were fourteen building berths up to 1,000 feet long. A total of 130 ships were built there between 1905 and 1930. In addition, around 400 locomotives were built at Dalmuir between 1920 and 1930.

The deepening recession after the Second World War affected all UK yards. Some, including Beardmore from 1930, were covenanted to cease building new ships. There were few new orders but Beardmore continued ship-repair work and marine engineering at Dalmuir until 1939.

Parts of the site were later used by Turner's Asbestos, Arnott Young (Ship Breakers), Babcock & Wilcox and others. In the 1980s Clydebank Enterprise Zone was created, led by the Scottish Development Agency, to attract new employment following the closure of the Singer factory, famed for sewing machines. Starting in 1991, a large private hospital and luxury hotel were built on the former yard in the zone for Middle East developers. This is the Golden Jubilee Hospital and Hotel, originally named the Beardmore Hotel.

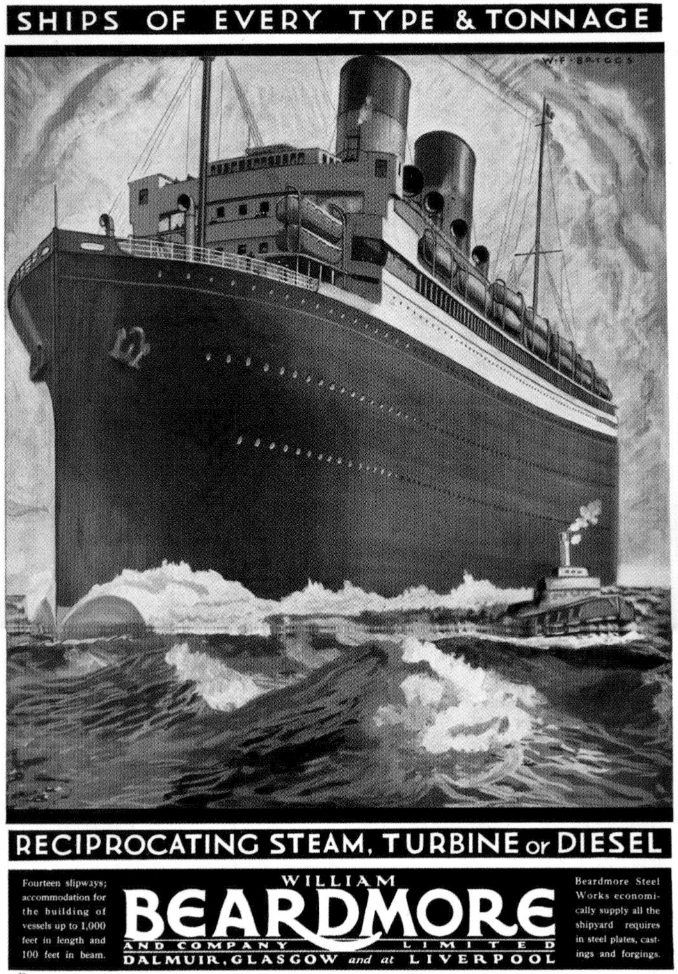

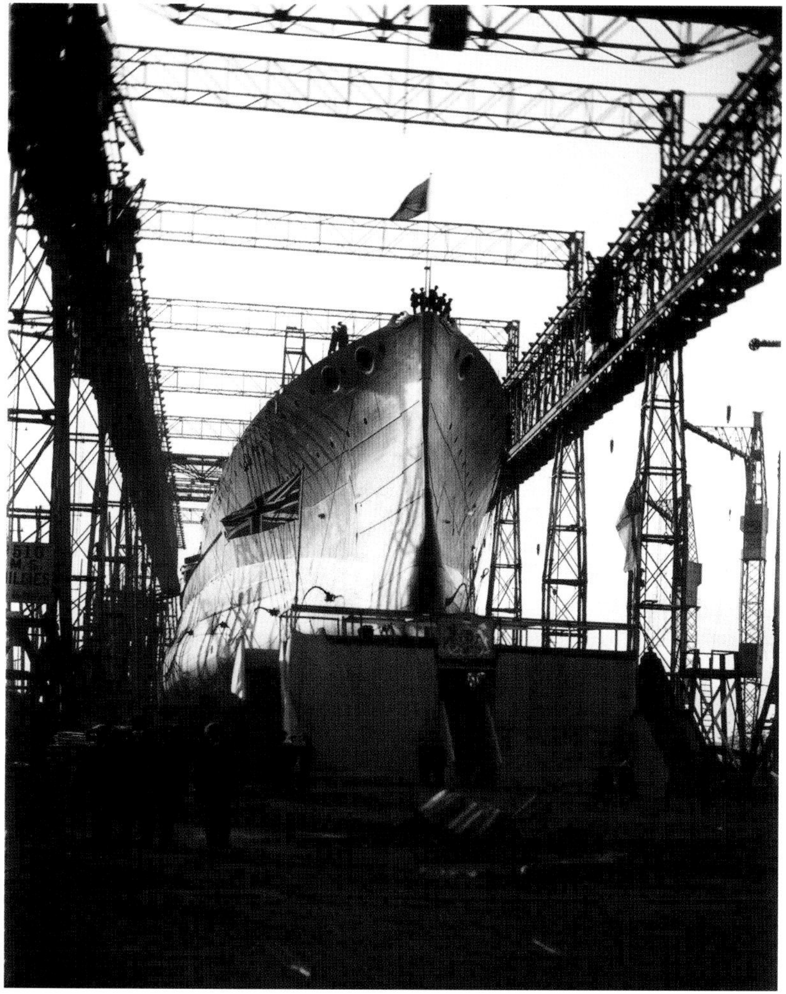

Preparation for launch day of dreadnought battleship HMS *Ramillies*.

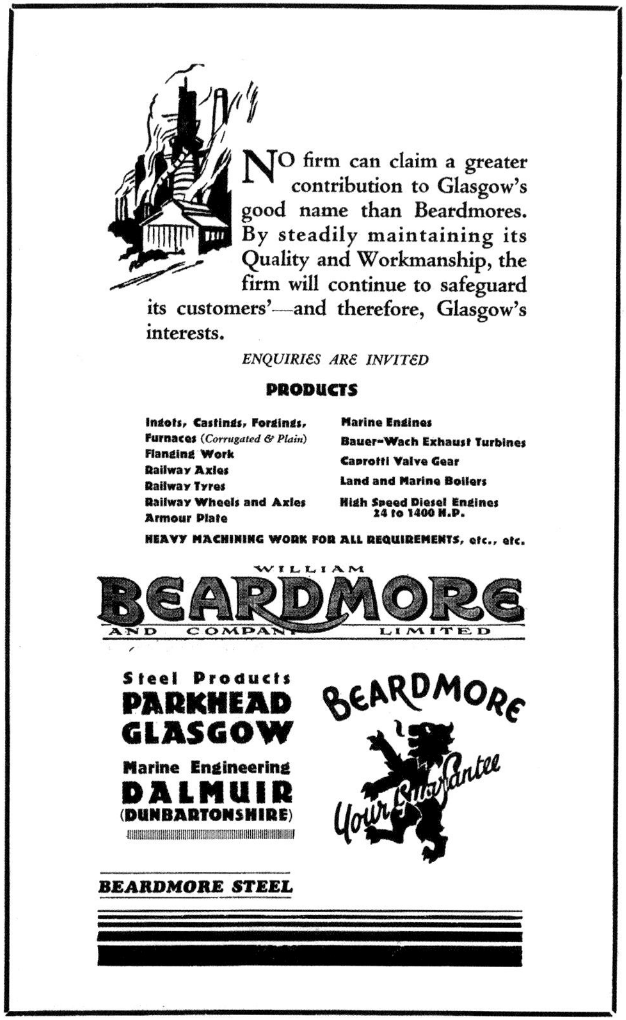

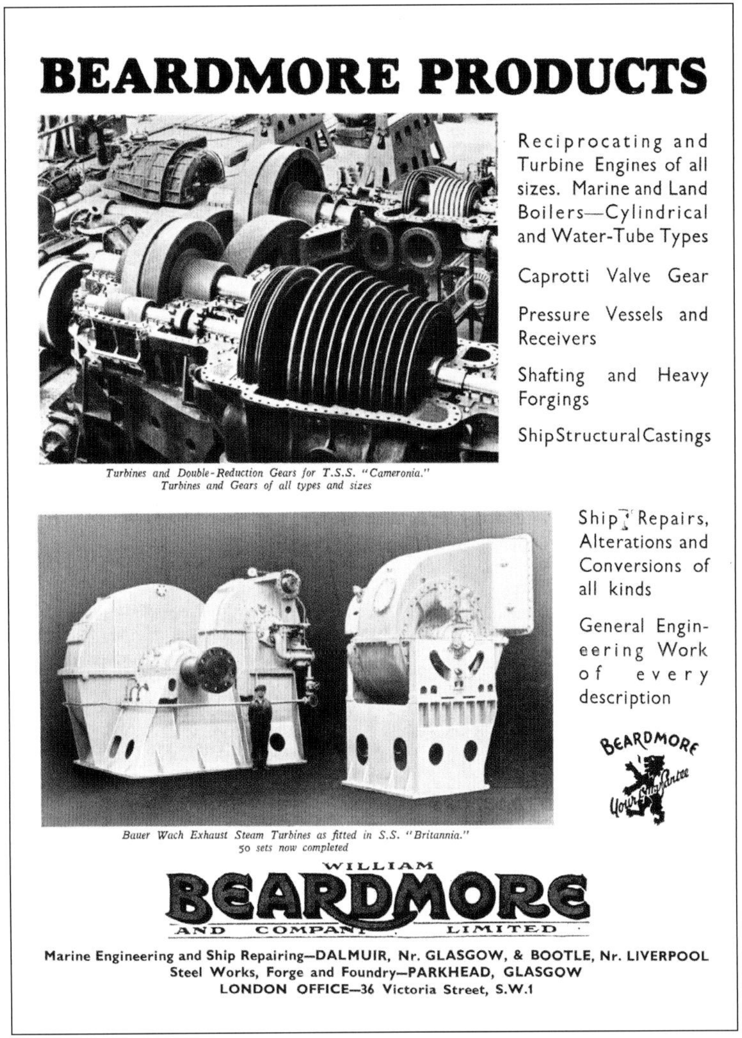
BEARDMORE PRODUCTS
Reciprocating and Turbine Engines of all sizes. Marine and Land Boilers—Cylindrical and Water-Tube Types
Caprotti Valve Gear
Pressure Vessels and Receivers
Shafting and Heavy Forgings
Ship Structural Castings
Turbines and Double-Reduction Gears for T.S.S. "Cameronia." Turbines and Gears of all types and sizes
Ship Repairs, Alterations and Conversions of all kinds
General Engineering Work of every description
BEARDMORE
Your Guarantee
Bauer Wach Exhaust Steam Turbines as fitted in S.S. "Britannia." 50 sets now completed
WILLIAM
BEARDMORE
AND COMPANY LIMITED
Marine Engineering and Ship Repairing—DALMUIR, Nr. GLASGOW, & BOOTLE, Nr. LIVERPOOL
Steel Works, Forge and Foundry—PARKHEAD, GLASGOW
LONDON OFFICE—36 Victoria Street, S.W.1

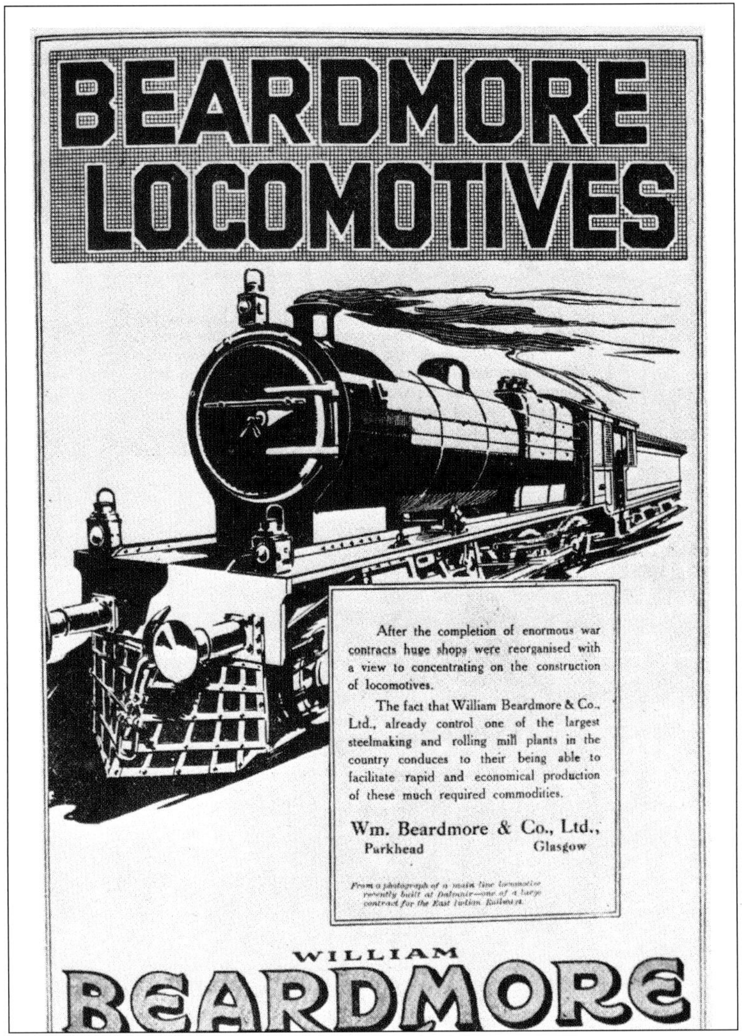
BEARDMORE LOCOMOTIVES
After the completion of enormous war contracts huge shops were reorganised with a view to concentrating on the construction of locomotives.
The fact that William Beardmore & Co., Ltd., already control one of the largest steelmaking and rolling mill plants in the country conduces to their being able to facilitate rapid and economical production of these much required commodities.
Wm. Beardmore & Co., Ltd.,
Parkhead
Glasgow
WILLIAM
BEARDMORE

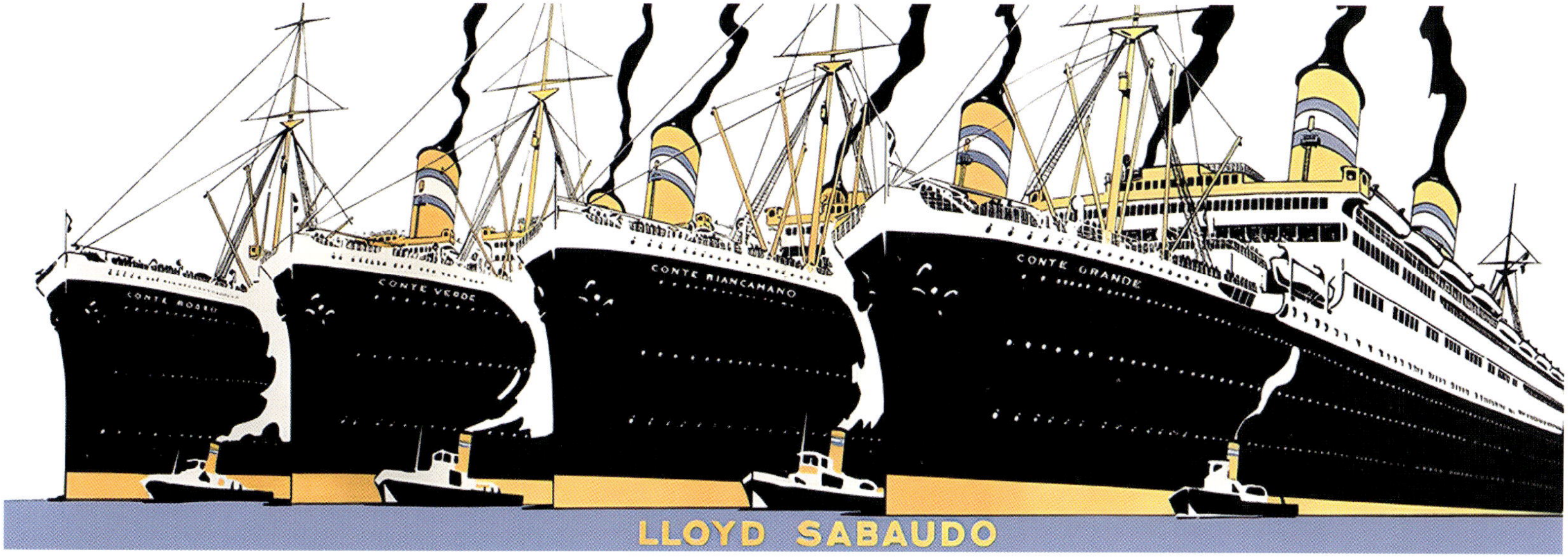

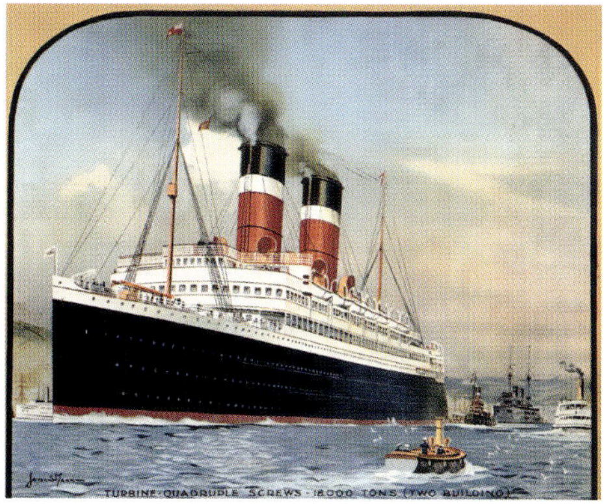

Above: Lloyd Sabaudo shipping line poster of Beardmore-built ships, left to right: *Conte Rosso*, *Conte Verde*, *Conte Biancamano* and *Conte Grande*.

Left: SS *Alsation*, built for the Allan Line.

Global Maritime Adventures

The top Glasgow writers of global maritime adventures are Alistair MacLean and Commodore Sir David Bone. Bone's father coined the phrase 'greyhound of the Atlantic' to describe the best of the long, lean and swift liners crossing the ocean.

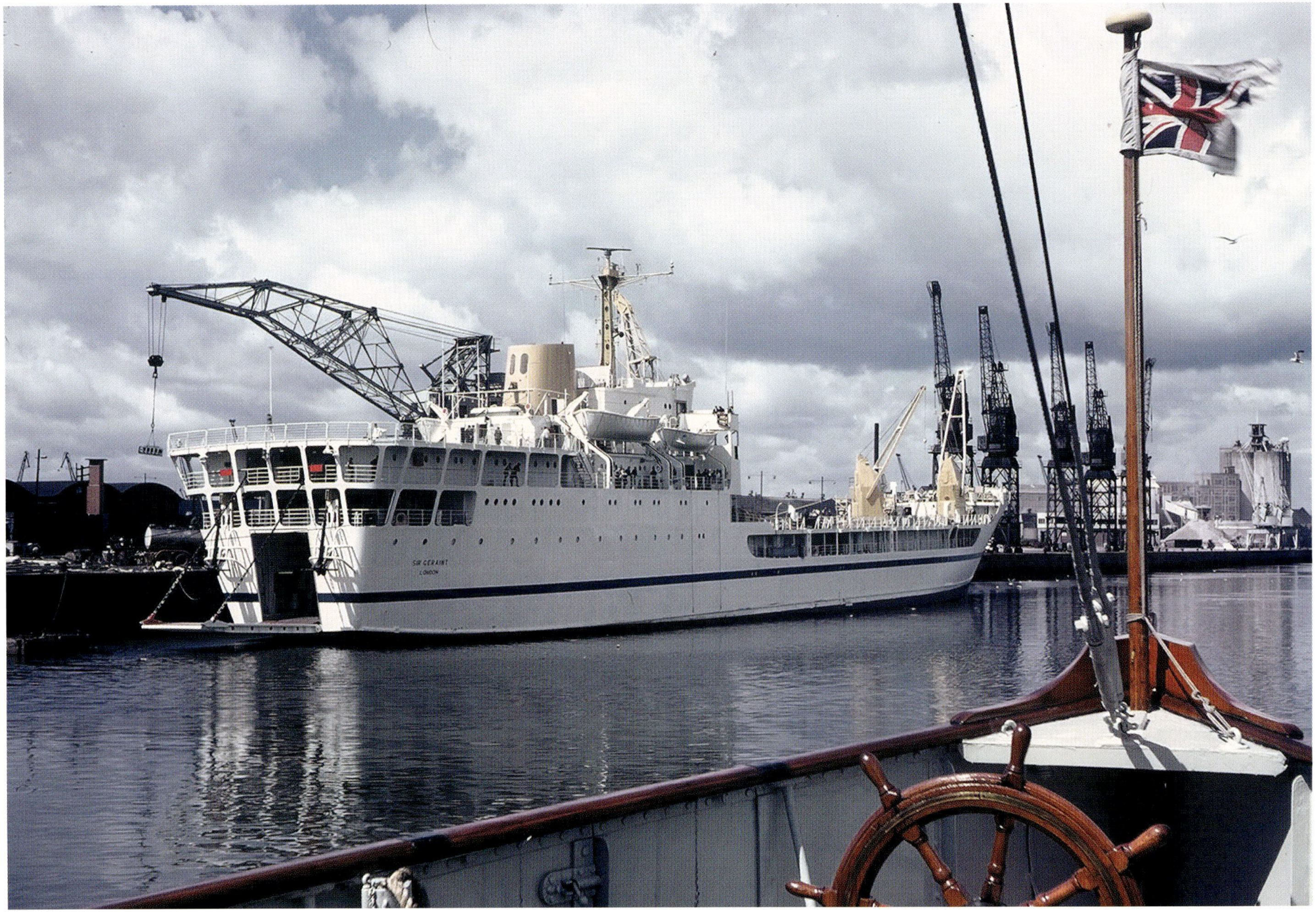

Sailing down the Clyde in the morning, passing Stephen's Shieldhall Wharf.

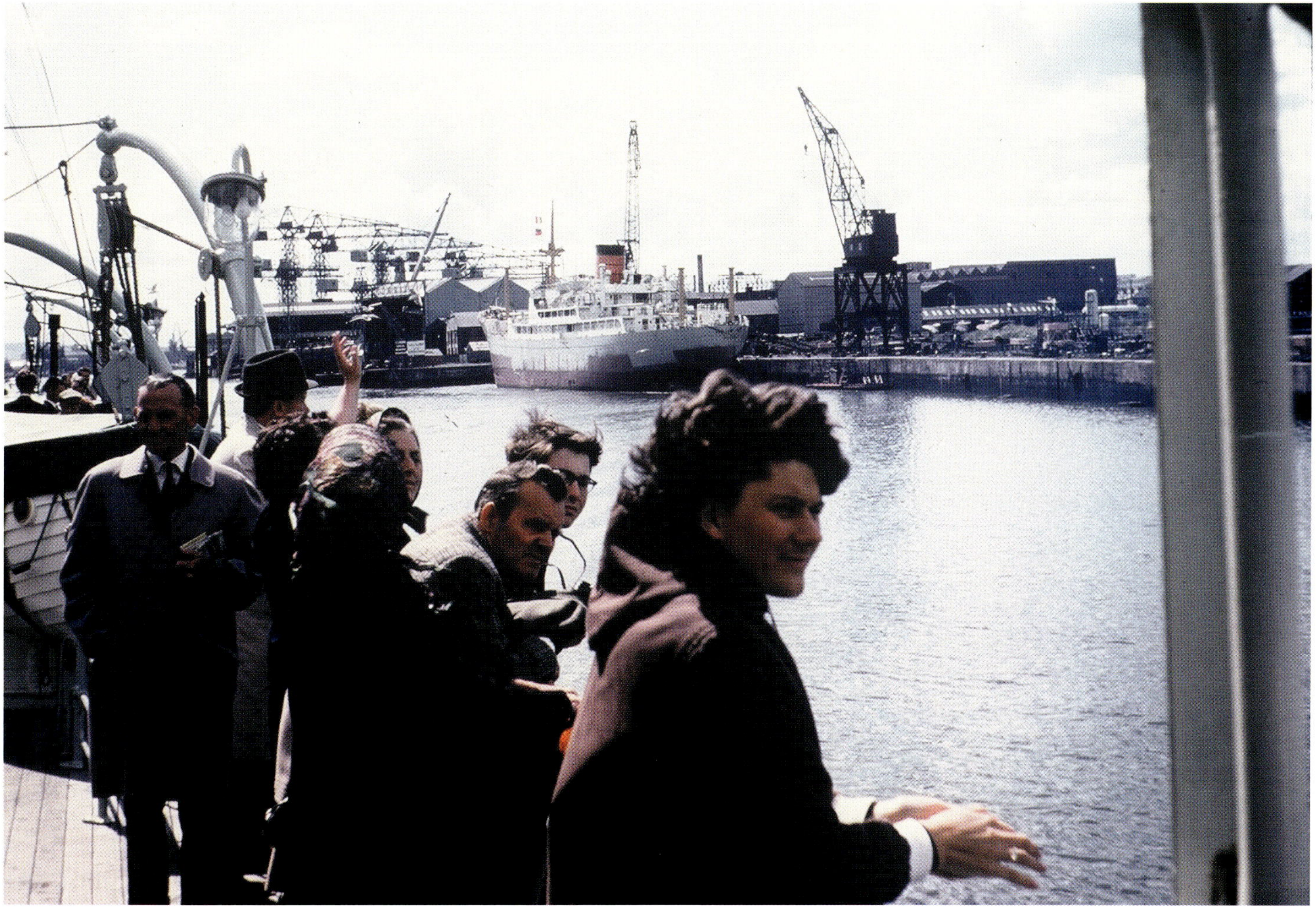

And back again in the evening, past Barclay Curle's shipyard.

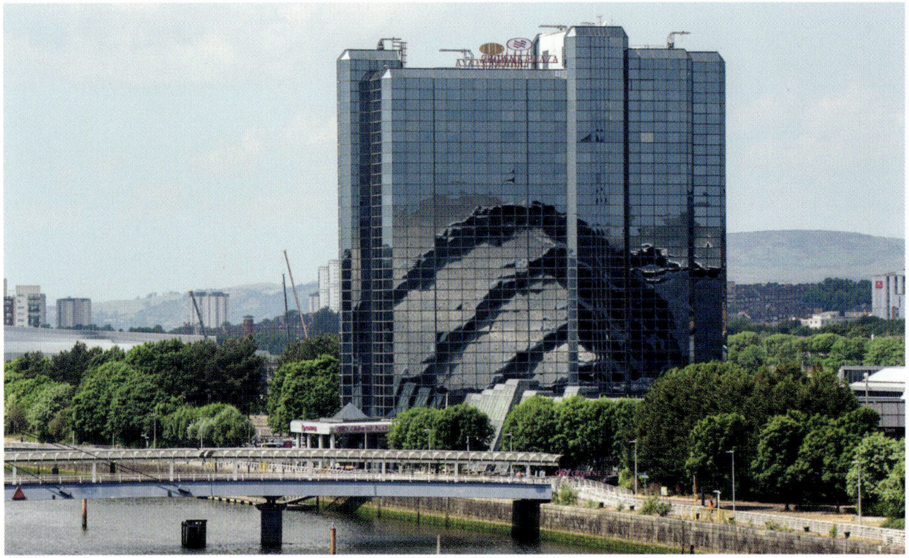

Reflections at Queen's Dock.

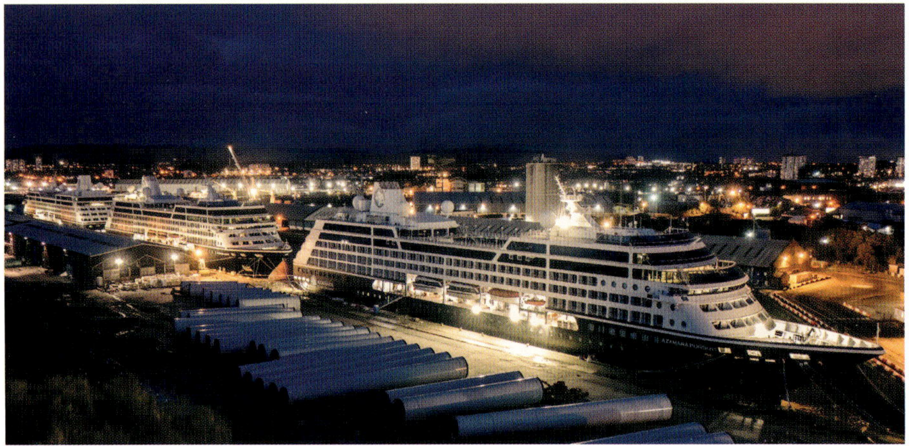

Azamara cruise liners in King George V Dock.